Switching Languages

EDITED BY STEVEN G. KELLMAN

Switching Languages

Translingual Writers Reflect on Their Craft

University of Nebraska Press
Lincoln and London

Acknowledgments for use of previously published material appear on pages 327–29, which constitute an extension of the copyright page.

∞

Library of Congress Cataloging-in-Publication Data
Switching languages : translingual writers reflect on their craft/ edited by Steven G. Kellman
p. cm. Includes bibliographical references and index.
ISBN 0-8032-2747-7 (cloth : alkaline paper) — ISBN 0-8032-7807-1 (paperback : alkaline paper)
1. Multilingualism and literature. I. Kellman, Steven G., 1947–
PN171.M93 S95 2003 809 — dc21 2002029133

Contents

Preface

Translingual authors – those who write in more than one language or in a language other than their primary one – are the prodigies of world literature. By expressing themselves in multiple verbal systems, they flaunt their freedom from the constraints of the culture into which they happen to have been born. And they challenge the pronouncement by George Santayana (who himself composed in English, not his native Spanish) that authentic poetry can be written only in the language of the lullabies the poet's mother sang. Though most of the world's population is at least *bi*lingual, few excel even in the native tongue.

No translingual is more dazzling than Vladimir Nabokov, who produced major work in Russian and in English. Prem Chand pioneered modern fiction in Urdu and then proceeded to do the same in Hindi, and Mendele Mokher Sforim is as important to the history of Yiddish literature as he is to that of Hebrew literature. Through his plays and novels, Samuel Beckett became a formidable figure in twentieth-century French literature, though, born in Dublin, he did not learn the language at his mother's knees. And Joseph Conrad, né Józef Teodor Konrad Korzeniowski, reinvented himself as a distinguished English novelist, though he came to English, after Polish and French, only in his twenties and, to his dying day, spoke the language with an accent so thick it was sometimes incomprehensible to his wife, Jessie.

But, as illustrated by the example of Andreï Makine, translinguals can be mistrusted and resented as much as admired. Born in Siberia in 1957, Makine grew up speaking Russian but adoring French, his "grandmaternal tongue"[1] – the language of his beloved grandmother and of the culture he cherished from afar. After emigrating to Paris in 1987, Makine wrote fiction, not in his native Russian but in French. However, attempts to get his work published were rebuffed. Protective of a language whose influence has waned since the reigns of Louis XIV, Napoleon, and Charles de Gaulle, editors in Paris dismissed Makine as, in the phrase he employs in his autobiographical fourth novel, *Dreams of My Russian Summers* (Le Testament français), "some funny little Russian who thought he could write in French."[2]

Determined to write and publish in French, Makine tried again, this time telling editors that his submission was a French translation of work he had originally written in Russian. The ruse worked, and the book was published and praised, especially for the quality of its "translation." When an editor insisted on checking the manuscript of Makine's second novel against the "original," the author hastily concocted a bogus source by translating his French into Russian. By 1995, when the prestigious publishing house Gallimard brought out *Dreams of My Russian Summers,* Makine ceased needing to pretend. He became the first non-Frenchman ever to win the Prix Goncourt, and his was the first book ever to win both the Prix Goncourt and the Prix Médicis. No longer a squalid secret, Makine's translingualism made his literary achievement seem all the more remarkable.

For the upstart Makine to have earned the highest honors in a culture, the French, that often defines itself through preserving, defending, and extolling its cherished but embattled national language was extraordinary. Yet talented translinguals have increasingly been forcing readers throughout the world to reconsider literary categories and loyalties. Though his work in English is not nearly as brilliant as in his native Russian, Joseph Brodsky served as poet laureate of the United States, and Ha Jin, an immigrant from China, won the National Book Award barely a dozen years after he took up English. Britain's most prestigious tribute for fiction, the Booker Prize, has been bestowed on several translinguals, including J. M. Coetzee, Keri Hulme, Kazuo Ishiguro, Ruth Prawer Jhabvala, Ben Okri, Arundhati Roy, and Salman Rushdie. And the most coveted literary award in the world, the Nobel Prize, has in recent decades gone to translinguals Gao Xingjian, Joseph Brodsky, Wole Soyinka, Elias Canetti, Samuel Beckett, and S. Y. Agnon.

It is difficult enough to write well in one's primary language. And it is reasonable to suspect fraud or genius from someone who writes in a second, third, or even fourth language. When Voltaire presented *Candide* as a translation from German, the prestige medium for serious philosophy, he was jesting. *Ossian,* James Macpherson's spurious specimen of third-century Gaelic verse, was probably the most notorious case of a translingual counterfeit. But when Nabokov, who grew up in St. Petersburg, published *Lolita* in exquisite American sentences (which he himself deprecated as "a second-rate brand of English"),[3] he was demonstrating brilliant dexterity and mock humility. In Russian, English, and even French, Nabokov was an extraordinary virtuoso of literary language.

So, too, was Apuleius, who emerged from the margins of the Roman Empire to master Latin prose. Born in Hippo, in what is now Algeria, Apuleius went on to study Greek before taking up Latin, the language in which he composed *The Golden Ass,* a matchless comic romp that refutes Virginia Woolf's contention that "Humour is the first of the gifts to perish in a foreign tongue."[4] It is precisely the luxuriance – the prodigious vocabulary and ornate syntax – of Apuleius's Latin that makes the original text of *The Golden Ass* such a challenge to the modern reader. As a linguistic interloper, Apuleius has much more to prove than native masters like Virgil or Horace, and he begins his famous book by pleading forgiveness – elegantly, disingenuously – for any crudeness in his use of Latin: "En ecce praefamur veniam, si quid exotici ac forensis sermonis rudis locutor offendero" (I first crave and beg your pardon, lest I should happen to displease or offend any of you by the rude and rustic utterance of this strange and foreign language).[5]

The case of Apuleius is a reminder that translingualism is as old as mythical Babel, where, fragmented among different tongues, human beings first found the need to use more than one. Much of ancient Latin literature was created by linguistic interlopers, authors – such as Lucan, Martial, Quintilian, and Seneca from Iberia; Ausonius from Gaul; and Augustine and Terence from Africa – who chose to appropriate the language of imperial Rome. Virtually all neo-Latin literature was written by translinguals, authors – including Petrarch, Descartes, Erasmus, and Milton – for whom Latin was the medium of a common European culture but not of their household. They, too, refute Santayana. Latin has not been the only imperial language, the authoritative form of discourse linking a far-flung and diverse population. Arabic, Mandarin, Persian, Russian, and Sanskrit have been others. During the period of European colonialism, aspiring authors in Africa, Asia, and the Americas advanced their ambitions by determining to write in English, French, Portuguese, or Spanish. Spanish literature of the Western hemisphere began, in fact, in translingualism, when Garcilaso de la Vega chose not to write *Comentarios reals* in his native Quechua. Of approximately five thousand languages currently spoken throughout the world, not many more than a couple of dozen are of practical value for establishing and sustaining a literary career. Though their mothers may have sung them to sleep in Berber, children who aim to get published are well advised to switch to Arabic or French. Because it was the dominant language of the Soviet Union, Fazil Iskander chose to write in Russian rather than his native Abkhazian. When Black Elk spoke, in his famous reminiscences, it was in Lakota, but what facilitated their fame is the fact that John G. Neihardt gave readers access to them in English.

War, disease, famine, political oppression, and economic hardship have contributed to an unprecedented movement of populations across the globe in recent decades; one estimate puts the current figure at more than 120 million migrants.[6] And migration is a powerful motive for translingualism, for assimilating to and through the language of a new environment. Clarice Lispector wrote in Portuguese not because of any special determination on her part, but because while still a young girl, she was taken by her parents from her native Ukraine to settle in Brazil. Though born Tomas Straussler in Czechoslovakia, Tom Stoppard became an English playwright because his father died and his mother then married a British officer who moved them all to England. And Phillis Wheatley, the first African American poet, switched languages, from Fulani to English, under duress, after being abducted from West Africa and sold to a Boston merchant at about the age of seven.

Yet for others translingualism is a way to vaunt their freedom. No external pressure compelled Beckett, who was already publishing important work in English, to switch to French, except the perverse challenge of renouncing the advantages of native fluency. Another Irishman, Oscar Wilde, wrote one of his plays, *Salomé,* in French precisely in order to be ornery, to disturb the British. "Français de sympathie, je suis Irlandais de race, et les Anglais m'ont condamné à parler le langage de Shakespeare" (French by sympathy, I am Irish by race, and the English have condemned me to speak the language of Shakespeare), he explained in French, rejecting the linguistic destiny cast for him by others.[7] When ambilinguals – writers fluent and accomplished in more than one language – commit themselves to one, it seems an affirmation of individual sovereignty. "I have no recollection whatever of a first language. So far as I am aware, I possess equal currency in English, French, and German," proclaims George Steiner, free to determine for himself the language of each literary project.[8] When Kamala Das decides each time between English and Malayalam, she is in the position of Mozart, free to compose his concerto for either oboe or flute, depending on the particular sonorities he wishes to explore at the moment. Just as Mozart later transcribed for flute a concerto he wrote for oboe, Isak Dinesen translated into Danish many of the stories she had conceived in English.

Recounting in her autobiography, *The Promised Land,* how she recreated herself in America, in English, Mary Antin erases any trace of anguish over abandoning her native Yiddish. Yet not every translingual act is triumphal. "I had to work like a coal-miner in his pit quarrying all my English sentences out of a black night," complained Conrad about the ordeal of writing in his adopted language.[9] "To change languages," quipped E. M. Cioran, who exchanged Romanian for French, "is to write a love letter with a dictionary."[10] Despite early success writing fiction in English, Yu Lihua, an immigrant to America, discovered constraints when she tried to express herself in a language alien to her community. "They [the publishers] were only interested in stories that fit the pattern of Oriental exoticism – the feet-binding of women and the addiction of opium-smoking men," she told an interviewer. "I didn't want to write that stuff. I wanted to write about the struggle of Chinese immigrants in American society."[11] And she did, more freely, by reverting to her native Chinese.

As much as flesh and blood, we are composed of and by words. If Homo sapiens is a species defined by language, then switching the language entails transforming the self. While it can be liberating, discarding one's native tongue is also profoundly unsettling; it means constructing a new identity syllable by syllable. Some authors – Julio Cortázar in Paris, Isaac Bashevis Singer in New York, Paul Bowles in Tangier, Nelly Sachs in Sweden, Ezra Pound in Italy, Alexander Solzhenitsyn in Vermont, Robert Graves in Majorca, Malcolm Lowry in Mexico, James Joyce in Trieste, Zurich, and Paris – stubbornly cling to their native tongues amid an alien ambience. Czeslaw Milosz's explanation for why he persists in using Polish as the medium of his poetry and prose even after five decades in California suggests some of the anxiety as well as exhilaration in translingual writing: "In my rejection of imposing a profound change on myself by going over to writing in a different language, I perceive a fear of losing my identity, because it is certain that when we switch languages we become someone else."[12]

Refusing to lose his identity as a Russian author, Isaac Babel lost his life instead. The case of Babel, five years older than Nabokov, testifies to the power of vectors resisting translingualism. By 1935, when he last visited his wife and daughter in exile in Paris, Babel was acutely aware of the brutal dangers awaiting him back in Stalin's Russia. Some of Babel's earliest stories, dating from his adolescence in Odessa, were written in French. Yet, incapable of imagining himself doing anything but writing, of writing in any language but Russian, and of writing Russian in any land but Russia, he chose to return to Moscow. Cynthia Ozick is accurate in her claim that, executed by firing squad on 27 January 1940, "Babel sacrificed his life to his language."[13]

It is not easy to pin down Proteus, and few generalizations about the protean experiences of translinguals are valid. But two powerful and antithetical forces seem to be at work when authors switch languages: populism and formalism. Authors try to trade in the common verbal currency, but some also aim to purify the tarnished words of the tribe. William Wordsworth revolutionized the writing of English poetry when, in his 1800 preface to *Lyrical Ballads,* he proclaimed that his intention was "to choose incidents and situations from common life, and to relate or describe them, throughout, as far as was possible, in a selection of language really used by men."[14] No longer would there be a specialized lexicon of "poetic language" – precious words like "forsooth," "verily," or "whilom" – that are deliberately appropriated to differentiate a text from ordinary speech. Embracing the vernacular, many authors of the past millennium (from Chaucer through Whitman and Twain to the latest slam poet) have tried to erase boundaries between written and spoken language. And it is toward that end, because code switching is common in conversations among contemporary Latinas, that Gloria Anzaldúa, Lorna Dee Cervantes, Sandra Cisneros, Angela de Hoyos, and others alternate between English and Spanish within a single written line. It was an urge toward verisimilitude that compelled John Sayles to teach himself enough of the language to render most of the dialogue in *Los gusanos* (1991), a novel about Cuban exiles, in Spanish, the language his characters would surely have used. Because he set it all somewhere south of Mexico, Sayles made virtually all of his film *Hombres armados/Men with Guns* (1997) in Spanish.

Dante began composing his *Commedia* in Latin but soon

switched to Italian, arguing in *De vulgari eloquentia* (in Latin!) that the tongue actually spoken in Florence could be at least as eloquent as the revered language of ancient Rome. The hegemony of Latin was shattered when, during the late Middle Ages and the Renaissance, authors throughout Europe began to employ their local vernaculars. The immediate consequence might have been to discourage translingualism; readers and writers in each country could now ignore Latin, once they as schoolboys (and very few schoolgirls) had survived compulsory instruction in its conjugations and declensions. But in the long term, the motive for literary language switching was strengthened. Even within the bounds of France alone, authors discovered a multitude of languages, dialects, and registers. To convey the life around them, it was not possible to rely on a standardized, frozen classical language or even a single native one. The bard of contemporary Queens, said to be the most ethnically diverse spot in the world, would sound ludicrous in Latin but also deficient if oblivious to Arabic, Chinese, Hindi, Korean, Russian, Spanish, and dozens of other languages spoken on the borough's streets. For his masterpiece of immigration fiction, *Call It Sleep* (1934), Henry Roth, whose first language was Yiddish, managed to create English prose supple enough to carry echoes of Yiddish, Polish, German, and Italian. Switching tongues is the natural way to negotiate a motley universe.

Yet many authors adopt their vocation and their style precisely because they wish to cultivate something *unnatural,* because they are intent on devising a written language that is distinct from the spoken ones. For much of the history of Japan, some of that nation's finest authors composed in Chinese, even during periods of political and cultural autonomy and even if they lacked any wish to emigrate to Xian. To create *kanshi* (poetry in Chinese) or *kambun* (prose in Chinese) was – somewhat like indulging in *ikebana,* the tradition of formal flower arrangement – to submit oneself to the discipline of a subtle art esteemed all the more for its artificiality. Nor did it preclude writing poetry and prose in Japanese as well. Translingualism became an exacting exercise in gratuitous creation.

Unlike Wordsworth, a modern poet in Tangiers, Cairo, or Damascus who employs classical Arabic is less concerned with demotic ambitions of simulating ordinary speech than with probing the exacting possibilities of inherited conventions. To the extent that it overtly differentiates itself from prose, poetry in many cultures deflects and distorts the language really used by men and women. Outside the privileged space of verse, few of us frame our thoughts in terza rima or anastrophe. Even free verse is inherently translingual, forging a new, unnatural language out of the shards of common speech. But the same could be said of crafted prose. The French language even reserves a special version of the preterite, called the *passé simple* and never employed in speech, to designate literary usage; its presence signals we are reading a novel or short story and in effect creates the separate literary language that Wordsworth rejected. When Hilda Doolittle, T. S. Eliot, James Joyce, and Ezra Pound plait their texts with swatches of Greek, Latin, French, German, Italian, Gaelic, Chinese, and Sanskrit, the translingualism is not driven by concern for verisimilitude. Nor is their polyglot project exclusively modern. In the twelfth century, the abbess and mystic Hildegard von Bingen was mixing German and Latin in an alphabet of her own invention to do what all poets essentially do: create their own verbal universe. But when Rolando Hinojosa-Smith jumps from Spanish to English in his *Klail City Death Trip,* a cycle of novels that traces Chicano experience in the Rio Grande Valley throughout the twentieth century, he is echoing actual speech, not patenting a new language.

All of which is to say that the aspirations and achievements of translingual authors are almost as varied as the languages they link. When I tried to survey the phenomenon in *The Translingual Imagination* (University of Nebraska Press, 2000), I looked at hundreds of examples and discovered that, though switching languages has a long antiquity, the business has been particularly brisk in recent years. André Aciman, Julia Alvarez, Edwidge Danticat, Assia Djebar, Ariel Dorfman, Rosario Ferré, Ursula Hegi, Aleksandar Hemon, Kazuo Ishiguro, Ha Jin, Milan Kundera, Chang-rae Lee,

Amin Maalouf, Andreï Makine, Anchee Min, Luc Sante, Vikram Seth, Ahduf Soueif, and Ilan Stavans are just a few of the many authors who have lately found readers in languages other than their primary ones. The switch from Spanish to English or from Arabic to French is not uncommon, but the ranks of contemporary translinguals also include Amma Darko, who writes in German though she grew up in Ghana, and Lulu Wang, a Chinese émigrée who writes fiction in Dutch.

Switching Languages is designed to allow translingual authors to speak for themselves, about their own experiences. Among materials available for inclusion and, if necessary, translation, texts were selected that represent the range of translingual experience – from Mary Antin's triumphal creation of a new self writing in American English to Marjorie Agosín's failure to feel at home in New England except when using Spanish. Texts have been organized to reflect a spectrum of responses to translingualism, from affirmation through lamentation to rejection. Languages represented by the authors in this collection include Afrikaans, Arabic, Chinese, Dutch, English, Esperanto, French, Frisian, German, Hebrew, Hindi, Igbo, Irish, Kannada, Kikuyu, Korean, Malayalam, Serer, Spanish, Urdu, Vietnamese, and Yiddish. None of the selections is more than a century old, because, in searching for appropriate material, I found that, though switching languages is nothing new, sustained discussion of the phenomenon is relatively recent. Like *The Translingual Imagination,* this anthology is offered in the hope of finding suitable language to animate that discussion.

I am grateful to the University of Nebraska Press for its support of my two-part project and to Ilan Stavans for encouraging me to assemble this collection. To express my gratitude to Wendy Barker, I lack appropriate language.

Notes

1. Andreï Makine, *Dreams of My Russian Summers,* trans. Geoffrey Strachan (New York: Arcade, 1997).

2. Makine, *Dreams of My Russian Summers,* p. 220.

3. Vladimir Nabokov, *Strong Opinions* (New York: McGraw-Hill, 1973), 15.

4. Virginia Woolf, "On Not Knowing Greek," *The Common Reader,* vol. 1 (London: Hogarth, 1925).

5. Apuleius, *The Golden Ass: Being the Metamorphoses of Lucius Apuleius, with an English Translation by W. Adlington* (Cambridge, Mass.: Harvard University Press, 1977), 2–3.

6. Peter Stalker, *Workers without Frontiers: The Impact of Globalization on Internal Migration* (Geneva: International Labour Organization, 2000).

7. Letter to Edmond de Goncourt, 17 December 1891; cited in Richard Ellmann, *Oscar Wilde* (New York: Alfred A. Knopf, 1988), 351.

8. George Steiner, *Extraterritorial: Papers on Literature and the Language Revolution* (New York: Atheneum, 1971), 115.

9. Letter to Edward Garnett, 28 August 1908; cited in C. Jean Aubry, ed., *Joseph Conrad: Life and Letters,* vol. 2 (New York: Doubleday, Page and Company, 1927), 82.

10. E. M. Cioran, *Anathemas and Admirations,* trans. Richard Howard (New York: Arcade, 1991), 82.

11. Cited in Xiao-huang Yin, *Chinese American Literature since the 1850s* (Urbana: University of Illinois Press, 2000), 169.

12. Czeslaw Milosz, *Milosz's ABC's,* trans. Madeline G. Levine (New York: Farrar, Straus and Giroux, 2001), 220.

13. Cynthia Ozick, "The Year of Writing Dangerously," *New Republic,* 8 May 1995.

14. William Wordsworth, "Preface to the Second Edition of Lyrical Ballads," in *Critical Theory since Plato,* ed. Hazard Adams (Fort Worth TX: Harcourt Brace Jovanovich, 1992), 438.

Proclamations

KAMALA DAS (1934–)

Born in Malabar to an affluent and eminent literary family, Kamala Nair grew up in Calcutta. At the age of fifteen, she married a relative, K. Madhava Das, a much older man to whom she bore three sons. Her autobiography, *My Story,* was published in 1976. Defying taboos on the behavior of upper-class married women, Das has been outspoken and controversial in her views on sexuality, politics, and other topics. She has painted, run – unsuccessfully – for public office, and written a widely read column. Das is trilingual – in Hindi, English, and Malayalam. She writes most of her fiction in Malayalam, under the pen name Madhavikutty, and most of her poetry in English, as Kamala Das. Her Malayalam fiction includes *Palayan* (1990), *Neypayasam* (1991), and *Dayarikkurippukal* (1992). In addition to the novel *The Alphabet of Lust* (1977), Das has published the following volumes of poetry in English: *Summer in Calcutta* (1965), *The Old Playhouse and Other Poems* (1973), and *The Anamalai Poems* (1985). "An Introduction," which comes from the 1967 collection *The Descendants,* is a confessional poem that celebrates Das's liberation through translingualism.

An Introduction

I don't know politics but I know the names
Of those in power, and can repeat them like
Days of week, or names of months, beginning with
Nehru. I am Indian, very brown, born in
Malabar, I speak three languages, write in
Two, dream in one. Don't write in English, they said,
English is not your mother-tongue. Why not leave
Me alone, critics, friends, visiting cousins,
Every one of you? Why not let me speak in
Any language I like? The language I speak
Becomes mine, its distortions, its queernesses
All mine, mine alone. It is half English, half
Indian, funny perhaps, but it is honest,
It is as human as I am human, don't
You see? It voices my joys, my longings, my
Hopes, and it is useful to me as cawing
Is to crows or roaring to the lions, it
Is human speech, the speech of the mind that is
Here and not there, a mind that sees and hears and
Is aware. Not the deaf, blind speech
of trees in storm or of monsoon clouds or of rain or the
Incoherent mutterings of the blazing
Funeral pyre. I was child, and later they
Told me I grew, for I became tall, my limbs
Swelled and one or two places sprouted hair. When
I asked for love, not knowing what else to ask

For, he drew a youth of sixteen into the
Bedroom and closed the door. He did not beat me
But my sad woman-body felt so beaten.
The weight of my breasts and womb crushed me. I shrank
Pitifully. Then . . . I wore a shirt and my
Brother's trousers, cut my hair short and ignored
My womanliness. Dress in sarees, be girl,
Be wife, they said. Be embroiderer, be cook,
Be a quarreler with servants. Fit in. Oh,
Belong, cried the categorizers, Don't sit
On walls or peep in through our lace-draped windows.
Be Amy, or be Kamala. Or, better
Still, be Madhavikutty. It is time to
Choose a name, a role. Don't play pretending games.
Don't play at schizophrenia or be a
Nympho. Don't cry embarrassingly loud when
Jilted in love . . . I met a man, loved him. Call
Him not by any name, he is every man
Who wants a woman, just as I am every
Woman who seeks love. In him . . . the hungry haste
Of rivers, in me . . . the oceans' tireless
Waiting. Who are you, I ask each and everyone,
The answer is, it is I. Anywhere and
Everywhere, I see the one who calls himself
I; in this world, he is tightly packed like the
Sword in its sheath. It is I who drink lonely
Drinks at twelve, midnight, in hotels of strange towns,
It is I who laugh, it is I who make love
And then, feel shame, it is I who lie dying
With a rattle in my throat. I am sinner,
I am saint. I am the beloved and the
Betrayed. I have no joys which are not yours, no
Aches which are not yours. I too call myself I.

IAN BURUMA (1951–)

Ian Buruma was born in The Hague, the Netherlands, to a Dutch father and a mother whose German Jewish family had settled in England. His wife is Japanese. He studied Chinese and Japanese literature at Leyden University in his native Holland and film at Nihon University in Tokyo. Buruma's translingualism and his extensive experience in Asia have enabled him to become a prominent commentator, a knowledgeable intermediary between Anglophonic readers and the cultures of Japan, Korea, Myanmar, and the Philippines. His books include *Behind the Mask: On Sexual Demons, Sacred Mothers, Transvestites, Gangsters, Drifters, and Other Japanese Cultural Heroes* (1984); *God's Dust: A Modern Asian Journey* (1989); *The Wages of Guilt: Memories of War in Germany and Japan* (1994); *The Missionary and the Libertine: Love and War in East and West* (2000); and *Bad Elements: Among the Rebels, Dissidents, and Democrats of Greater China* (2001). In "The Road to Babel," which first appeared in the *New York Review of Books,* to which he is a frequent contributor, Buruma uses his own background in Dutch, Frisian, and English to survey contemporary translingualism.

The Road to Babel

1

In 1951 there was a riot in the northern Dutch province of Friesland. It was not much of a riot, really, but the reasons for it, and the consequences, were interesting. The trouble started when a judge refused to hear the testimony of a local veterinarian in Frisian. The judge couldn't understand Frisian, an old Germanic language related to Dutch, German, and English, and in any case Dutch was the official language of public affairs in Friesland. So the judge, though perhaps a little tactless, was within his rights.

Things were stirred up, however, by the editor of a local newspaper named Fedde Schurer, who wrote a scorching attack against the judge, comparing him to the "Saxon gang" which invaded Friesland from Germany at the end of the fifteenth century. Schurer was prosecuted for contempt of court. A mob gathered in protest in the central square of Leeuwarden, the provincial capital. Schurer was carried around on the shoulders of his supporters. The police charged with truncheons; the fire brigade pulled out the water hoses. Schurer, the people's hero, fell through a glass window and scratched his arm. The national press began to pay attention. Metropolitan arrogance was condemned. And as a result, Frisian was recognized in 1956 as a language that could be used in the courts for the first time since the sixteenth century, when Friesland became a province of the Dutch Republic.

The idea of Frisian as a kind of national language was, like so much else, a product of nineteenth-century Romanticism. It had not been used in government, schools, or churches for hundreds of years. But in the late 1800s, folk poets emerged to promote the native tongue. The first Bible translation was only completed in the 1940s. Teaching the language in primary schools has been permitted since 1937 and in higher education since 1980. About 400,000 people now know Frisian – that is to say, about half the people in Friesland have at least a passive knowledge of it. You can hear it spoken on radio stations. This revival has come as a reaction against the uniformity of standard Dutch, an assertion of local identity, rather like Welsh, Irish, or Catalan.

There is a price to pay for too much regional chauvinism. At least all Frisians are educated in Dutch. But the Catalans are so keen to defend their language that Castillian Spanish is often neglected; some even prefer to learn English. As a result, Barcelona is in danger of becoming a more provincial city than it should be, isolated in a linguistic fog.

My paternal grandfather spoke Frisian at home. But he moved to Amsterdam to study theology, a common intellectual pursuit among gifted provincials. My father does not speak a word of Frisian. All that is left of our Frisian heritage is our name; a perverse pride in the fact that twelve hundred years ago Frisians murdered an eighty-year-old English priest named Boniface who had no business converting natives to the Roman faith; and the imperfect mastery of one sentence in Frisian, used during the old struggles against the Saxon gang, when a legendary hero named Big Pier swung his club with devastating effect. It was a password meant to weed out alien infiltrators. It goes, in English translation: "Butter, bread, and green cheese, if you can't say that, you're not a real Fries" (Bûter, brea en griene tsiis, wa't dat net sizze kin is gjin oprjochte Fries).

*

One of the main attractions of a native tongue, or dialect, or slang, indeed the main reason for reviving or inventing one, is the fact that outsiders don't get it. In a sense the entire language is a kind of password. If you understand, you pass. From a strictly regional point of view, my father and I have lost an "identity." We don't get it anymore either, we don't pass, in Friesland. That is the way of the world. Once you head for the metropole, mud of the old soil does not stick to your boots for long. I can still speak and write in Dutch, but make a living by writing in English, my mother's language. For me the metropole has shifted even farther afield than Amsterdam. This is hardly unusual either. I am just one in a crowd of Bengalis, Chinese, Germans, Cubans, Russians, Belgians, Poles, and whatnot who have gone the same route.

Whether we like it or not, North America has become, in a linguistic sense, the metropole of the world; the rest is periphery, even though almost a billion people – 15 percent of the world's population – speak Mandarin Chinese, and 266 million speak Spanish. English is the lingua franca of international business, pop music, computer technology, airline travel, and much else besides. The French don't like it, but English is now the main language spoken in meetings of the European Commission in Brussels. English is the language of Hollywood movies, the common currency of worldwide entertainment. And in more and more countries, English is becoming the language of science and higher education too, replacing Latin as the lingua franca of learning.

A Dutch minister of education seriously suggested some years ago that English should be the language of instruction at all Dutch universities. The idea is not new. An education minister of the Meiji government in nineteenth-century Japan had a similar, though more radical, suggestion: only after English had replaced Japanese as the national language would Japan become a modern and civilized nation. His idea did not bear fruit. But as for Holland, another former Dutch minister of education recently told me he was convinced that English would be the nation's primary language in two or three generations. If he is right, Dutch will go the way of Frisian, a badge of nostalgic identity, but nothing more than that. And the danger, in that event, would be that the Dutch would become like Singaporeans, proficient in several languages, masters of none. And where the Dutch go, others might follow.

The domination of a metropolitan language, whether Dutch,

English, Castilian, or Chinese, can indeed be a fearful thing. Identities are threatened. But in fact mastery of the native language is often a password even in the metropole itself. I am convinced that my maternal grandfather, the son of an immigrant, and thus more British than the British, deliberately mispronounced his French, lest he be mistaken for a foreigner. So language is clearly a sensitive issue; and yet I believe the fears are often misplaced, and, when they are manipulated for political ends, sinister.

Some are so worried about the domination of English that they use such phrases as "killer language," as though English were a kind of epidemic disease striking all people dumb in their own languages. The pathological terminology is no coincidence. Those who speak of killer languages, and deplore the extinction of Mbabaran in Australia or Wappo in the American West, also use terms such as "biolinguistic diversity" and link the survival of languages to larger ecological concerns: the disappearance of rain forests, animal life, and rare flora. Native habitats, ecolinguists claim, sometimes with good reason, are ruined by "biological waves" of Europeans and Americans crashing through the dense but fragile world of tribes and small peoples. Experts say there are still about six thousand languages spoken, of which only about three thousand are expected to survive very long.

*

Guardians of more robust languages, such as the members of the French Academy, worry less about extinction than pollution. Words such as *le weekend* or *le fax* make them ill. And if you think Franglais is bad, take note of Japanese, which absorbs a huge mangled vocabulary from English, as it did before from Chinese, and even Portuguese and Dutch. A strike is a *suto,* from *sutoraiki;* to quit a health-threatening habit is to make a *dokuta sutoppu* (doctor's stop); to sexually harass is to commit *seku-hara.* A personal computer is a *paso-kon,* a golfing handicap a *hande,* and so on. Creative linguistic pilfering is easy to do in Japanese, for a new verb can be created by simply sticking the verb ending *ru* at the end of any borrowed phrase, as in, say, *makuru,* to eat a McDonald's hamburger – *maku,* short for *Makudonarudo,* and *ru.* (The equivalent in French, by the way, is *bouffer un macdo.*) The interesting thing is that the Japanese, like my British grandfather, are notoriously bad at learning foreign languages, partly, I believe, for xenophobic reasons, as though paralyzed by the thought that speaking a foreign language too well would sully the purity of one's Japaneseness.

Keeping a language pure of outside influences is always a losing battle, for no language was ever pure in the first place. Old English was changed enormously by Norman French, but Old English was itself a mixture of Frisian, Anglian, and various Saxon dialects. The Japanese writer Tanizaki Junichiro once promoted the idea that only pure Japanese, stripped clean of Chinese loanwords, would be fine enough to convey the deepest literary expressions. Since almost 60 percent of the Japanese language consists of Chinese loanwords, this was an impractical suggestion. But he made it in the 1930s, a time of overheated nationalism, and such drives toward purification are invariably inspired more by political than literary concerns.

The French have been worried about Anglo-Saxon pollution for a long time. Charles Maurras, a gifted prose stylist and a poisonous philosopher who founded the ultra-right Action Française, was a grumpy spectator at the first modern Olympic Games in Athens in 1896. He was particularly incensed by the sound of English spoken around him, especially American English, that "disgusting patois." Indeed, he thought international sports were a bad thing, for they infected the world with noxious Anglo-Saxon expressions. Maurras, a great defender of French classical purity, took a biological view of things, just like the ecolinguists. English was rootless, cosmopolitan, and infectious, like a disease. Naturally, he was a raving anti-Semite too.

Flemish Belgians have waged a long battle against foreign pollution, except that in their case the linguistic enemy is French, the language of the Walloons, who used to be richer and more powerful than the Flemish speakers. Flemish, a dialect of Dutch, was full of French words, just as English is, but for political reasons official

Flemish pedagogues did their best to find Dutch equivalents for every French loanword. The results are rich in comic absurdity, at least to the Dutch ear. Helicopter thus becomes *wentelwiek,* literally "wheeling wing." The other result is that more and more Flemings refuse to learn French. And since few Walloons know Dutch, two Belgians meeting in Antwerp or Liège will often find themselves speaking in English.

*

The main danger, however, of linguistic purism is not absurdity so much as stagnation and lifelessness. The example of Singapore is a warning less against using English as the main language of instruction in a country where most people speak something else as well than against too much engineering. The former prime minister, Lee Kuan Yew, has been a ferocious watchdog in this regard, trying to ban Chinese dialects in public life, or issuing public warnings against using Sino-Malay slang while speaking English. One reason so many Singaporeans cannot speak any language really well is their self-consciousness. Forced to speak an affected 1950s BBC English in public, they lapse into a looser, slangier hybrid tongue called Singlish in private, almost as though to spite the stern headmaster. Too stiff or too slangy – neither is likely to produce great literature.

Singaporean BBC English is not the only example of a model frozen in time. Filipino newspapers still use American journalese of the 1930s – "Prexie nixes solons" – and the Indian English-language press can still read like the prewar *Manchester Guardian.* In fact, of course, BBC English as a model of how the Queen's language should be spoken no longer exists. British radio and television announcers speak in a variety of regional accents, encouraged since the 1960s, when dialect became cool. And standard English has become something known as Thames Estuary, after the eastern suburbs of London and beyond. It is a nasal, almost whining, southern middle-class English with shades of cockney. Tony Blair tends to lapse into it. Mick Jagger has spoken a *faux*-cockney version for years. Even the Queen's speech last Christmas bore traces of it.

In any case English, as a lingua franca of business, information technology, and entertainment, will continue to creep into other languages, just as French used to do, or German, Chinese, Sanskrit, Arabic, and Persian. English is also mutating into professional dialects that consist of nothing but jargon. Inside the institutions of the European Union, something one might call Brussels English is taking shape with its own peculiar jargon and even spelling. Airline pilots across the globe converse in an English that is comprehensible only to themselves. In some cases, it is the only English they know. This has been known to cause problems in emergencies. It is one of the reasons Japan Airlines started hiring foreign pilots.

2

Jargon English is ugly, but hardly a mortal threat to the continued existence of other major languages. And even where English, mostly by reason of imperial conquest, has become a main language, the effect on native identities is by no means as clear-cut as some people suppose, or fear. India is one obvious example. English is the common language of Indian elites and the government. It is in fact the only truly national language of all India, even though it is spoken only by about 5 percent of the population. Indeed, the modern sense of Indian nationhood found one of its first and most eloquent expressions in English, in the writings of Nehru. English was the language of the colonial masters, but also of many nationalists who fought for independence. And English is the language of some of the finest Indian writers today, not just those who write nostalgically from London or New York, but Indians living in Delhi, Calcutta, and Bombay.

To be sure, Nehru and others wanted to make Hindi into the national language. But they chose a rather artificial form of Hindi, heavily encrusted with archaic terms borrowed from Sanskrit. Some of the main proponents of this national language were not native Hindi speakers but Hindu intellectuals from Gujarat and Bengal. And in the south Hindi was not spoken at all. So it never really took hold. And few people wish to revive it, even though there are proponents of a more popular Hindi, as an official alternative to English. They have not gotten very far either.

The problem was put well by a south Indian, whose article, in English, was plucked by a friend of mine from the Internet. The author, named Rajeev Srinivasan, is a native speaker of Malayalam, the language of Kerala, about which he has all the Romantic sentiments of a nineteenth-century idealist. He writes: "As someone who is completely bilingual in English and Malayalam, I can say with certainty that for me, Malayalam is the language of the heart, and English of the head." Neither Hindi, nor English, he continues, could possibly express the "distinct Malayali ethos, with its melancholy, brooding ways that contrast so markedly with the exuberant, tropical landscape."

Then, to clinch his argument about languages of the heart and the head, he quotes a poem by Sir Walter Scott:

> Breathes there the man, with soul so dead,
> Who never to himself hath said,
> This is my own, my native land!

But even if Sir Walter Scott's words can only appeal to his head, Rajeev Srinivasan still prefers English to Hindi, for at least English connects you to the wider world, not to mention the World Wide Web, whereas Hindi would make Malayalam speakers feel like second-class citizens. Hindi, he says, is "a conquering language." The language of one old empire, then, can be useful in staving off the advances of another.

There are examples elsewhere of the same phenomenon. The people of East Timor, whose common language now is Indonesian, or Bahassa Indonesian, wish to have another national language. The only one they can think of is Portuguese. Meanwhile, people in Irian Jaya have a difficult time rising against their Indonesian masters because their many tribal languages are mutually incomprehensible. They, too, could do with a national language in their struggle for autonomy. Dutch, perhaps?

The Philippines is an interesting case, for it went from being a European colony to an American one. The first great Filipino novel, *Noli me tangere* by José Rizal – the bible, as it were, of Filipino identity and independence, a book drenched in modern national sentiment – was written in Spanish. More than one twentieth-century Filipino writer, expressing himself in English, has deplored the loss of Spanish as the national tongue. Some writers would like to use Tagalog. But most readers of Tagalog, mainly on the island of Luzon, prefer comic books to literary novels, however expressive of deep national sentiments. So English remains the language of the elite, and thus of most Filipino literature – though not of the movies, a more popular art.

*

Tagalog will survive for a long time, just as I expect Malayalam will. But many smaller languages continue to disappear, not all because of English. A gentleman named Tefvik Esenc, the last speaker of a Caucasian language called Ubykh, died on his farm in Turkey in 1992. Red Thundercloud, from South Carolina, ran out of people to converse with in Catawba Sioux, and died in 1996. Australia used to have 250 aboriginal languages. Soon there may be none. Yiddish is dying, certainly as a literary language, and Ladino is almost dead. Deaths are always sad events. But I am not sure the ecolinguists always deplore these losses for the right reasons.

When languages die because the speakers are massacred or forced to change, this is indeed deplorable, but the ecolinguists think diversity is a good thing per se, and the loss of any language, no matter how small, and whatever the circumstances of its demise, a loss to humanity. For as Daniel Nettle and Suzanne Romaine, the authors of *Vanishing Voices,* argue: "Each language is a living museum, a monument to every culture it has been vehicle to." This is no doubt true. And living museums are fascinating for linguists and other enthusiasts. But should every living museum be preserved for its own sake? Literature may have an intrinsic value, but do spoken languages? The ecolinguists argue that they do, partly for environmental reasons. Languages, claim Nettle and Romaine, "are like the miner's canary: where languages are in danger, it is a sign of environmental distress."

Is this always true? The Inuit of Nunavut, formerly known as Eskimos, are indeed a threatened community, not by the Canadian government but because they are a dwindling group on the edge of the world. Their suicide rate is horrendous. But they do still speak their native language. Another expression of their identity is shooting rare bowhead whales with .50 caliber hunting rifles. The point here is not to be facetious. The hunts are not just for the meat. They are defended on cultural grounds: shooting whales is deemed essential for the preservation of identity. This, surely, is not what the ecolinguists have in mind.

One reason minority languages have been threatened during the last two centuries is the rise of nationalism. France used to be a country of many languages. But the republican idea of liberty, equality, and fraternity has meant that all French citizens – and preferably the rest of the world as well – should speak French. This has been both a good and a bad thing. A common language strengthened a common sense of citizenship, which, in principle, if not always in practice, transcended race or religion. It was bad in the sense that a common language was forced on Bretons and other minorities to the detriment of their own. This was based on the fallacy that people should speak only one language, as though multilingualism should necessarily tear up the nation.

Nettle and Romaine say we "need to divest ourselves of the traditional equation between language, nation, and state." In fact, the word "traditional" here makes little sense. Most nation-states are not very old, and certainly not eternal. But they are right in that many languages are older than the states which adopted them. The ecolinguists prefer to think of most languages as expressions of culture, local, even tribal culture, languages of the heart, so to speak, rooted in a particular soil. The metropolitan or "global languages," on the other hand, are for "communicating beyond local levels and expressing ourselves as citizens of the world" – that is, they are languages of the head.

This, too, is a questionable claim. German was the main language of the Austro-Hungarian Empire. More citizens of Budapest in the early twentieth century read German-language newspapers than Hungarian ones. German was presumably the language of the head. And yet some of the greatest literature and poetry to emerge from the empire was written in German by people who had no "local" Germanic roots at all. Many of them were Jews, the so-called rootless cosmopolitans, and thus perhaps the most loyal citizens of Franz Joseph's realm: Kafka, Joseph Roth, Musil.

*

To equate language with the state may be wrong, but to equate it entirely with a specific local culture or common ancestry is equally wrong. Another ecolinguist, David Crystal, has a balanced view of culture and language. Language, he says, is a preeminent but not exclusive badge of identity; cultures can continue even after shifting to another language. But then, by way of assessing the catastrophic consequences of losing a language, he asks us to imagine what would have happened if Norman French had displaced Old English after 1066: no Chaucer, Shakespeare, Wordsworth, Dickens. True enough. But that is to assume that Shakespeare could only have expressed himself in English. One might as well turn this imaginary example the other way around. What if English had not displaced Irish as the main language of Ireland? No Joyce, Yeats, Wilde, Shaw. And what are we to make of Beckett, who wrote in French and English, and who, when asked whether he was British, answered "Au contraire"?

Literary genius remains a mystery. The emergence of a Nabokov or Beckett cannot be rationally explained, but ancestry or nationhood surely has very little to do with it. It is generally true, of course, that you gain a feeling for the rhythm and expressiveness of a language by growing up with it, by learning nursery rhymes as a child and talking with other children at school. Literate native speakers can spot a cliché when they hear one. But none of this is essential. A Joseph Conrad can switch languages and still be great, and not because he was expressing "Polishness," let alone "Englishness."

When Conrad began to write his famous novels, English was the lingua franca of a great empire, but not yet of the world. Will the dominance of English produce more Conrads? One of the more interesting literary events of the last few years has been the success of Ha Jin, a Chinese writer in English. Ha was in his twenties when he came to the United States. He is perhaps no Conrad, but his prose is arresting. One of its characteristics is a kind of cultural minimalism, entirely lacking literary or cultural allusions. His novel *Waiting* was set in China, so allusions connected to the English-speaking world would have looked out of place anyway. And yet one wonders whether Ha Jin's work is a harbinger of a new international English style, in which culture and language are entirely disconnected. Kazuo Ishiguro, born in Japan but raised in Britain, did not consciously switch languages (he does not speak Japanese), but he tries to avoid any allusions which can be understood only by native English speakers. He claims to write for the world. The password quality of language, in other words, is deliberately discarded.

The current generation of writers in English with a non-English background is living in a different world from the one inhabited by Conrad, Nabokov, or Arthur Koestler. Before World War II, writers and their readers, whether they came from London, St. Petersburg, or Budapest, still shared cultural references. Literate people had a working knowledge of the Old and New Testaments and classical mythology. There was still such a thing as European, or even Western, civilization. There is much less of that now. The common references today are both global and parochial, that is to say, they are by and large American: Hollywood, pop music, airline and computer jargon. And the consequences of this may be worse, in some respects, for Americans than for speakers of more minor languages.

*

The one big advantage of speaking Dutch or Danish, or even German or Bengali, is that one is forced to be proficient in at least one other language if one is going to function in the modern world. Even the most ardent ecolinguists do not argue for monolingualism. David Crystal speaks of "healthy bilingualism," a somewhat dubious term perhaps (the word "healthy" should be used with care), but his meaning is clear: the native tongue is about history, culture, identity, and literature, while the metropolitan language is for communicating with the wider world. The distinction can be overstated, as I said, but the ability to speak and read more than one language is surely a good thing. Reading another language allows you to understand not only what people from a different place think, but how they think. Not that thoughts or feelings are determined by language. Indeed, the more one learns to understand other languages, the more a common humanity comes into view. This does not resolve human conflict. Wars would still occur even if the whole world spoke English or Esperanto. But you can only understand your own cultural, political, and social place in the world if you understand the world of others, and for that it helps to comprehend what they say.

In some respects, then, the metropole can be a more provincial place than the periphery. With only one language at one's disposal, even if it is the language of the world, others will look either very strange or deceptively similar. They speak English, eat McDonald's hamburgers, and watch Hollywood films, so they must be just like Americans. This can be as misleading as the assumption that because we cannot understand what people say, their thoughts must be foreign to us too.

English is the password language of an international elite, far larger in scale than French or Latin ever was. This is the result of history, of empire building, and the power of the United States. There is nothing about the English language itself that predestined it to dominate. In some distant future, the lingua franca of business and culture could be Chinese – difficult to imagine, perhaps, but theoretically possible.

Millions and millions aspire to join the Anglophone elite. Perhaps one day there will be almost universal comprehension of

English. But the ambition to be understood by everyone will surely be matched by an equally tenacious desire to guard one's own passwords, which cannot be so readily understood. Unlike the retired Dutch education minister, I do not expect Dutch to disappear soon as a primary language. On the contrary, I believe that the superficial uniformity of globalization will provoke the Frisian effect in many places. The Internet, which links the whole world, is seen as an imperialist bastion of English, but in fact is slowly turning into an electronic free-for-all, where people can use any language they like. Indeed the Internet is becoming a repository not just of existing languages, but of virtually extinct languages too. For it is only there, on audio links to cyberspace, that you can still hear such rare Australian Aboriginal languages as Jiwarli, whose last native speaker died in 1986. And that is why I believe that just as we cannot stop ourselves from rebuilding the Tower of Babel, it will be knocked down again and again.

Artificial languages represent the most willful case of switching tongues. Languages that evolve naturally within a culture are usually not an option for those who grow up within that culture; if a Spaniard speaks Spanish, it is probably not the consequence of deliberate choice, the way it would be if the Spaniard spoke Korean. Particularly during the past 150 years, numerous systems – including Balta, Bopal, Dil, Idiom Neutral, Interlingua, Lingua Franca Nova, Mondolingue, Novial, Pasilingua, Spelin, Veltparl, and Volapük – have been invented in the hope that individuals would decide to adopt them as a supplement to the natural languages that define and divide their speakers throughout the world.

"One who hopes" is a translation of the name given to the most successful of the artificial languages, Esperanto, from the pseudonym that its inventor, Ludwig Lazarus Zamenhof (1859–1917), devised for himself. In 1887, Zamenhof, an oculist living in Warsaw, published in Russian a treatise introducing his linguistic concoction. Convinced that the plethora of languages impedes communication and exacerbates strife, Zamenhof hoped that a new, impartial language would promote world peace. And if the imbalance of power among existing languages conferred privilege on speakers of favored languages and handicapped speakers of others, might not Esperanto encourage equality? Within China, Uigur, a Turkic language spoken in Sinkiang Province, lacks the prestige of Mandarin, but if Esperanto became lingua franca, bigotry based on linguistics might not have a chance.

With a limited vocabulary, phonetic spelling, and rationalized grammar, Esperanto is much easier to learn than most natural languages. Zamenhof was a Jew born to a Russian-speaking family in Bialystok. His father taught German and French, and he himself ended up speaking Russian, Yiddish, Hebrew, German, Polish, and French. Exposed to the perils of ethnic and linguistic rancor, Zamenhof hoped that Esperanto would offer neutral ground for universal harmony. It is naïve to believe that violence ends when all speak alike; bitter antagonists share languages in Northern Ireland, Bosnia, and Rwanda. And if anyone is choosing to learn another language in the hope of universal communication, a natural one (e.g., English, Hindi, Chinese, Spanish, Arabic) might be a more efficient investment of time and energy. Yet the number of Esperanto speakers is now, by some estimates, about 2 million. None is monolingual, and, except for a very few whose zealous parents might have taught them Zamenhof's contraption first, virtually all Esperantists are willful translinguals. Many practice and promote their adopted tongue in centers throughout the world and at international conferences. They have made Esperanto a medium for original expression and for translation of canonical world literature. Yet none of the thousands of books published in the language has attracted much readership outside Esperantist circles, nor has the only feature film made in the language, *Incubus* (1965), been a hit. The United Nations has never seriously considered adopting Esperanto as an official language. In July 1996, the Eighty-First World Esperanto Congress met in the Czech Republic and produced *The Prague Manifesto,* which, reproduced below in its original form and in English translation, proclaims the importance of switching to Esperanto.

Manifesto de Prago

Ni, anoj de la tutmonda movado por la progresigo de Esperanto *direktas* ĉi tiun manifeston al ĉiuj registaroj, internaciaj organizoj kaj homoj de bona volo; *deklaras* nian intencon firmvole plulabori por la celoj ĉi tie esprimitaj; kaj *invitas* ĉiun unuopan organizaĵon kaj homon aliĝi al nia strebado. Lanĉita en 1887 kiel projekto de helplingvo por internacia komunikado, kaj rapide evoluinta en vivoplenan, nuancoriĉan lingvon, Esperanto jam de pli ol jarcento funkcias por kunligi homojn trans lingvaj kaj kulturaj baroj. Intertempe, la celoj de ĝiaj parolantoj ne perdis gravecon kaj aktualecon. Nek la tutmonda uzado de kelkaj naciaj lingvoj, nek progresoj en la komunikad-tekniko, nek la malkovro de novaj metodoj de lingvoinstruado verŝajne realigos jenajn principojn, kiun ni konsideras esencaj por justa kaj efika lingva ordo.

1. DEMOKRATIO. Komunika sistemo, kiu tutvive privilegias iujn homojn samtempe postulante de aliaj ke ili investu jarojn da penoj por atingi malpli altan gradon de kapablo, estas fundamente maldemokratia. Kvankam, kiel ĉiu lingvo, Esperanto ne estas perfekta, ĝi ege superas ĉiun rivalon en la sfero de egaleca tutmonda komunikado. Ni asertas ke lingva malegaleco sekvigas komunikan malegalecon je ĉiuj niveloj, inkluzive de la internacia nivelo. Ni estas movado por demokratia komunikado.

2. TRANSNACIA EDUKADO. Ĉiu etna lingvo estas ligita al difinita kulturo kaj naci(ar)o. Ekzemple, lernejano kiu studas la anglan lernas pri la kulturo, geografio kaj politiko de la anglalingvaj landoj, precipe Usono kaj Britio. La lernejano kiu studas Esperanton lernas pri mondo sen limoj, en kiu ĉiu lando prezentiĝas kiel hejmo.

Ni asertas ke la edukado per iu ajn etna lingvo estas ligita al difinita perspektivo pri la mondo. Ni estas movado por transnacia edukado.

3. PEDAGOGIA EFIKECO. Nur malgranda procentaĵo el tiuj, kiuj studas fremdan lingvon, ekmastras ĝin. Plena posedo de Esperanto eblas eĉ per memstudado. Diversaj studoj raportis propedeŭtikajn efikojn al la lernado de aliaj lingvoj. Oni ankaŭ rekomendas Esperanton kiel kerna ero en kursoj por la lingva konsciigo de lernantoj. Ni asertas ke la malfacileco de la etnaj lingvoj ĉiam prezentos obstaklon por multaj lernantoj, kiuj tamen profitus el la scio de dua lingvo. Ni estas movado por efika lingvoinstruado.

4. PLURLINGVECO. La Esperanto-komunumo estas unu el malmultaj mondskalaj lingvokomunumoj kies parolantoj estas senescepte du- aŭ plurlingvaj. Ĉiu komunumano akceptis la taskon lerni almenaŭ unu fremdan lingvon ĝis parola grado. Multokaze tio kondukas al la scio de kaj amo al pluraj lingvoj kaj ĝenerale al pli vasta persona horizonto. Ni asertas ke la anoj de ĉiuj lingvoj, grandaj kaj malgrandaj, devus disponi pri reala ŝanco por alproprigi duan lingvon ĝis alta komunika nivelo. Ni estas movado por la provizo de tiu ŝanco.

5. LINGVAJ RAJTOJ. La malegala disdivido de potenco inter la lingvoj estas recepto por konstanta lingva malsekureco, aŭ rekta lingva subpremado, ĉe granda parto de la monda loĝantaro. En la Esperanto-komunumo, la anoj de lingvoj grandaj kaj malgrandaj, oficialaj kaj neoficialaj, kunvenas sur neŭtrala tereno, dank' al la reciproka volo kompromisi. Tia ekvilibro inter lingvaj rajtoj kaj respondecoj liveras precedencon por evoluigi kaj pritaksi aliajn solvojn al la lingva malegaleco kaj lingvaj konfliktoj. Ni asertas ke la vastaj potencodiferencoj inter la lingvoj subfosas la garantiojn, esprimitajn en tiom da internaciaj dokumentoj, de egaleca traktado sendistinge pri la lingvo. Ni estas movado por lingvaj rajtoj.

6. LINGVA DIVERSECO. La naciaj registaroj emas konsideri la grandan diversecon de lingvoj en la mondo kiel baron al komunikado kaj evoluigo. Por la Esperanto-komunumo, tamen, la lingva diverseco estas konstanta kaj nemalhavebla fonto de riĉeco. Sekve,

ĉiu lingvo, kiel ĉiu vivaĵospecio, estas valora jam pro si mem kaj inda je protektado kaj subtenado. Ni asertas ke la politiko de komunikado kaj evoluigo, se ĝi ne estas bazita sur respekto al kaj subteno de ĉiuj lingvoj, kondamnas al formorto la plimulton de la lingvoj de la mondo. Ni estas movado por lingva diverseco.

7. HOMA EMANCIPIĜO. Ĉiu lingvo liberigas kaj malliberigas siajn anojn, donante al ili la povon komuniki inter si, barante la komunikadon kun aliaj. Planita kiel universala komunikilo, Esperanto estas unu el la grandaj funkciantaj projektoj de la homa emancipiĝo – projekto por ebligi al ĉiu homo partopreni kiel individuo en la homara komunumo, kun firmaj radikoj ĉe sia loka kultura kaj lingva identeco, sed ne limigita de ili. Ni asertas ke la ekskluziva uzado de naciaj lingvoj neeviteble starigas barojn al la liberecoj de sinesprimado, komunikado kaj asociiĝo. Ni estas movado por la homa emancipiĝo.

The Prague Manifesto (English Translation)

We, members of the worldwide movement for the promotion of Esperanto, address this manifesto to all governments, international organizations and people of good will; declare our unshakeable commitment to the objectives set out here; and call on all organizations and individuals to join us in working for these goals. For more than a century Esperanto, which was launched in 1887 as a project for an auxiliary language for international communication and quickly developed into a rich living language in its own right, has functioned as a means of bringing people together across the barriers of language and culture. The aims that inspire the users of Esperanto are still as important and relevant as ever. Neither the worldwide use of a few national languages, nor advances in communications technology, nor the development of new methods of language teaching is likely to result in a fair and effective language order based on the following principles, which we hold to be essential.

1. DEMOCRACY. Any system of communication which confers lifelong privileges on some while requiring others to devote years of effort to achieving a lesser degree of competence is fundamentally antidemocratic. While Esperanto, like any language, is not perfect, it far outstrips other languages as a means of egalitarian communication on a world scale. We maintain that language inequality gives rise to communicative inequality at all levels, including the international level. We are a movement for democratic communication.

2. GLOBAL EDUCATION. All ethnic languages are bound to certain cultures and nations. For example, the child who learns

English learns about the culture, geography and political systems of the English-speaking world, primarily the United States and the United Kingdom. The child who learns Esperanto learns about a world without borders, where every country is home. We maintain that education in any language is bound to a certain view of the world. We are a movement for global education.

3. EFFECTIVE EDUCATION. Only a small percentage of foreign-language students attain fluency in the target language. In Esperanto, fluency is attainable even through home study. Various studies have shown that Esperanto is useful as a preparation for learning other languages. It has also been recommended as a core element in courses in language awareness. We maintain that the difficulties in learning ethnic languages will always be a barrier for many students who would benefit from knowing a second language. We are a movement for effective language learning.

4. MULTILINGUALISM. The Esperanto community is almost unique as a worldwide community whose members are universally bilingual or multilingual. Every member of the community has made the effort to learn at least one foreign language to a communicative level. In many cases this leads to a love and knowledge of several languages and to broader personal horizons in general. We maintain that the speakers of all languages, large and small, should have a real chance of learning a second language to a high communicative level. We are a movement for providing that opportunity to all.

5. LANGUAGE RIGHTS. The unequal distribution of power between languages is a recipe for permanent language insecurity, or outright language oppression, for a large part of the world's population. In the Esperanto community the speakers of languages large and small, official and unofficial, meet on equal terms through a mutual willingness to compromise. This balance of language rights and responsibilities provides a benchmark for developing and judging other solutions to language inequality and conflict. We maintain that the wide variations in power among languages undermine the guarantees, expressed in many international instruments,

of equal treatment regardless of language. We are a movement for language rights.

6. LANGUAGE DIVERSITY. National governments tend to treat the great diversity of languages in the world as a barrier to communication and development. In the Esperanto community, however, language diversity is experienced as a constant and indispensable source of enrichment. Consequently every language, like every biological species, is inherently valuable and worthy of protection and support. We maintain that communication and development policies which are not based on respect and support for all languages amount to a death sentence for the majority of languages in the world. We are a movement for language diversity.

7. HUMAN EMANCIPATION. Every language both liberates and imprisons its users, giving them the ability to communicate among themselves but barring them from communication with others. Designed as a universally accessible means of communication, Esperanto is one of the great functional projects for the emancipation of humankind – one which aims to let every individual citizen participate fully in the human community, securely rooted in his or her local cultural and language identity yet not limited by it. We maintain that exclusive reliance on national languages inevitably puts up barriers to the freedoms of expression, communication and association. We are a movement for human emancipation.

Prague, July 1996

LÉOPOLD SÉDAR SENGHOR (1906–2001)

Léopold Sédar Senghor grew up speaking Serer in his native Joal, Senegal. Though he did not learn his first words of French, at a local Roman Catholic mission school, until he was seven, he became one of the leading French poets of the twentieth century. In 1928, Senghor received a partial scholarship to study in Paris, and by 1935, after becoming the only African to pass the rigorous *agrégation* requirements, he was teaching French to French students in Tours. Senghor was an officer in the French army during World War II when he was captured by the Germans and sent to a concentration camp. He later served as a deputy from Senegal in the National Assembly and, advocating an African brand of socialism, was a persuasive voice for granting independence to the peoples of French West Africa. When Senegal became independent, Senghor was elected its first president, and he continued serving in that position until the middle of his fifth elected term, in 1980.

Along with Aimé Césaire of Martinique and Léon Damas of Guiana, Senghor championed the concept of Négritude, an affirmation of the unity and validity of black experience throughout the world. In 1947, he cofounded *Présence africaine,* an influential journal of black culture, and a poetry anthology that he edited in 1948, *Anthologie de la nouvelle poésie nègre et malgache,* was instrumental in spreading knowledge of the continent's poetry. Collections of his own poetry include *Chants d'ombre* (Songs of shadow, 1945); *Hosties noires* (Black offerings, 1948); *Ethiopiques* (1956); *Nocturnes* (1961); and *Elégies majeures* (Major elegies, 1979). In 1984, Senghor became the first black ever inducted into the French Academy.

Though he translated some African poetry from indigenous languages, French is Senghor's principal medium of expression. In numerous forums, including the November 1962 issue of the journal *Esprit,* where this essay first appeared, he has praised French, the lingua franca of Francophone nations spread throughout the world, as an instrument of enlightenment. Senghor's embrace of the French language has been mocked and scorned by some postcolonialist critics, but a careful reading of his essay makes it clear that the author is not oblivious to the imperfections and abuses of French society. However, French, Senghor's adopted language, represents for him an ideal of universal civilization.

French, Language of Culture

It was in 1937. I had then been teaching French, along with the classical languages, for two years, at the Lycée Descartes in Tours. During vacation in my native Senegal, I was invited to give a talk. As my topic, I had chosen "The Cultural Problem in French West Africa." A crowd of the "sophisticated," white and black together, was packed into the large hall of the Dakar Chamber of Commerce. They were expecting to hear me extol Greco-Roman culture, or at least French culture. In front of the astonished governor general, I launched a vigorous attack against *assimilation* and extolled *Négritude,* advocating a return to our roots: to the black African languages. It was a *succès de scandale,* more, all things considered, among the Africans than among the Europeans. "Now that he has learned Latin and Greek," murmured the former, "he wants to drag us back to Wolof."

Despite political independence – or autonomy – proclaimed, two years earlier, in all the former "Overseas Territories," despite the popularity enjoyed by Négritude in the Francophone sub-Saharan states, *French* had lost none of its prestige. It was everywhere proclaimed the *official language* of the state, and its radiance was only spreading, even in Mali, even in Guinea. Moreover, following Ghana, itself no fan of France, the Anglophone nations one after another introduced French into their secondary school curricula, sometimes even making it a requirement.

How can we explain this favor, this fervor, particularly this *disjunction* between French politics and culture? That is the focus of my remarks.

Let me make a preliminary observation. This disjunction is more apparent than real. *Decolonization,* which General de Gaulle pursued steadily and achieved brilliantly in Algeria, did not count for nothing. In Africa, the mind does not submit to *dichotomy.* Unlike Europeans, Africans do not separate *culture* from *politics.* The conflict in Bizerte almost drove French out of Tunisian schools.

Thus, if the teaching of French is introduced or maintained in Africa, if it is strengthened, it is, first of all, because of political reasons. In Anglophone Africa more than anywhere else. To all other reasons, add the following: that the majority of African states are Francophone and, at the UN, a third of the delegations speak French. In 1960, after the massive admission of new African nations into the international organization, Habib Bourguiba drew the logical conclusion: It was necessary to strengthen the teaching of French in Tunisia. In practice, Hassan II has not pursued a different policy. Morocco alone counts nine thousand French "educators," more than half of those who serve abroad.

However, the principal reason for the expansion of French beyond the metropolis, for the birth of a *Francophonia,* is a cultural matter. This is the place to answer the question posed to me personally by *Esprit:* "What does the use of French represent for a black writer?" Of course, I shall not refrain from answering later. But allow me just to expand the discussion, to answer in the name of all the black elites, of the politicians as well as of the writers. If so, I am convinced that part of the discussion applies as well to the North Africans – I am thinking in particular about the late Jean Amrouche – although they are better qualified than I to speak for themselves.

There is, first of all, a de facto reason. Among the elites, many, thinking in French, speak French better than their mother tongue, diluted as it is with Francisms, at least in the cities. To take a national example, at Radio Dakar, the broadcasts in French are purer than the broadcasts in the vernaculars. Moreover, it is not always easy, for the uninitiated, to distinguish the voices of the Senegalese from the voices of the French.

Second reason: the richness of French vocabulary. Because of its series of twins, either popular or learned in origin, it contains a multiplicity of *synonyms.* I am well aware that, contrary to what the average Frenchman believes, the black African languages possess remarkable richness and flexibility. But where the Frenchman employs a Latin word to designate a tree, a paraphrase to designate an action, the black African employs a single noun or a single verb. As noted by André Davesne, in *Croquis de brousse,* there are, in Wolof, seven words to designate a woman of ill repute while "to seek is translated by eleven words and to sing by twenty." But what, on first view, constitutes the strength of black African languages at the same time constitutes their weakness. They are *poetic languages.* Their words, almost always concrete, are *pregnant* with images. The arrangement of words within clauses, of clauses within sentences, is a function more of sensibility than intelligibility, of the heart than of the reason. What in the final analysis proves the superiority of French in this matter is that it also provides us with a technical and scientific vocabulary that is unsurpassed. Finally, a profusion of those *abstract* words that our languages lack.

Third reason: French syntax. Because it is stocked with an abundant vocabulary, thanks, in part, to its reserves of Latin and Greek, French is a concise language. By the same token, it is a precise and nuanced language, therefore clear. It is, consequently, a *discursive* language, which puts every fact, every argument in its place, without neglecting any. *A language of analysis,* French is no less *a language of synthesis.* One cannot analyze without synthesizing; one cannot differentiate without recombining; one cannot expose a contradiction without transcending it. If French has not retained all its technical rigor from Latin, it has inherited an entire series of cornerstone words, cement words, linchpin words. *Implement words,* conjunctions and conjunctive locutions link one proposition to another, one idea to another, subordinating them to one another. They indicate the stages necessary for active thought, for reasoning. Proof of this is that black intellectuals have had to borrow these tools from French in order to *bolster* their vernaculars. To the *syntax of juxtaposition* of the black African languages is opposed the *syntax of subordination* of French; to the syntax of the lived concrete, that of the abstract conceived: in short, the syntax of reason to that of emotion.

Fourth reason: French stylistics. French style could be defined as a *symbiosis* of Greek subtlety and Latin rigor, a symbiosis enlivened by Celtic passion. It is *ordination* more than order. Its genius is to reach into the vast dictionary of the universe in order to construct – out of materials thus assembled, facts, emotions, ideas – a new world: that of *Man.* An ideal world, and at the same time real, because it derives from Man, where everything, arranged in its place, converges interdependently toward the same goal.

It is thus that French prose – and the poem until the time of the Surrealists – has taught us to rely on facts and ideas in order to elucidate the universe; indeed, in order to express the internal world through coherent *restructuration* of the universe.

Fifth reason: French Humanism. It is, precisely, of this elucidation, of this *re-creation,* that French Humanism consists. For it has Man as object of its activity. Whether it is a question of Law, Literature, Art, indeed of Science, the mark of the French genius remains this concern with Man. French expresses, always, a moral code. From that derives its quality of *universality,* which serves as a corrective to its taste for individualism.

I know the criticism leveled at this humanism of the *honnête homme,* the reasonable man: it is a closed, static system that is based on *equilibrium.* A few years ago, I gave a talk entitled "The Humanism of the French Union." My purpose was to show how, in contact with "colonial" realities, that is, the overseas territories, French humanism was enriched, deepening and enlarging itself, in order to integrate the *values* of those civilizations. How it had passed *from assimilation to cooperation:* to symbiosis. From a static morality to the morality of movement dear to Pierre Teilhard de Chardin. As Jean Daniel noted about Algeria, in the *Express* of 28 June 1962, Colonizers and Colonized are, in reality, reciprocally colonized: "It [the nation of France] is so fully impregnated by the civilizations that it intended to dominate that the colonized today create for it a different fate, seeing in this executioner a powerful victim, in this alienator an alienated, in this enemy an accomplice." I just want to note here the positive contribution of Colonization, which is apparent at the dawn of independence. Yesterday's enemy is an accomplice who enriches us while enriching itself by contact with us.

Yet before finishing, I need to address the question that was posed to me personally. For these reasons are as much those of the politicians, who want to direct both the economic and the cultural development of their peoples in order to assure them more than well-being, *best-being. What does the use of French represent for me, a black writer?* The question deserves a response all the more in that it is addressed to a *Poet* and I defined the black African languages as *"poetic languages."*

In response, I return to the de facto argument. I think in French; I express myself better in French than in my mother tongue.

There is also the fact that any child placed young enough within a foreign country will learn its language as easily as do the natives. That testifies to the resiliency of the human mind and to the fact that any language can express the entirety of the human soul. Each simply emphasizes one or another aspect of that soul while translating it in *its* manner.

Yet it is the case that French is, contrary to what has been said, *an eminently poetic language.* Not because of its clarity, but because of its richness. Certainly, it was, until the nineteenth century, a language of moralists, jurists, and diplomats: "A language of courtesy and honor." But it was then that along came Victor Hugo, who, overthrowing Malherbe's noble and austere arrangement, put "a red stocking cap on the old dictionary." In the same blow, he liberated a throng of taboo words: jumbled together, concrete words and abstract words, learned words and technical words, popular words and exotic words. And then, a century later, came the Surrealists, who were not content with tossing the *discursive poem* out of the French garden. They discarded all the linchpin words, delivering to us naked poems, panting with the very rhythm of the soul. They had rediscovered the *black syntax of juxtaposition,* where words, telescoped, burst forth in flames of metaphor: of *symbol.* The groundwork, as we see, had been laid for a *black poetry in the French language.*

Of course, they tell me, but what has been the advantage of French for those who have command of a black African language? The advantage was, essentially, the richness of vocabulary and the fact that French is a language with an *international audience.* Let's put aside this last fact, which is obvious enough that it needs no explication. The advantage of French was – is – to offer us a choice: "The Black," writes André Davesne in *Croquis de brousse,* "is thus prepared, by his verbal traditions, to distinguish, in the words that the French language provides him, two values: one abstract and intellectual, signification; the other concrete and sensuous, musicality. If he therefore, without hesitation, undertakes apprenticeship in our language, he will draw upon a double treasury of words: one group that designates something that is tangible, an object, for example, and whose meaning cannot be deflected; another whose use is less consistent and whose meaning is too mysterious or too 'intellectual' to become definite in the use to which it is put but which deserves to be used because of tonality and resonance."

Out of what is instinctive among illiterates, we have been able to make a *poetics,* a deliberate method of creation. The problem is, after all, more complex than Davesne admits. It is all the French words that, through violation and recovery, are able to light the flame of metaphor. All that is necessary is to uproot the most "intellectual" words, excavating their etymologies, in order to deliver them to the sunshine of the symbol.

As we have seen, vocabulary alone does not exhaust the virtues of French. Stylistics, in particular, provides the opportunity for miraculous finds. To get back to the music of words, French offers a variety of timbres from which every effect can be drawn; from the sweetness of the trade winds at night against the lofty palms, to the violence of lightning flashing over the tops of the baobabs. Even the rhythms of French offer unsuspected resources. The binary rhythm of classical verse can, after all, render the despotic panting of the tom-tom. It is sufficient to jostle it slightly for contretemps and syncopations to surge up out of the base rhythm.

What can we conclude from all of this if not that we, black politicians, we, black writers, feel at least as free within French as within our mother tongues. More free, in truth, since *Freedom* is measured by the power of the tool: by the force of creation.

It is not a question of renouncing the African languages. For centuries, perhaps millennia, they will still be spoken, expressing the vast immensities of *Négritude.* We shall continue to fish for *archetype images* in them: fish of great depths. It is a question of expressing our *authenticity* as cultural hybrids, as men of the twentieth century. At the moment when, through *totalization* and *socialization,* the *Civilization of the Universal* is constructed, it is, in a word, a matter of our using this marvelous tool, found within the ruins of the colonial regime. This tool that is the French language.

Francophonie is that *integral Humanism* that is woven into the earth: that *symbiosis* of "dormant energies" of all the continents, all the races, awakening to their complementary ardor. "France," an FLN [Algerian National Liberation Front] representative was saying to me, "is you, is me: It is French Culture." Let's reverse the proposition in order to be complete: *Négritude, Arabism,* they are also you, you metropolitan French. *Our* values give vigor, now, to the books that you read, the language that you speak: *French,* the Sun that shines beyond the Metropolis.

Translated by Steven G. Kellman

GLORIA ANZALDÚA (1942–)

Born in the Rio Grande Valley of South Texas, Gloria Anzaldúa is an educator and activist who presents herself as a Chicana, feminist, and lesbian. Bilingual in Spanish and English and adept at different registers of each of those two languages, she demonstrates and celebrates her hybrid identity through frequent code switching, the blending of different languages within the same text. Anzaldúa has published an autobiographical novel, *La prieta* (1997), as well as the bilingual children's book *Friends from the Other Side/Amigos del otro lado* (1993) and the compilation *Interviews/Entrevistas* (2000). "How to Tame a Wild Tongue" is reprinted from *Borderlands/La frontera: The New Mestiza* (1987), a mixed genre collection that proclaims the author's defiant pride in her eclectic heritage.

How to Tame a Wild Tongue

"We're going to have to control your tongue," the dentist says, pulling out all the metal from my mouth. Silver bits plop and tinkle into the basin. My mouth is a motherlode.

The dentist is cleaning out my roots. I get a whiff of the stench when I gasp. "I can't cap that tooth yet, you're still draining," he says.

"We're going to have to do something about your tongue," I hear the anger rising in his voice. My tongue keeps pushing out the wads of cotton, pushing back the drills, the long thin needles. "I've never seen anything as strong or as stubborn," he says. And I think, how do you tame a wild tongue, train it to be quiet, how do you bridle and saddle it? How do you make it lie down?

> Who is to say that robbing a people of
> its language is less violent than war?
> – Ray Gwyn Smith[1]

I remember being caught speaking Spanish at recess – that was good for three licks on the knuckles with a sharp ruler. I remember being sent to the corner of the classroom for "talking back" to the Anglo teacher when all I was trying to do was tell her how to pronounce my name. "If you want to be American, speak 'American.' If you don't like it, go back to Mexico where you belong."

"I want you to speak English. *Pa' hallar buen trabajo tienes que saber hablar el inglés bien. Qué vale toda tu educación si todavía hablas inglés con un* 'accent,'" my mother would say, mortified that I spoke English like a Mexican. At Pan American University, I and all Chicano students were required to take two speech classes. Their purpose: to get rid of our accents.

Attacks on one's form of expression with the intent to censor are a violation of the First Amendment. *El Anglo con cara de inocente nos arrancó la lengua.* Wild tongues can't be tamed, they can only be cut out.

Overcoming the Tradition of Silence

Ahogadas, escupimos el oscuro.
Peleando con nuestra propia sombra
el silencio nos sepulta.

En boca cerrada no entran moscas. "Flies don't enter a closed mouth" is a saying I kept hearing when I was a child. *Ser habladora* was to be a gossip and a liar, to talk too much. *Muchachitas bien criadas,* well-bred girls, don't answer back. *Es una falta de respeto* to talk back to one's mother or father. I remember one of the sins I'd recite to the priest in the confession box the few times I went to confession: talking back to my mother, *hablar pa' 'tras, repelar. Hocicona, repelona, chismosa,* having a big mouth, questioning, carrying tales are all signs of being *mal criada.* In my culture they are all words that are derogatory if applied to women – I've never heard them applied to men.

The first time I heard two women, a Puerto Rican and a Cuban, say the word "*nosotras,*" I was shocked. I had not known the word existed. Chicanas use "*nosotros*" whether we're male or female. We are robbed of our female being by the masculine plural. Language is a male discourse.

And our tongues have become
dry   the wilderness has
dried out our tongues   and
we have forgotten speech.
– Irena Klepfisz[2]

Even our own people, other Spanish speakers *nos quieren poner candados en la boca.* They would hold us back with their bag of *reglas de academia.*

Oyé como ladra: El lenguaje de la frontera

Quien tiene boca se equivoca. – Mexican saying

"*Pocho,* cultural traitor, you're speaking the oppressor's language by speaking English, you're ruining the Spanish language," I have been accused by various Latinos and Latinas. Chicano Spanish is considered by the purist and by most Latinos deficient, a mutilation of Spanish.

But Chicano Spanish is a border tongue which developed naturally. Change, *evolución, enriquecimiento de palabras nuevas por invención o adopción* have created variants of Chicano Spanish, *un nuevo lenguaje. Un lenguaje que corresponde a un modo de vivir.* Chicano Spanish is not incorrect, it is a living language.

For a people who are neither Spanish nor live in a country in which Spanish is the first language; for a people who live in a country in which English is the reigning tongue but who are not Anglo; for a people who cannot entirely identify with either standard (formal, Castillian) Spanish nor standard English, what recourse is left to them but to create their own language? A language which they can connect their identity to, one capable of communicating the realities and values true to themselves – a language with terms that are neither *español ni inglés,* but both. We speak a patois, a forked tongue, a variation of two languages.

Chicano Spanish sprang out of the Chicanos' need to identify ourselves as a distinct people. We needed a language with which we could communicate with ourselves, a secret language. For some of us, language is a homeland closer than the Southwest – for many Chicanos today live in the Midwest and the East. And because we are a complex, heterogeneous people, we speak many languages. Some of the languages we speak are:

1. Standard English
2. Working-class and slang English
3. Standard Spanish
4. Standard Mexican Spanish
5. North Mexican Spanish dialect
6. Chicano Spanish (Texas, New Mexico, Arizona and California have regional variations)
7. Tex-Mex
8. *Pachuco* (called *caló*)

My "home" tongues are the languages I speak with my sister and brothers, with my friends. They are the last five listed, with 6 and 7 being closest to my heart. From school, the media and job situations, I've picked up standard and working-class English. From Mamagrande Locha and from reading Spanish and Mexican literature, I've picked up Standard Spanish and Standard Mexican Spanish. From *los recién llegados,* Mexican immigrants, and *braceros,* I learned the North Mexican dialect. With Mexicans I'll try to speak either Standard Mexican Spanish or the North Mexican dialect. From my parents and Chicanos living in the Valley, I picked up Chicano Texas Spanish, and I speak it with my mom, younger brother (who married a Mexican and who rarely mixes Spanish with English), aunts and older relatives.

With Chicanas from *Nuevo México* or *Arizona* I will speak Chicano Spanish a little, but often they don't understand what I'm saying. With most California Chicanas I speak entirely in English (unless I forget). When I first moved to San Francisco, I'd rattle off something in Spanish, unintentionally embarrassing them. Often it is only with another Chicana *tejana* that I can talk freely.

Words distorted by English are known as anglicisms or *pochismos.* The *pocho* is an anglicized Mexican or American of Mexican origin who speaks Spanish with an accent characteristic of North Americans and who distorts and reconstructs the language according to the influence of English.[3] Tex-Mex, or Spanglish, comes most naturally to me. I may switch back and forth from English to Spanish in the same sentence or in the same word. With my sister and my brother Nune and with Chicano *tejano* contemporaries I speak in Tex-Mex.

From kids and people my own age I picked up *Pachuco. Pachuco* (the language of the zoot suiters) is a language of rebellion, both against Standard Spanish and Standard English. It is a secret language. Adults of the culture and outsiders cannot understand it. It is made up of slang words from both English and Spanish. *Ruca* means girl or woman, *vato* means guy or dude, *chale* means no, *simón* means yes, *churro* is sure, talk is *periquiar, pigionear* means petting, *que gacho* means how nerdy, *ponte águila* means watch out, death is called *la pelona.* Through lack of practice and not having others who can speak it, I've lost most of the *Pachuco* tongue.

Chicano Spanish

Chicanos, after 250 years of Spanish/Anglo colonization, have developed significant differences in the Spanish we speak. We collapse two adjacent vowels into a single syllable and sometimes shift the stress in certain words such as *maíz/maiz, cohete/cuete.* We leave out certain consonants when they appear between vowels: *lado/lao, mojado/mojao.* Chicanos from South Texas pronounce *f* as *j* as in *jue* (*fue*). Chicanos use "archaisms," words that are no longer in the Spanish language, words that have been evolved out. We say *semos, truje, haiga, ansina,* and *naiden.* We retain the "archaic" *j,* as in *jalar,* that derives from an earlier *h* (the French *halar* or the Germanic *halon,* which was lost to standard Spanish in the sixteenth century), but which is still found in several regional dialects such as the one spoken in South Texas. (Due to geography, Chicanos from the Valley of South Texas were cut off linguistically from other Spanish speakers. We tend to use words that the Spaniards brought over from Medieval Spain. The majority of the Spanish colonizers in Mexico and the Southwest came from Extremadura – Hernán Cortés was one of them – and Andalucía. Andalucians pronounce *ll* like a *y,* and their *d*'s tend to be absorbed by adjacent vowels: *tirado* becomes *tirao.* They brought *el lenguaje popular, dialectos y regionalismos.*)[4]

Chicanos and other Spanish speakers also shift *ll* to *y* and *z* to *s.*[5] We leave out initial syllables, saying *tar* for *estar, toy* for *estoy, hora* for *ahora* (*cubanos* and *puertorriqueños* also leave out initial letters of some words). We also leave out the final syllable such as *pa* for *para.* The intervocalic *y,* the *ll* as in *tortilla, ella, botella,* gets replaced by *tortia* or *tortiya, ea, botea.* We add an additional syllable at the beginning of certain words: *atocar* for *tocar, agastar* for *gastar.* Sometimes we'll say *lavaste las vacijas,* other times *lavates* (substituting the *ates* verb endings for the *aste*).

We use anglicisms, words borrowed from English: *bola* from ball, *carpeta* from carpet, *máchina de lavar* (instead of *lavadora*) from washing machine. Tex-Mex argot, created by adding a Spanish sound at the beginning or end of an English word such as *cookiar* for cook, *watchar* for watch, *parkiar* for park, and *rapiar* for rape, is the result of the pressures on Spanish speakers to adapt to English.

We don't use the word *vosotros/as* or its accompanying verb form. We don't say *claro* (to mean yes), *imagínate,* or *me emociona,* unless we picked up Spanish from Latinas, out of a book, or in a classroom. Other Spanish-speaking groups are going through the same, or similar, development in their Spanish.

Linguistic Terrorism

> *Deslenguadas. Somos los del español deficiente.* We are your linguistic nightmare, your linguistic aberration, your linguistic *mestisaje,* the subject of your *burla.* Because we speak with tongues of fire we are culturally crucified. Racially, culturally and linguistically *somos huérfanos* – we speak an orphan tongue.

Chicanas who grew up speaking Chicano Spanish have internalized the belief that we speak poor Spanish. It is illegitimate, a bastard language. And because we internalize how our language has been used against us by the dominant culture, we use our language differences against each other.

Chicana feminists often skirt around each other with suspicion and hesitation. For the longest time I couldn't figure it out. Then it dawned on me. To be close to another Chicana is like looking into the mirror. We are afraid of what we'll see there. *Pena.* Shame. Low estimation of self. In childhood we are told that our language is wrong. Repeated attacks on our native tongue diminish our sense of self. The attacks continue throughout our lives.

Chicanas feel uncomfortable talking in Spanish to Latinas, afraid of their censure. Their language was not outlawed in their countries. They had a whole lifetime of being immersed in their native tongue; generations, centuries in which Spanish was a first language, taught in school, heard on radio and TV, and read in the newspaper.

If a person, Chicana or Latina, has a low estimation of my native tongue, she also has a low estimation of me. Often with *mexicanas y latinas* we'll speak English as a neutral language. Even among Chicanas we tend to speak English at parties or conferences. Yet, at the same time, we're afraid the other will think we're *agringadas* because we don't speak Chicano Spanish. We oppress each other trying to out-Chicano each other, vying to be the "real" Chicanas, to speak like Chicanos. There is no one Chicano language just as there is no one Chicano experience. A monolingual Chicana whose first language is English or Spanish is just as much a Chicana as one who speaks several variants of Spanish. A Chicana from Michigan or Chicago or Detroit is just as much a Chicana as one from the Southwest. Chicano Spanish is as diverse linguistically as it is regionally.

By the end of this century, Spanish speakers will comprise the biggest minority group in the United States, a country where students in high schools and colleges are encouraged to take French classes because French is considered more "cultured." But for a language to remain alive it must be used.[6] By the end of this century

English, and not Spanish, will be the mother tongue of most Chicanos and Latinos.

So, if you want to really hurt me, talk badly about my language. Ethnic identity is twin skin to linguistic identity – I am my language. Until I can take pride in my language, I cannot take pride in myself. Until I can accept as legitimate Chicano Texas Spanish, Tex-Mex and all the other languages I speak, I cannot accept the legitimacy of myself. Until I am free to write bilingually and to switch codes without having always to translate, while I still have to speak English or Spanish when I would rather speak Spanglish, and as long as I have to accommodate the English speakers rather than having them accommodate me, my tongue will be illegitimate.

I will no longer be made to feel ashamed of existing. I will have my voice: Indian, Spanish, white. I will have my serpent's tongue – my woman's voice, my sexual voice, my poet's voice. I will overcome the tradition of silence.

> My fingers
> move sly against your palm
> Like women everywhere, we speak in code.
> —Melanie Kaye/Kantrowitz[7]

"Vistas," corridos, y comida: My Native Tongue

In the 1960s, I read my first Chicano novel. It was *City of Night* by John Rechy, a gay Texan, son of a Scottish father and a Mexican mother. For days I walked around in stunned amazement that a Chicano could write and could get published. When I read *I Am Joaquín*,[8] I was surprised to see a bilingual book by a Chicano in print. When I saw poetry written in Tex-Mex for the first time, a feeling of pure joy flashed through me. I felt like we really existed as a people. In 1971, when I started teaching high school English to Chicano students, I tried to supplement the required texts with works by Chicanos, only to be reprimanded and forbidden to do so by the principal. He claimed that I was supposed to teach "American" and English literature. At the risk of being fired, I swore my students to secrecy and slipped in Chicano short stories, poems, a play. In graduate school, while working toward a Ph.D., I had to "argue" with one adviser after the other, semester after semester, before I was allowed to make Chicano literature an area of focus.

Even before I read books by Chicanos or Mexicans, it was the Mexican movies I saw at the drive-in – the Thursday night special of $1.00 a carload – that gave me a sense of belonging. *"Vámonos a las vistas,"* my mother would call out and we'd all – grandmother, brothers, sister and cousins – squeeze into the car. We'd wolf down cheese and bologna white bread sandwiches while watching Pedro Infante in melodramatic tearjerkers like *Nosotros los pobres,* the first "real" Mexican movie (that was not an imitation of European movies). I remember seeing *Cuando los hijos se van* and surmising that all Mexican movies played up the love a mother has for her children and what ungrateful sons and daughters suffer when they are not devoted to their mothers. I remember the singing-type "westerns" of Jorge Negrete and Miquel Aceves Mejía. When watching Mexican movies, I felt a sense of homecoming as well as alienation. People who were to amount to something didn't go to Mexican movies, or *bailes* or tune their radios to *bolero, rancherita,* and *corrido* music.

The whole time I was growing up, there was *norteño* music, sometimes called North Mexican border music, or Tex-Mex music, or Chicano music, or *cantina* (bar) music. I grew up listening to *conjuntos,* three- or four-piece bands made up of folk musicians playing guitar, *bajo sexto,* drums and button accordion, which Chicanos had borrowed from the German immigrants who had come to Central Texas and Mexico to farm and build breweries. In the Rio Grande Valley, Steve Jordan and Little Joe Hernández were popular, and Flaco Jiménez was the accordion king. The rhythms of Tex-Mex music are those of the polka, also adapted from the Germans, who in turn had borrowed the polka from the Czechs and Bohemians.

I remember the hot, sultry evenings when *corridos* – songs of love and death on the Texas-Mexican borderlands – reverberated out of cheap amplifiers from the local *cantinas* and wafted in through my bedroom window.

Corridos first became widely used along the South Texas/Mexican border during the early conflict between Chicanos and Anglos. The *corridos* are usually about Mexican heroes who do valiant deeds against the Anglo oppressors. Pancho Villa's song, "*La cucaracha*," is the most famous one. *Corridos* of John F. Kennedy and his death are still very popular in the Valley. Older Chicanos remember Lydia Mendoza, one of the great border *corrido* singers who was called *la Gloria de Tejas*. Her "*El tango negro*," sung during the Great Depression, made her a singer of the people. The ever-present *corridos* narrated one hundred years of border history, bringing news of events as well as entertaining. These folk musicians and folk songs are our chief cultural myth-makers, and they made our hard lives seem bearable.

I grew up feeling ambivalent about our music. Country-western and rock-and-roll had more status. In the 1950s and 1960s, for the slightly educated and *agringado* Chicanos, there existed a sense of shame at being caught listening to our music. Yet I couldn't stop my feet from thumping to the music, could not stop humming the words, nor hide from myself the exhilaration I felt when I heard it.

There are more subtle ways that we internalize identification, especially in the forms of images and emotions. For me food and certain smells are tied to my identity, to my homeland. Woodsmoke curling up to an immense blue sky; woodsmoke perfuming my grandmother's clothes, her skin. The stench of cow manure and the yellow patches on the ground; the crack of .22 rifle and the reek of cordite. Homemade white cheese sizzling in a pan, melting inside a folded *tortilla*. My sister Hilda's hot, spicy *menudo, chile colorado* making it deep red, pieces of *panza* and hominy floating on top. My brother Carito barbequing *fajitas* in the backyard. Even now and 3,000 miles away, I can see my mother spicing the ground beef, pork and venison with *chile*. My mouth salivates at the thought of the hot steaming *tamales* I would be eating if I were home.

Si le preguntas a mi mamá, "¿Qué eres?"

> Identity is the essential core of who
> we are as individuals, the conscious
> experience of the self inside.
> – Kaufman[9]

Nosotros los Chicanos straddle the borderlands. On one side of us, we are constantly exposed to the Spanish of the Mexicans; on the other side we hear the Anglos' incessant clamoring so that we forget our language. Among ourselves we don't say *nosotros los americanos, o nosotros los españoles, o nosotros los hispanos.* We say *nosotros los mexicanos* (by *mexicanos* we do not mean citizens of Mexico; we do not mean a national identity, but a racial one). We distinguish between *mexicanos del otro lado* and *mexicanos de este lado.* Deep in our hearts we believe that being Mexican has nothing to do with which country one lives in. Being Mexican is a state of soul – not one of mind, not one of citizenship. Neither eagle nor serpent, but both. And like the ocean, neither animal respects borders.

> *Dime con quien andas y te diré quien eres.*
> (Tell me who your friends are and
> I'll tell you who you are.)
> – Mexican saying

Si le preguntas a mi mamá, "¿Qué eres?" te dirá, "Soy mexicana." My brothers and sister say the same. I sometimes will answer, *"soy mexicana,"* and at others will say, *"soy Chicana" o "soy tejana."* But I identified as *"Raza"* before I ever identified as *"mexicana"* or "Chicana."

As a culture, we call ourselves Spanish when referring to ourselves as a linguistic group and when copping out. It is then that we forget our predominant Indian genes. We are 70–80 percent Indian.[10] We call ourselves Hispanic[11] or Spanish-American or Latin American or Latin when linking ourselves to other Spanish-speaking peoples of the Western hemisphere and when copping out. We call ourselves Mexican-American[12] to signify we are neither Mexican nor American, but more the noun "American" than the adjective "Mexican" (and when copping out).

Chicanos and other people of color suffer economically for not acculturating. This voluntary (yet forced) alienation makes for psychological conflict, a kind of dual identity – we don't identify with the Anglo-American cultural values and we don't totally identify with the Mexican cultural values. We are a synergy of two cultures with various degrees of Mexicanness or Angloness. I have so internalized the borderland conflict that sometimes I feel like one cancels out the other and we are zero, nothing, no one. *A veces no soy nada ni nadie. Pero hasta cuando no lo soy, lo soy.*

When not copping out, when we know we are more than nothing, we call ourselves Mexican, referring to race and ancestry; *mestizo* when affirming both our Indian and Spanish (but we hardly ever own our black ancestry); Chicano when referring to a politically aware people born and/or raised in the United States; *Raza* when referring to Chicanos; *tejanos* when we are Chicanos from Texas.

Chicanos did not know we were a people until 1965, when Cesar Chavez and the farmworkers united and *I Am Joaquin* was published and *la Raza Unida* party was formed in Texas. With that recognition, we became a distinct people. Something momentous happened to the Chicano soul – we became aware of our reality and acquired a name and a language (Chicano Spanish) that reflected that reality. Now that we had a name, some of the fragmented pieces began to fall together – who we were, what we were, how we had evolved. We began to get glimpses of what we might eventually become.

Yet the struggle of identities continues, the struggle of borders is our reality still. One day the inner struggle will cease and a true integration take place. In the meantime, *tenémos que hacer la lucha. ¿Quién está protegiendo los ranchos de mi gente? ¿Quién está tra-*

tando de cerrar la fisura entre la india y el blanco en nuestra sangre? El Chicano, si, el Chicano que anda como un ladrón en su propia casa.

Los Chicanos, how patient we seem, how very patient. There is the quiet of the Indian about us.[13] We know how to survive. When other races have given up their tongue, we've kept ours. We know what it is to live under the hammer blow of the dominant *norteamericano* culture. But more than we count the blows, we count the days the weeks the years the centuries the eons until the white laws and commerce and customs will rot in the deserts they've created, lie bleached. *Humildes* yet proud, *quietos* yet wild, *nosotros los mexicanos-Chicanos* will walk by the crumbling ashes as we go about our business. Stubborn, persevering, impenetrable as stone, yet possessing a malleability that renders us unbreakable, we, the *mestizas* and *mestizos,* will remain.

Notes

1. Ray Gwyn Smith, "Moorland Is Cold Country," unpublished book.

2. Irena Klepfisz, "*Di rayze aheym*/The Journey Home," in *The Tribe of Dina: A Jewish Women's Anthology,* ed. Melanie Kaye/Kantrowitz and Irena Klepfisz (Montpelier VT: Sinister Wisdom Books, 1986), 49.

3. R. C. Ortega, *Dialectología del barrio,* trans. Hortencia S. Alwan (Los Angeles CA: R. C. Ortega, 1977), 132.

4. Eduardo Hernández-Chávez, Andrew D. Cohen, and Anthony F. Beltramo, *El lenguaje de los Chicanos: Regional and Social Characteristics of Language Used by Mexican Americans* (Arlington VA: Center for Applied Linguistics, 1975), 39.

5. Hernández-Chávez, Cohen, and Beltramo, *El lenguaje de los Chicanos,* xvii.

6. Irena Klepfisz, "Secular Jewish Identity: Yidishkayt in America," in Kaye/Kantrowitz and Klepfisz, eds., *The Tribe of Dina,* 43.

7. Melanie Kaye/Kantrowitz, "Sign," in *We Speak in Code: Poems and Other Writings* (Pittsburgh PA: Motheroot Publications, 1980), 85.

8. Rodolfo Gonzales, *I Am Joaquín/Yo soy Joaquín* (New York: Bantam Books, 1972). It was first published in 1967.

9. Gershen Kaufman, *Shame: The Power of Caring* (Cambridge MA: Schenkman Books, 1980), 68.

10. Hernández-Chávez, Cohen, and Beltramo, *El lenguaje de los Chicanos,* 88–90.

11. "Hispanic" is derived from *Hispanis* (*España,* a name given to the Iberian Peninsula in ancient times, when it was a part of the Roman Empire) and is a term designated by the U.S. government to make it easier to handle us on paper.

12. The Treaty of Guadalupe Hidalgo created the Mexican-American in 1848.

13. Anglos, in order to alleviate their guilt for dispossessing the Chicano, stressed the Spanish part of us and perpetrated the myth of the Spanish Southwest. We have accepted the fiction that we are Hispanic, that is Spanish, in order to accommodate ourselves to the dominant culture and its abhorrence of Indians. Hernández-Chávez, Cohen, and Beltramo, *El lenguaje de los Chicanos,* 88–91.

Conversions

MARY ANTIN (1881–1949)

Born Maryashe Antin to a Jewish family in Polotzk, Russia, Mary Antin was part of the massive wave of European immigration at the turn of the twentieth century that transformed the society of the United States. When she arrived in Boston in 1894, she became one of more than 18 million new Americans between 1890 and 1920. A long letter describing her voyage across the Atlantic Ocean that Antin composed in Yiddish and sent to her uncle back in Russia was eventually revised and published in English, as – misspelling the name of her native town – *From Plotzk to Boston* (1899).

"I was born, I have lived, and I have been made over," Antin declares in the opening sentence of *The Promised Land,* the autobiography that she published in 1912. The book both celebrated the assimilationist ideal of the United States as a melting pot and, in its popular success, demonstrated that an indigent foreigner could master the language well enough to be taken seriously as an American author. Antin was not oblivious to the hardships of starting a new life in a strange land and, through an energetic campaign of essays and lectures and a book titled *They Who Knock at Our Gates* (1914), became a prominent advocate of immigrant rights. But, despite darker moments, *The Promised Land* is a story of individual triumph over adversity, a portrait of the artist as an earnest young American. In this excerpt, Antin, who does not admit any distress over abandonment of her native Yiddish, recounts a crucial moment in her childhood when she discovered that she could write effectively in English.

Initiation

It is not worth while to refer to voluminous school statistics to see just how many "green" pupils entered school last September, not knowing the days of the week in English, who next February will be declaiming patriotic verses in honor of George Washington and Abraham Lincoln, with a foreign accent, indeed, but with plenty of enthusiasm. It is enough to know that this hundred-fold miracle is common to the schools in every part of the United States where immigrants are received. And if I was one of Chelsea's hundred in 1894, it was only to be expected, since I was one of the older of the "green" children, and had had a start in my irregular schooling in Russia, and was carried along by a tremendous desire to learn, and had my family to cheer me on.

I was not a bit too large for my little chair and desk in the baby class, but my mind, of course, was too mature by six or seven years for the work. So as soon as I could understand what the teacher said in class, I was advanced to the second grade. This was within a week after Miss Nixon took me in hand. But I do not mean to give my dear teacher all the credit for my rapid progress, nor even half the credit. I shall divide it with her on behalf of my race and my family. I was Jew enough to have an aptitude for language in general, and to bend my mind earnestly to my task; I was Antin enough to read each lesson with my heart, which gave me an inkling of what was coming next, and so carried me along by leaps and bounds. As for the teacher, she could best explain what theory she followed in teaching us foreigners to read. I can only describe the method, which was so simple that I wish holiness could be taught in the same way.

There were about half a dozen of us beginners in English, in age from six to fifteen. Miss Nixon made a special class of us, and aided us so skillfully and earnestly in our endeavors to "see-a-cat," and "hear-a-dog-bark," and "look-at-the-hen," that we turned over page after page of the ravishing history, eager to find out how the common world looked, smelled, and tasted in the strange speech. The teacher knew just when to let us help each other out with a word in our own tongue, – it happened that we were all Jews – and so, working all together, we actually covered more ground in a lesson than the native classes, composed entirely of the little tots.

But we stuck – stuck fast – at the definite article; and sometimes the lesson resolved itself into a species of lingual gymnastics, in which we all looked as if we meant to bite our tongues off. Miss Nixon was pretty, and she must have looked well with her white teeth showing in the act; but at the time I was too solemnly occupied to admire her looks. I did take great pleasure in her smile of approval, whenever I pronounced well; and her patience and perseverance in struggling with us over that thick little word are becoming to her even now, after fifteen years. It is not her fault if any of us to-day give a buzzing sound to the dreadful English *th*.

I shall never have a better opportunity to make public declaration of my love for the English language. I am glad that American history runs, chapter for chapter, the way it does; for thus America came to be the country I love so dearly. I am glad, most of all, that the Americans began by being Englishmen, for thus did I come to inherit this beautiful language in which I think. It seems to me that in any other language happiness is not so sweet, logic is not so clear. I am not sure that I could believe in my neighbors as I do if I thought about them in un-English words. I could almost say that my conviction of immortality is bound up with the English of its promise. And as I am attached to my prejudices, I must love the English language!

Whenever the teachers did anything special to help me over my private difficulties, my gratitude went out to them, silently. It meant so much to me that they halted the lesson to give me a lift, that I needs must love them for it. Dear Miss Carrol, of the second grade, would be amazed to hear what small things I remember, all because I was so impressed at the time with her readiness and sweetness in taking notice of my difficulties.

Says Miss Carrol, looking straight at me:

"If Johnnie has three marbles, and Charlie has twice as many, how many marbles has Charlie?"

I raise my hand for permission to speak.

"Teacher, I don't know vhat is tvice."

Teacher beckons me to her, and whispers to me the meaning of the strange word, and I am able to write the sum correctly. It's all in the day's work with her; with me, it is a special act of kindness and efficiency.

She whom I found in the next grade became so dear a friend that I can hardly name her with the rest, though I mention none of them lightly. Her approval was always dear to me, first because she was "Teacher," and afterwards, as long as she lived, because she was my Miss Dillingham. Great was my grief, therefore, when, shortly after my admission to her class, I incurred discipline, the first, and next to the last, time in my school career.

The class was repeating in chorus the Lord's Prayer, heads bowed on desks. I was doing my best to keep up by the sound; my mind could not go beyond the word "hallowed," for which I had not found the meaning. In the middle of the prayer a Jewish boy across the aisle trod on my foot to get my attention. "You must not say that," he admonished in a solemn whisper; "it's Christian." I whispered back that it wasn't, and went on to the "Amen." I did not know but what he was right, but the name of Christ was not in the prayer, and I was bound to do everything that the class did. If I had any Jewish scruples, they were lagging away behind my interest in school affairs. How American this was: two pupils side by side in the schoolroom, each holding to his own opinion, but both submitting to the common law; for the boy at least bowed his head as the teacher ordered.

But all Miss Dillingham knew of it was that two of her pupils whispered during morning prayer, and she must discipline them. So I was degraded from the honor row to the lowest row, and it was many a day before I forgave that young missionary; it was not enough for my vengeance that he suffered punishment with me. Teacher, of course, heard us both defend ourselves, but there was a time and place for religious arguments, and she meant to help us remember that point.

I remember to this day what a struggle we had over the word "water," Miss Dillingham and I. It seemed as if I could not give the sound of *w;* I said "vater" every time. Patiently my teacher worked with me, inventing mouth exercises for me, to get my stubborn lips to produce that *w;* and when at last I could say "village" and "water" in rapid alternation, without misplacing the two initials, that memorable word was sweet on my lips. For we had conquered, and Teacher was pleased.

Getting a language in this way, word by word, has a charm that may be set against the disadvantages. It is like gathering a posy blossom by blossom. Bring the bouquet into your chamber, and these nasturtiums stand for the whole flaming carnival of them tumbling over the fence out there; these yellow pansies recall the velvet crescent of color glowing under the bay window; this spray of honeysuckle smells like the wind-tossed masses of it on the porch, ripe and bee-laden; the whole garden in a glass tumbler. So it is with one who gathers words, loving them. Particular words remain associated with important occasions in the learner's mind. I could thus write a history of my English vocabulary that should be at the same time an account of my comings and goings, my mistakes and my triumphs, during the years of my initiation.

If I was eager and diligent, my teachers did not sleep. As fast as my knowledge of English allowed, they advanced me from grade to grade, without reference to the usual schedule of promotions. My father was right, when he often said, in discussing my prospects, that ability would be promptly recognized in the public schools. Rapid as was my progress, on account of the advantages with which I started, some of the other "green" pupils were not far behind me; within a grade or two, by the end of the year. My brother, whose childhood had been one hideous nightmare, what with the stupid rebbe, the cruel whip, and the general repression of life in the Pale, surprised my father by the progress he made under intelligent, sympathetic guidance. Indeed, he soon had a reputation in the school that the American boys envied; and all through the school course he more than held his own with pupils of his age. So much for the right and wrong way of doing things.

There is a record of my early progress in English much better than my recollections, however accurate and definite these may be. I have several reasons for introducing it here. First, it shows what the Russian Jew can do with an adopted language; next, it proves that vigilance of our public-school teachers of which I spoke; and last, I am proud of it! That is an unnecessary confession, but I could not be satisfied to insert the record here, with my vanity unavowed.

This is the document, copied from an educational journal, a tattered copy of which lies in my lap as I write – treasured for fifteen years, you see, by my vanity.

Editor "Primary Education": –

This is the uncorrected paper of a Russian child twelve years old, who had studied English only four months. She had never, until September, been to school even in her own country and has heard English spoken *only* at school. I shall be glad if the paper of my pupil and the above explanation may appear in your paper.

M. S. Dillingham.

Chelsea, Mass.

SNOW

Snow is frozen moisture which comes from the clouds. Now the snow is coming down in feather-flakes, which makes nice snow-balls. But there is still one kind of snow more. This kind of snow is called snow-crystals, for it comes down in little curly balls. These snow-crystals aren't quiet as good for snow-balls as feather-flakes, for they (the snow-crystals) are dry: so they can't keep together as feather-flakes do.

The snow is dear to some children for they like sleighing.

As I said at the top – the snow comes from the clouds.

Now the trees are bare, and no flowers are to see in the fields and gardens, (we all know why) and the whole world seems like asleep without the happy birds songs which left us till spring. But the snow which drove away all these pretty and happy things, try, (as I think) not to make us at all unhappy; they covered up the branches of the trees, the fields, the gardens and houses, and the whole world looks like dressed in a beautiful white – instead of green – dress, with the sky looking down on it with a pale face.

And so the people can find some joy in it, too, without the happy summer.

Mary Antin.

And now that it stands there, with *her* name over it, I am ashamed of my flippant talk about vanity. More to me than all the praise I could hope to win by the conquest of fifty languages is the association of this dear friend with my earliest efforts at writing; and it pleases me to remember that to her I owe my very first appearance in print. Vanity is the least part of it, when I remember how she called me to her desk, one day after school was out, and showed me my composition – my own words, that I had written out of my own head – printed out, clear black and white, with my name at the end! Nothing so wonderful had ever happened to me before. My whole consciousness was suddenly transformed. I suppose that was the moment when I became a writer. I always loved to write – I wrote letters whenever I had an excuse – yet it had never occurred to me to sit down and write my thoughts for no person in particular, merely to put the word on paper. But now, as I read my own words, in a delicious confusion, the idea was born. I stared at my name: MARY ANTIN. Was that really I? The printed characters composing it seemed strange to me all of a sudden. If that was my name, and those were the words out of my own head, what relation did it all have to *me,* who was alone there with Miss Dillingham, and the printed page between us? Why, it meant that I could write again, and see my writing printed for people to read! I could write many, many, many things; I could write a book! The idea was so huge, so bewildering, that my mind scarcely could accommodate it.

JULIA ALVAREZ (1950–)

Born in the Dominican Republic, Julia Alvarez emigrated to New York at the age of ten when her parents, prominent opponents of the dictatorship of General Raphael Leonidas Trujillo, were forced to flee their Caribbean homeland. "What made me into a writer was coming to this country," she has written, "all of a sudden losing a culture, a homeland, a language, a family." Beginning with *Homecoming* (1984), her first volume of poetry, Alvarez established herself as a writer in English. Her first novel, *How the García Girls Lost Their Accents,* was published in 1991, to wide acclaim. Other works of fiction by Alvarez are *In the Time of the Butterflies* (1994), *¡Yo!* (1997), and *In the Name of Salomé* (2000). Though she has lived for many years in Vermont and is now much more fluent in English than Spanish, Dominican landscapes and the ordeal of acculturation continue to haunt her writing. Included in the essay collection *Something to Declare* (1998) is this description of how Alvarez began to lose her accent, how she switched from Spanish to "My English."

My English

Mami and Papi used to speak it when they had a secret they wanted to keep from us children. We lived then in the Dominican Republic, and the family as a whole spoke only Spanish at home, until my sisters and I started attending the Carol Morgan School, and we became a bilingual family. Spanish had its many tongues as well. There was the castellano of Padre Joaquín from Spain, whose lisp we all loved to imitate. Then the educated español my parents' families spoke, aunts and uncles who were always correcting us children, for we spent most of the day with the maids and so had picked up their "bad Spanish." Campesinas, they spoke a lilting, animated campuno, *ss* swallowed, endings chopped off, funny turns of phrases. This campuno was my true mother tongue, not the Spanish of Calderón de la Barca or Cervantes or even Neruda, but of Chucha and Iluminada and Gladys and Ursulina from Juncalito and Licey and Boca de Yuma and San Juan de la Maguana. Those women yakked as they cooked, they storytold, they gossiped, they sang – boleros, merengues, canciones, salves. Theirs were the voices that belonged to the rain and the wind and the teeny, teeny stars even a small child could blot out with her thumb.

Besides all these versions of Spanish, every once in a while another strange tongue emerged from my papi's mouth or my mami's lips. What I first recognized was not a language, but a tone of voice, serious, urgent, something important and top secret being said, some uncle in trouble, someone divorcing, someone dead. *Say it in English so the children won't understand.* I would listen, straining to understand, thinking that this was not a different language but just another and harder version of Spanish. *Say it in English so the children won't understand.* From the beginning, English was the sound of worry and secrets, the sound of being left out.

I could make no sense of this "harder Spanish," and so I tried by other means to find out what was going on. I knew my mother's face by heart. When the little lines on the corners of her eyes crinkled, she was amused. When her nostrils flared and she bit her lip, she was trying hard not to laugh. She held her head down, eyes glancing up, when she thought I was lying. Whenever she spoke that gibberish English, I translated the general content by watching the Spanish expressions on her face.

*

Soon, I began to learn more English, at the Carol Morgan School. That is, when I had stopped gawking. The teacher and some of the American children had the strangest coloration: light hair, light eyes, light skin, as if Ursulina had soaked them in bleach too long, to' deteñío. I did have some blond cousins, but they had deeply tanned skin, and as they grew older, their hair darkened, so their earlier paleness seemed a phase of their acquiring normal color. Just as strange was the little girl in my reader who had a *cat* and a *dog,* that looked just like un gatito y un perrito. Her mami was *Mother* and her papi *Father.* Why have a whole new language for school and for books with a teacher who could speak it teaching you double the amount of words you really needed?

Butter, butter, butter, butter. All day, one English word that had particularly struck me would go round and round in my mouth and weave through all the Spanish in my head until by the end of the day, the word did sound like just another Spanish word. And so I would say, "Mami, please pass la mantequilla." She would scowl and say in English, "I'm sorry, I don't understand. But would you be needing some butter on your bread?"

Why my parents didn't first educate us in our native language by enrolling us in a Dominican school, I don't know. Part of it was that Mami's family had a tradition of sending the boys to the States to boarding school and college, and she had been one of the first girls to be allowed to join her brothers. At Abbot Academy, whose school song was our lullaby as babies ("Although Columbus and Cabot never heard of Abbot, it's quite the place for you and me"), she had become quite Americanized. It was very important, she kept saying, that we learn our English. She always used the possessive pronoun: *your* English, an inheritance we had come into and must wisely use. Unfortunately, my English became all mixed up with our Spanish.

Mix-up, or what's now called Spanglish, was the language we spoke for several years. There wasn't a sentence that wasn't colonized by an English word. At school, a Spanish word would suddenly slide into my English like someone butting into line. Teacher, whose face I was learning to read as minutely as my mother's, would scowl but no smile played on her lips. Her pale skin made her strange countenance hard to read, so that I often misjudged how much I could get away with. Whenever I made a mistake, Teacher would shake her head slowly, "In English, YU-LEE-AH, there's no such word as *columpio*. Do you mean a *swing?*"

I would bow my head, humiliated by the smiles and snickers of the American children around me. I grew insecure about Spanish. My native tongue was not quite as good as English, as if words like *columpio* were illegal immigrants trying to cross a border into another language. But Teacher's discerning grammar-and-vocabulary-patrol ears could tell and send them back.

Soon, I was talking up an English storm. "Did you eat English parrot?" my grandfather asked one Sunday. I had just enlisted yet one more patient servant to listen to my rendition of "Peter Piper picked a peck of pickled peppers" at breakneck pace. "Huh?" I asked impolitely in English, putting him in his place. *Cat got your tongue? No big deal! So there! Take that! Holy Toledo!* (Our teacher's favorite "curse word.") *Go jump in the lake! Really dumb. Golly. Gosh.* Slang, clichés, sayings, hot-shot language that our teacher called, ponderously, idiomatic expressions. Riddles, jokes, puns, conundrums. *What is yellow and goes click-click? Why did the chicken cross the road? See you later, alligator.* How wonderful to call someone an alligator and not be scolded for being disrespectful. In fact, they were supposed to say back, *In a while, crocodile.*

There was also a neat little trick I wanted to try on an English-speaking adult at hone. I had learned it from Elizabeth, my smart-alecky friend in fourth grade, whom I alternately worshiped and resented. I'd ask her a question that required an explanation, and she'd answer, "Because . . ." "Elizabeth, how come you didn't go to Isabel's birthday party?" "Because . . ." "Why didn't you put your name in your reader?" "Because . . ." I thought that such a cool way to get around having to come up with answers. So, I practiced saying it under my breath, planning for the day I could use it on an unsuspecting English-speaking adult.

One Sunday at our extended family dinner, my grandfather sat down at the children's table to chat with us. He was famous, in fact, for the way he could carry on adult conversations with his grandchildren. He often spoke to us in English so that we could practice speaking it outside the classroom. He was a Cornell man, a United Nations representative from our country. He gave speeches in English. Perfect English, my mother's phrase. That Sunday, he asked me a question. I can't even remember what it was because I wasn't really listening but lying in wait for my chance. "Because . . . ," I answered him. Papito waited a second for the rest of my sentence and then gave me a thumbnail grammar lesson, "*Because* has to be followed by a clause."

"Why's that?" I asked, nonplussed.

"Because," he winked, "Just because."

A beginning wordsmith, I had so much left to learn; sometimes it was disheartening. Once Tío Gus, the family intellectual, put a speck of salt on my grandparents' big dining table during Sunday dinner. He said, "Imagine this whole table is the human brain. Then this teensy grain is all we ever use of our intelligence!" He enumerated geniuses who had perhaps used two grains, maybe three: Einstein, Michelangelo, da Vinci, Beethoven. We children believed him. It was the kind of impossible fact we thrived on, proving as it did that the world out there was not drastically different from the one we were making up in our heads.

Later, at home, Mami said that you had to take what her younger brother said "with a grain of salt." I thought she was still referring to Tío Gus's demonstration, and I tried to puzzle out what she was saying. Finally, I asked what she meant. "Taking what someone says with a grain of salt is an idiomatic expression in English," she explained. It was pure voodoo is what it was – what later I learned poetry could also do: a grain of salt could symbolize both the human brain and a condiment for human nonsense. And it could be itself, too: a grain of salt to flavor a bland plate of American food.

When we arrived in New York, I was shocked. A country where everyone spoke English! These people must be smarter, I thought. Maids, waiters, taxi drivers, doormen, bums on the street, all spoke this difficult language. It took some time before I understood that Americans were not necessarily a smarter, superior race. It was as natural for them to learn their mother tongue as it was for a little Dominican baby to learn Spanish. It came with "mother's milk," my mother explained, and for a while I thought a mother tongue was a mother tongue because you got it from your mother's breast, along with proteins and vitamins.

Soon it wasn't so strange that everyone was speaking in English instead of Spanish. I learned not to hear it as English, but as sense. I no longer strained to understand, I understood. I relaxed in this second language. Only when someone with a heavy southern or British accent spoke in a movie, or at church when the priest droned his sermon – only then did I experience that little catch of anxiety. I worried that I would not be able to understand, that I wouldn't be able to "keep up" with the voice speaking in this acquired language. I would be like those people from the Bible we had studied in religion class, whom I imagined standing at the foot of an enormous tower that looked just like the skyscrapers around me. They had been punished for their pride by being made to speak different languages so that they didn't understand what anyone was saying.

But at the foot of those towering New York skyscrapers, I began to understand more and more – not less and less – English. In sixth grade, I had one of the first in a lucky line of great English teachers who began to nurture in me a love of language, a love that had been there since my childhood of listening closely to words. Sister Maria Generosa did not make our class interminably diagram sentences from a workbook or learn a catechism of grammar rules. Instead, she asked us to write little stories imagining we were snowflakes, birds, pianos, a stone in the pavement, a star in the sky. What would it feel like to be a flower with roots in the ground? If the clouds could talk, what would they say? She had an expressive, dreamy look that was accentuated by the wimple that framed her face.

Supposing, just supposing . . . My mind would take off, soaring into possibilities, a flower with roots, a star in the sky, a cloud full of sad, sad tears, a piano crying out each time its back was tapped, music only to our ears.

Sister Maria stood at the chalkboard. Her chalk was always snapping in two because she wrote with such energy, her whole habit shaking with the swing of her arm, her hand tap-tap-tapping on the board. "Here's a simple sentence: 'The snow fell.'" Sister pointed with her chalk, her eyebrows lifted, her wimple poked up. Sometimes I could see wisps of gray hair that strayed from under her headdress. "But watch what happens if we put an adverb at the beginning and a prepositional phrase at the end: 'Gently, the snow fell on the bare hills.'"

I thought about the snow. I saw how it might fall on the hills, tapping lightly on the bare branches of trees. Softly, it would fall on the cold, bare fields. On toys children had left out in the yard, and on cars and on little birds and on people out late walking on the streets. Sister Maria filled the chalkboard with snowy print, on and on, handling and shaping and moving the language, scribbling all over the board until English, those verbal gadgets, those tricks and turns of phrases, those little fixed units and counters, became a charged, fluid mass that carried me in its great fluent waves, rolling and moving onward, to deposit me on the shores of my new homeland. I was no longer a foreigner with no ground to stand on. I had landed in the English language.

HA JIN (1956–)

Born in Jinzhou, in northern China, Xuefei Jin adopted Ha Jin as nom de plume in homage to the city of Harbin, where he lived for several years, and because the name was easier for Americans to pronounce. During the Cultural Revolution (1966–1976), which closed down schools and sent city dwellers to work as peasants in the countryside, his early formal education was spotty. Jin served in the People's Liberation Army, along the border with Russia, from ages fourteen to nineteen. A daily radio program provided his first instruction in English. When he enrolled at Hilongjiang University in Harbin, Jin was willy-nilly assigned to study English, and he graduated with a B.A. in it in 1981.

After receiving an M.A. from Shandong University in 1984, Jin traveled to Massachusetts to study for the doctorate he eventually received from Brandeis University in 1993. Although his original intention was to return to teach in China after concluding his studies at Brandeis, the Tiananmen Square massacre in 1989 convinced Jin to stay in the United States. His first book, a volume of poems he wrote in English called *Between Silences,* was published in 1990. Jin's commitment to the writing life was fortified in 1993, when he was hired to teach poetry at Emory University. In 2002, he took up a position at Boston University. Jin's prolific output includes the poetry collections *Facing Shadows* (1996) and *Wreckage* (2001); two volumes of short stories, *Ocean of Words* (1996) and *The Bridegroom* (2000); and the novels *In the Pond* (1998), *Waiting* (1999), and *The Crazed* (2002). With *Waiting,* Ha Jin became the third non-native speaker of English – after Isaac Bashevis Singer and Jerzy Kozinski – to win the National Book Award. Other honors he has received include the PEN/Hemingway Award, the Flannery O'Connor Award for Short Fiction, and a Guggenheim Fellowship.

In this interview, conducted by the editor via electronic mail in July 2001, Ha Jin discusses his adoption of English as his literary medium.

Interview with Ha Jin

SGK: Vladimir Nabokov, a translingual author for whom you have expressed admiration, claimed that it was not important to him whether he wrote in Russian, French, or English, that the medium of his imagination was images, not words. Does the particular language in which you write determine how and what you write?

HJ: Nabokov might indeed think through images, but he must have had to handle Russian differently from the way he wrote in English. The linguistic differences would produce a different effect in his writing. In fact, he mentioned that to him, English was poetically inferior to Russian. As for me, a different language doesn't determine what I write but does affect how I write, because the feeling, the sound, the sentiment of English differ a great deal from Chinese. Also, English has a different literary tradition and a different reference system that's culturally bound. All these cannot help but influence my way of writing.

SGK: You first read Walt Whitman, whom you mention in *Waiting*, and other American authors in Chinese translation. In what ways did the filter of Chinese syntax and vocabulary shape your experience of American literature?

HJ: Chinese doesn't depend on syntactic manipulation most of the time. By contrast, English, especially Whitman's lines, has the syntactic abundance and eloquence that can rarely be found in Chinese. There are some words Chinese does not have; likewise, some Chinese words are absent from English. Some concepts cannot be fully understood by just reading American fiction and poetry. You have to have an ID card in your hand to understand the idea "identity."

SGK: When and how did you begin writing in English? Did you initially think in Chinese and then transpose your thoughts into English?

HJ: Two stages. I wrote my first English book between 1987 and 1988, but I thought this was just an excursion and I would eventually write in Chinese. After 1989, specifically the Tiananmen massacre, I decided to immigrate and to write in English exclusively. Afterwards, I forced myself to write in the adopted language. When I write, I think in English only, though Chinese will appear from time to time. When the characters begin talking, at times they speak Chinese, which I have to adapt into English.

SGK: Is there anything intrinsic to the English language itself that drew you to write in it, or was it simply the language of the country in which you had found refuge and were trying to earn a living?

HJ: In the beginning I was assigned to study English at college, but for the first two years I didn't work hard at all. I didn't like the language. Even when I decided to write in English a decade later, I viewed it merely as a tool. But as I continued, I grew to love English, which has become a part of my existence. I decided to use Chinese to supplement English in my work.

SGK: There is an active Chinese-language press in the United States. Were you ever inclined to participate in its culture?

HJ: I am kind of involved, but not as an insider. Languages are like fences – English seems to have walled me into a different territory. But occasionally I participate in their activities.

SGK: Your first publications in English were poems. Does prose fiction pose greater challenges to an author writing in a second language?

HJ: Poetry poses more challenges. To produce significant poetry, one has to write with the full weight of English. This kind of mastery is harder for a writer like me. In fact, Nabokov tried to write poetry in English, but he is a great novelist, not a great poet.

SGK: In your fiction, do you consciously try to create an English style that simulates the Chinese spoken by your characters?

HJ: Yes. I want to make the language sound authentic and purposely avoid standard English. Also, this is an opportunity to see how much English can absorb the distortion. In this respect, English is pliantly robust. I believe that to put something new into a language, however tiny the new elements may be, is a way to express one's love for the language, because English has always gotten its vitality from alien sources.

SGK: In which language(s) do you do most of your reading? Were you reading intensively in English when you began writing in that language?

HJ: Most of the time I read in English, but I read some Chinese-language newspapers and ancient Chinese poetry.

SGK: I understand that some of your writing has recently been published in Taiwan. How does its reconfiguration into Chinese affect the nature of the work?

HJ: The books have been well received in Taiwan. I believe that literature should speak truth to everyone. In this sense, it shouldn't be diminished through translation. I hope the Chinese readers can say about my books, "This is honest work."

SGK: The novelist Anton Shammas has stated that he writes fiction in Hebrew rather than his native Arabic because "You cannot write about the people whom you love in a language that they understand; you can't write freely. In order not to feel my heroes breathing down my neck all the time, I used Hebrew." Has English provided you with a similar freedom? If, as you have stated, you intend eventually to write fictions set in America, will English, a language that your characters understand, infringe on your freedom?

HJ: English does give me a lot of freedom, but of a different kind, closer to solitude. The language enables me to be independent and work alone. This kind of loneness will be altered when I begin to write about the American experience. Many characters will be English speakers, and technically different kinds of requirements will have to be met. I will have to depend on the American idiom and the natural speech. A huge task and a lot of labor, but I have no other choice and have to try.

ANDREW LAM (1964–)

Andrew Lam was born in 1964 in Saigon. He was eleven years old in 1975, when the Vietnam War ended and he emigrated to California, part of the mass exodus of more than 165,000 Vietnamese to the United States after the fall of the American-supported Saigon regime. Lam received a B.A. in biochemistry from the University of California at Berkeley and an M.A. in creative writing from San Francisco State University. He is currently an associate editor with the Pacific News Service in San Francisco and a regular commentator on NPR's *All Things Considered.* He is working on his first collection of short stories. English is, after Vietnamese and French, Lam's third language, and in "My American Beginning," he recounts his conversion to Anglophonia.

My American Beginning

On my writing desk there sits a framed little card, yellow now with age, and it tells of my American beginning. It's a picture of a sloop, and under it, the words "Sail Boat" are written. Mr. Kaesleau, my first teacher in America, gave it to me along with a deck of similar cards almost twenty-five years ago when I was eleven, fresh from Vietnam, not speaking a word of English.

Mr. Kaesleau taught English. He had a kind face and a thick mustache that was quite expressive, especially when he smiled and wiggled his eyebrows like Groucho. He gave me A's (which didn't count) before I could put a sentence together, "to encourage me," as he would say, and at lunchtime, I was one of a handful of privileged kids who were allowed to eat in his classroom and play games. It was a sanctuary for the small kids who would sometimes get jumped by the bullies.

For a while I became his echo. Every day at lunchtime, he would spend time teaching me new vocabularies. "Sail boat," he would say while holding the card up in front of me, and "sail boat" I would repeat after him, copying his inflection and facial gesture. "Hospital," he would say. And "hospital," I would yell back, as if a little parakeet.

Then within a few months, I began to speak English freely, albeit haltingly and outgrew the cards. I began to banter and joke with my new friends with my funny way of talking. I made them laugh. And I flirted with the girls and made them blush. Speaking English, I had a new personality, a sunny, sharp-tongued kid, and often Mr. Kaesleau would shake his head in wonder at the change.

How could he have known that I was desperately in love with my new tongue?

I embraced it the way a drowning person embraced a life saver. At home, in the crowded refugee apartment my family shared with my aunt's family, we were a miserable bunch. I remember the smell of fish sauce wafting in the air and the sounds of the adults talking of what's gone and past. Vietnamese was spoken there and often only in whispers and occasionally in exploded exchanges when the crowded conditions became too much for us to bear. In that apartment I fell silent, became essentially a mute, overwhelmed by sadness and confusions.

In school, however, I was someone else. Each morning before school in the shower, I would open my mouth and say certain words I learned the day before and listen to their vibrations. I could almost see the words with their sharp edges and round arches taking shape in the steamy air. In school among friends, words flowed freely from my tongue, my lips, turning into a swift flowing river, and I, filled with ardor for a newfound self, sailed its iridescent waters toward Spring.

By the end of that school year, Mr. Kaesleau gave me the cards to take home as mementos, knowing full well that I didn't need them anymore. That day I remember taking a shortcut over a hill and on the way down, I tripped and fell. The cards flew out of my hand to scatter like a flock of playful butterflies on the verdant slope. Though I skinned my knees, I laughed. Then, as I scampered to retrieve each one of them, I found myself yelling out ecstatically the name of each image on the cards, as if for the first time.

"School." "Cloud." "Bridge." "House." "Dog."

When I looked up, I saw, far in the distance, San Francisco's downtown, its high-rises resembling a fairytale castle made of glittering diamonds whose backdrop was a lovely green sea.

"City," I said. "My beautiful city." And the words slipped into my bloodstream and made it real and me intensely happy for the first time in a long time. For it was then that I saw that I, sad and confused and full of longing, through my new love for the new language, and through the renaming of things, could too claim my stake in the New World.

CHANG-RAE LEE (1965–)

Born in Seoul, South Korea, in 1965, Chang-rae Lee and his mother and sister emigrated to the United States when he was three. His father, who had preceded the family to America, began a new career in psychiatry, the talking cure, and Lee credits his father, who had to learn a new language in order to pursue his calling, with the inspiration to master English. He grew up in the Westchester County suburbs of New York City and graduated from Yale University with a degree in English. Lee earned an M.F.A. in creative writing from the University of Oregon. He served as director of the M.F.A. program at Hunter College of the City University of New York until joining the faculty of Princeton University in 2002.

If nothing else, the titles of the two novels, *Native Speaker* and *A Gesture Life,* that Lee has thus far published announce language as the author's theme, if not his trial. Published in 1995, *Native Speaker* was an auspicious debut, winning both the American Book Award and the PEN/Hemingway Award. *A Gesture Life* followed in 1999, and so did continuing acclaim.

The editor conducted the following interview with Chang-rae Lee, speaking from his home in New Jersey, by telephone on 17 August 2001.

Interview with Chang-rae Lee

SGK: When and how did you begin writing in English? Did you initially think in Korean and then transpose your thoughts into English?

CRL: I learned English in the first grade here. I spoke Korean through kindergarten, and, though I did not speak it until a few months into first grade, English became my only written language. I didn't start writing creatively until high school and college, so I had very little Korean to work with as a writer. I used to answer in Korean to my parents, but my grasp of the language is now passive. Unless I am thinking of a specific Korean term, it doesn't enter into my writing.

SGK: How active is your command of Korean? Do you read Korean literature?

CRL: If you were to ask me the word for "vacuum cleaner" or "cantaloupe" in Korean, I would not be able to call it forth. I don't use my Korean day to day. I don't live in a Korean community. I do not read much Korean literature, and what I do read has all been translated. I can read a menu in Korean, but I can't really read Korean literary prose.

SGK: Might you have become a writer in Korean if your family had never left Seoul?

CRL: For me, that is a cultural more than a linguistic question. My situation in the United States is much different than it was in Korea, where I had much less of a chance to be a writer. In America, my father was able to send me to a prep school, and, while that was not the only influence determining my career, it was a catalyst in my becoming a writer. In Korea, that opportunity would never have presented itself.

SGK: Vladimir Nabokov claimed that it was not important to him whether he wrote in Russian, French, or English, that the medium of his imagination was images, not words. Does the particular language in which you write determine how and what you write?

CRL: My position is exactly the opposite of Nabokov's. I devote a lot of care and time to the rhythm and sound of my sentences. The image for me comes after the words; it is always secondary. What is most compelling and most interesting for me about the process of writing is the specific combination of words. I was always very conscious of other people's language. My first novel is very much about how language influences our lives. For me, language is the primary force defining the self and the culture.

SGK: In what ways, if any, has the filter of Korean syntax and vocabulary shaped your experience as both a reader and writer in English?

CRL: I think it must have had some kind of effect, though not necessarily through anything as specific as syntax and vocabulary. My English sentences echo a certain Korean feeling – a sense of mourning, a lament. The words I don't know, but the tune I do. And maybe a certain Korean sensibility has been carried into my English prose a little bit.

SGK: Is there anything intrinsic to the English language itself that drew you to write in it, or was it simply the language of the country in which you grew up and in which it was easier to publish?

CRL: English is in effect the only language I have. I do delight in it, as someone who is an outsider. I do not know that I would not delight in another language – if I grew up in French, for example. But English is the language that inspires me. Maybe that's an immigrant mode, but my delight in language is that of the serious traveler who delights in the native language of wherever he happens to be.

SGK: There is an active Korean-language press in the United States. Were you ever inclined to participate in its culture?

CRL: No. My parents read Korean-language publications, but they didn't mean anything to me. I have made connections with other Korean Americans, but not with Korean-language culture in the United States.

SGK: You have stated elsewhere that, before writing *A Gesture Life,* you traveled to Korea to interview former "comfort women," Koreans who during World War II were conscripted into prostitution by the invading Japanese military. Did you conduct these interviews in Korean, and did you consciously try to create an English style that simulates the Korean – and/or Japanese – spoken by your characters?

CRL: The interviews were conducted through an interpreter, though a lot of times I didn't really need a translation. I didn't really try to create an English style that echoed the language of the characters. I didn't consciously think of Franklin Hata as speaking Japanese. I was more focused on his thoughts than his speech. His dialogue in the novel is plain and straightforward, so perhaps in that respect a reflection of his newness to the language.

SGK: Both Henry Park, narrator of *Native Speaker,* and Franklin Hata, narrator of *A Gesture Life,* are taciturn outsiders for whom language is problematic. To what extent do you share their relationship to English?

CRL: I definitely do. This stems from an early feeling that I was never going to learn English. It was a genuine fear that I have never entirely dispelled. As a writer, I'm constantly trying to stretch my English. I sometimes wonder whether English is my language, though it is of course, and I have virtually no other. I quarrel with English a lot and test it a lot. I think that has defined me as a writer.

SGK: I understand that *Native Speaker,* at least, has been published in Korea. How does its reconfiguration into Korean affect the nature of the work?

CRL: Both books have been translated into Korean. I am not fluent enough in Korean to be able to make a judgment, but those who can tell me that *Native Speaker* was not well translated. Yet the novel contains odd formulations that would be a challenge to any translator. In both it and *A Gesture Life,* American idioms create problems for a Korean version. I have been received well in Italy and France, so I assume that their translators were successful.

SGK: You have stated that your next book will focus on Americans living in Korea during the Korean War. In what way is language an issue and a challenge in that novel?

CRL: It is actually one of the books that I am working on, and it might not be the first to appear in print. In it, I am approaching language a little differently than I have before. My American characters do not speak the local language, but in their colonial situation they don't need to. While Park and Hata try very hard to adapt to the language of the country they are in, the Americans in this book are feeling out the power of the language that they bring with them to Korea.

Between Languages

BAAL-MAKHSHOVES (1873–1924)

Baal-Makhshoves, which is Yiddish for thinker, is the pen name of Israel Isidor Elyashev, who was born in Kovno in 1873. He studied medicine in Heidelberg and Berlin and practiced it in Vilna, Riga, Warsaw, and St. Petersburg. But literature was his true calling, if not trade, and, though he also wrote in German and Russian, Baal-Makhshoves, who briefly edited the Yiddish journal *Klal-Velag,* pioneered the creation of serious literary criticism in Yiddish. During his lifetime, Yiddish, a Germanic language with Hebrew and Slavic elements, was the daily language of millions of Jews in eastern and central Europe. Mendele Mokher Sforim, I. L. Peretz, and Sholem Aleichem were kneading it into a supple medium of brilliant fiction, but Hebrew, a Semitic language, remained the sacred Jewish literary tongue, the medium of the Book. In this essay Baal-Makhshoves describes the diglossia of Yiddish and Hebrew within Jewish culture and how translingualism was the norm for Jews throughout their long Diaspora.

One Literature in Two Languages

1

Bees give us honey, and literati give us – literature. Don't look to bees for that specific purpose. They gratify people with their sweet honey involuntarily. They are not aware that their honey brings relief to ailing lungs. And who knows? If bees could talk, perhaps we might hear the deep sighs and oaths with which they curse their bitter luck at being made to give up their sweet honey.

What is the relevance of all this? It is relevant with regard to our literature of these last few years.

A new type of person has developed among us who is a writer not only on Mondays and on Tuesdays, but all year round. This new type has made a firm commitment to produce literature. His eyes see only whatever has the marks of a literary theme. His heart beats only when it is moved by a literary impression upon it, and everything mundane assumes a literary form. Such a person produces, intentionally or not, with great effort and hardship what is termed "literature." They have me to thank for the appearance among us, from time to time, of a hefty volume of slender booklets entitled *Sifrut* (Literature) today, *Literarishe Monatshriften* (Literary monthlies) tomorrow, and the day after tomorrow *Kunst und Leben* (Art and life); a *M'orer* in London, a *Revivim* in Lemberg, a *Reshifim* in Warsaw, and a *Ha'atid* in Berlin-Cracow.

My friends, don't look for some sort of unified direction in all these essay collections. Dr. Joseph Klausner, S. Y. Horowitz, and his regular adversary, Haradetsky, are all seated around one table at *Ha'atid;* Hillel Zeitlin and Reuven Breinin are united with David Frishman in the *Sifrut* camp. Chaim Brenner in his *M'orer* and

Revivim mixes together Moshe Kleinman with M. Y. Berdyczewski. In the *Literarishe Monatshriften* three singers from three different Yiddish factions – A. Veiter, S. Gorelick, and S. Niger – have united into a single choir. And in the *Birnboim Wochenblatt,* I. L. Peretz has met up with one A. Kleinman and with Birnboim himself. *Hashiloah* was the only journal that for a time remained pure as gold and did not, Heaven forbid, mingle with anyone else. And since Nahum Sokolov appeared in what was formerly Ahad Ha'am's house organ he too has lost his innocence and his distinctiveness in such collections.

2

Many people complain that our literary undertakings are nipped in the bud. There is grief for the young *M'orer,* which departed this world too soon, and for the *Literarishe Monatshriften,* which did not survive beyond its infancy. But as a loyal reader, I don't share these views. I am convinced that we have lost nothing. Only the names and the languages of our publications have changed, and our writers have not disappeared at all. If the writers' bad luck brought about the demise of one of the publications, these writers promptly regathered in another, which distinguished itself from the first only by its name and language. If the bright halls of the "literary monthlies" are closed to these writers, they come together in yet another collection, a Hebrew one – and they write in Hebrew. If one publisher closes down his Yiddish shop, another opens up immediately with the same material in Hebrew. If a Zeitlin offers his fiery moralizing articles in Yiddish in the *Heint* today, he will submit the identical piece in the language of the prophets in *Reshifim* tomorrow. Chaim Brenner's articles in *Revivim* can be found in *Heint* under the new heading of "Quiet Words." Namberg does not find it necessary even to change his name when he writes in Hebrew what he had formerly written in Yiddish. What appeared in *Der Yud* under the title of "Oyf Ein Kvartir" (In one lodging) now appears in *Sifrut* as "B'maon akhad."

Jewish literature is not going under – Heaven forbid. It is *one* and its name is *one.* It simply comes before the reader in two forms which, like the pans on a scale, swing in opposite directions. Just as nothing is absolutely balanced in nature, so the scales move up and down: sometimes one is at the top, sometimes the other. Today Brenner comes to us in a Yiddish garment. Tomorrow Sholem Aleichem comes in a Hebrew one. Last year Namberg was a Hebraist in *Ha Zman.* Today he is a Yiddishist in *Unzer Leben* and in *Romantseitung.* Does the name, typography, or publisher of a journal really matter? In recent years it has come to be required that a Jewish writer, just like a correspondent in an office, must know at least *two* languages in order to create freely. To commemorate the jubilee of I. L. Peretz, two editions of his *Collected Works* were published, one in Hebrew and one in Yiddish. And when the celebrant himself was asked in which of these volumes one could find the real Peretz, he answered modestly that the sparks of his spirit were scattered in both *Collected Works,* and that in order to comprehend the greatness and unity of his vision you would have to immerse yourself in both collections. At present, plans call for the publication of a Yiddish collected works of David Frishman. And I am sure that when Reb Mendele reaches his seventy-fifth birthday, some will want to proclaim him a Hebraist and publish his collected works in Hebrew. Sholem Aleichem himself has said recently that as long as all of his works have not been translated into Hebrew, the Angel of Death will not be able to overpower him! Nahum Sokolov is not certain whether he, too, will take on a Yiddish guise. His articles in the *Telegraph* could fill a volume no thinner than a *Gemara.* Our literature contains in its inner chambers a Yiddish Bialik, a Yiddish Berdyczewski, and even a Yiddish . . . Klausner. Ahad Ha'am is the lone exception. Yet Ahad Ha'am has said about himself that he is not a writer (see his *Al Parashat Drakhim*) and therefore his *Truth from the Land of Israel* does not have a Yiddish title, although in Yiddish it would appear in almost exactly the same words.

3

Some impassioned readers among us will not admit that our one and only literature has a double language. After the Czernowitz conference,[1] one of our Hebrew writers (now living in America) swore that from that day on he would not stain his pen with a single Yiddish word! And for him such an oath was not a small matter. For with that oath he severed the bond between himself and his mother, who lives in Russia and to whom he is a truly devoted son. And I have also learned that after Sholem Asch's address to the conference, an impassioned Yiddishist began to teach his little boy the *Modeh ani*[2] in pure Yiddish. This response was no less difficult for the father than the Hebrew writer's oath was for him, for the *Modeh ani* is without taste in Yiddish, lacking both salt and pepper. Furthermore, their fanaticism did not last long. The Hebrew writer rapidly became the editor of a Zionist paper, and the fanatic Yiddishist has joined a Hebrew teachers' organization, where, everyone knows, only the purest Hebrew is taught.

The Czernowitz resolution faded away like smoke. At the Czernowitz conference, 90 percent of whose participants were writers, it was forgotten temporarily that there actually are writers among Jews. These writers themselves suddenly forgot that it is their fate to gather straw for two kinds of goats, to acquire two languages. It is an old story that participants in conferences are intense idealists and have a tendency to be somewhat sentimental. That is no small matter! After all, they represent all Jews, and they are fighting for national progress! Doctors determined a long time ago that the pulse of a conference participant beats ten times harder than it would under normal circumstances, and that the participant's imagination works 5 percent harder than usual. American doctors are of the opinion that cold massages, a trip in a hot air balloon, and participation in conferences are the best remedies for tired nerves and anemia.

The average person cannot imagine what a pleasure it is to discard one's own problems for a few days a year and for a change worry about someone else's. For example, if Sholem Asch had not been in such a hurry to write his *Shabtai Zvi* before the conference, when he was so wrapped up in himself and his translators, who needed seventy translations of his newest work, and if he had written his work on the day of the conference, at a time when his soul was full of ideals, his work might well have turned out much better, or, more likely, it might never have seen the light of day. I return to my earlier point. The average person simply has no idea how delightful it is to forget one's own literary problems for a while and to agonize over someone else's woes! If the Czernowitz writers had thought more about themselves than about other people's business, they would, first of all, have taken a strong oath to write in only *one* language; second, they would have boycotted those writers who appear in Hebrew papers; third, they would have pressured Hebrew papers not to publish Yiddish articles in anything but the original. In a word, they should have been faithful to Yiddish and consequently have reduced their own chances for receiving a poor residual honorarium for publishing the same thing twice – in Yiddish and in Hebrew. They should repress the urge to appear in *Sifrut* today and in the *Literarishe Monatshriften* tomorrow.[3] But it is much harder to make such a commitment than it is to pass a resolution stating that Yiddish is our national language. It is easier to be the cause of bloodied scalps among the Czernowitz students, who would sacrifice themselves for a Czernowitz resolution, rather than decide not to contribute simultaneously to *Teater Velt, Yugent Velt,* and *Sifrut.* Of course, it is much easier for a *writer* to push another writer to the wall with a resolution than to decline an honorarium from a poor Yiddish paper.

I don't mean to stain anyone's honor – Heaven forbid; I just want to demonstrate that the Czernowitz group, acting out of great ideals and equally great love for the people, forgot momentarily that first and foremost they are Jewish writers, and they live and breathe between two languages, even as a bridegroom is escorted to the bridal canopy by two parents.

4

And does the writer live and breathe between two languages only? Don't our better critics carry within them the spirit of the German language? And in our younger writers, who were educated in the Russian language, can't we discern the spirit of Russian? And don't we hear echoes of French among our colleagues, the Palestinian writers (Ben-Ami, Hermoni)?

True, we have among us language artists – such as Bialik, Sokolov, Abramovitch, Sholem Aleichem – who occasionally write in a language that might cause one to conclude that not one word has crept into Jewish literature that is not thoroughly Jewish in nationality. There are probably likely to be among us talented writers who strive to create the spirit of a Hebrew language that should be the natural convergence of Biblical language, prophetic language, Mishnaic language, Midrash, and the juridical, philosophical, and mystical language of the *Gemara,* medieval philosophy, Kabbalah, and Hasidism. Ahad Ha'am, Berdyczewski, Zeitlin, and And – these are the talented writers who strive to achieve such a blending of the various pure elements in the Hebrew language. However, Hebrew is also a mixture of the spirit of many other languages. And I continue to have great doubts whether the generation of writers in Eretz Israel (who are already as far removed from Russian as from a Russian pogrom) can really understand the language of Brenner, Shafman, and And.

The spirit of the German language is the same everywhere. It does not matter who uses it: a German, a German American, or a Swiss. The same is true for the French language even though the Belgians, the French Swiss, and the French themselves originate from different peoples. Not so with the Hebrew language, whose spirit is different in every country. For the spirit of a strange language peeks out from under the mask of words. As for Yiddish, it is even worse. Its purity is a thousand times more suspect than that of the Hebrew language. For besides the present, Hebrew has a history and a literature of thousands of years, and thanks to which one can still hope some day to create a language with a pure national spirit. But Yiddish has only a *present.* It would never occur to anyone to make a synthesis of *Ze'ena u'Re'ena,*[4] Isaac Meyer Dik, Aksenfeld, Ettinger, Shomer, Yiddish folk songs, Alikum Zunser, the Zionists, Bundist brochures, and American literature. If we were to compare the Hebrew language to an island in a sea of foreign languages that would engulf it, to what can we compare Yiddish? Perhaps to an inn along a dirt road, where people stop over as if they were at home, but where no one stays longer than a short while? Only the present can make Yiddish a literary language, only from the present does it derive its existence. But our present is such that it cannot and will not create anything genuine. The creation of a language, or of any new enterprise, can take place only in an atmosphere of calm and quiet, into which the cries of the marketplace and the sighs of want do not penetrate. But a wandering people cannot construct such a quiet environment. Not only can it contribute nothing to its language but it also impoverishes and weakens that language by its eternal wandering.

*

And what, in a nutshell, is the point? It is that we have two languages and a dozen echoes from other foreign languages, but that we have only *one* literature. And therefore the reader who seeks to become acquainted with the currents of Jewish life, to comprehend the spirit of the Jewish individual and multitude and how they find expression in Jewish literature, that reader dares not separate Hebrew writers from Yiddish ones, Mendele, Bialik, Sholem Aleichem, Berdyczewski, Feierberg, and others – all are representatives of our literature, all embody a piece of Jewish life in their writing; all of them are Jewish artists, even though they do not all use both languages to express their artistic motifs.

5

On the wide streets of a southern Russian city the crowd festively carried the picture of Shevchenko, crowned with laurels and encircled with Ukrainian flags. From a distance it appeared to be a religious procession bearing the holy icons of the church or of the Virgin Mary. In this fashion the newly liberated nations in Russia pay homage to their spiritual representatives, the originators of a national literature.

For the significance of literature at this very moment cannot be sufficiently appreciated. On the surface it signals differentiation, but at the core lies the sign of collective bonding. Everything that separates – binds, and whatever binds naturally, organically, has the right to demand that it be viewed as something that *should* and *must* develop freely.

As long as a people has no literature, it can be considered mute. The individual may speak, but the people are silent. A genuine literature is the magic box that contains the spirit of the people with all its sorrows, hopes, and ideals, future and present. Literature is the oral scripture that becomes the written one, and that far surpasses that first Bible. Those who keep exclusively to their oral scripture soon turn to stone and are erased from the book of nations. The Karaites provide the best example: they seem to have the same origin as we; one of them might nowadays well be able to trace his lineage back to King David. Yet no one considers the Karaites to be a nation. At the constituent assembly, in the choir of nations, their voice will not join in song.[5]

The literature of oppressed peoples has always been their own territory, where they feel entirely at home. At the very least it has proved a kind of ex-territoriality, something like Franz Josef's palace or an English embassy in a foreign land. On the threshold of the building the foreign country's authority ends. Behind the walls of such a building, be it in Turkey or Persia, a man could live as if he were entirely at home, with no one having any power over him except his own national community.

We Jews have been able to survive history because of this exterritoriality. Heine once likened the Bible to a fatherland for the Jew, one that he carries along in his baggage. And the term "People of the Book," with which history has crowned us, clearly contains the notion that our earth, our very home, has always been literature.

Obviously, we must take the term *literature* in its broadest sense. Everything that expresses the spiritual movements of a people, be it science, philosophy, journalism, or poetry, and that *is accepted by the people,* makes up what can be proudly called *national literature.*

6

From its inception our literature has nearly always been a *bilingual* one, and those among us who cannot separate literature from language – that is, the cultural values that have been accepted by the masses from the languages spoken by the intellectuals and the people – can in no way come to terms with this fact. They do not want to acknowledge that, for us, bilingualism is such an old ailment that it has long ceased to pose a threat to the Jewish organism. They close their eyes to something that has been recognized by every Jew who is familiar with the history of our two-thousand-year-old literature.

For this bilingualism is already present in the Bible. When, in the course of his studies, the heder boy reaches the books of Daniel and Nehemiah, he suddenly falls into the Chaldean of the Persian Jewish historian trying to tell his story. And when he studies the sections in *The Ethics of the Fathers,* one of the finest chapters in Jewish literature, he must also come to a stop before words in Aramaic. And when this youngster begins to study the *Gemara,* he comes to experience what has always been characteristic for Jews – speaking in two languages as a matter of course. And out of the modest little Mishnah grows the voluminous Talmud, all in Aramaic.

This same bilingualism infiltrates all corners of Jewish cultural and religious life. The Onkelos translation of the Bible into Aramaic makes up one-third of the sacred ceremony of the Torah reading,[6] as every Jew is obliged to read the weekly Torah portion twice in the language of Moses and once in the Aramaic translation. And we also find Aramaic in the songs and liturgy of the prayer book.

Later, when the Jews were thrust into the Arab world, a whole

Jewish philosophical literature came into being in Arabic. Even Maimonides's renowned *Guide for the Perplexed,* which until recently played such an important role in Jewish spiritual life, though almost as old as Methuselah, was written in Arabic.

From the fifteenth century on, an inspirational literature developed in the second language – Yiddish. Just as the Jews once adapted Arabic at first for their daily business and later for their intellectual interests, so they later adapted the old German tongue, for their wanderings caused them to become strongly bound up to the Germans.

Also from the fifteenth century on, the finest Jewish intellectuals sought to give the people books in Yiddish. Writers from Eliahu Bachur to Abramovitch strove to provide for the Jewish masses even a small portion of what has always delighted the Jewish mind. And with time the *Ze'ena u'Re'ena* became for the people what the Onkelos Bible had been for the Jews before the Second Destruction of the Temple, when the masses of people could no longer understand Hebrew and therefore had to be given translations in their synagogues.

From these little-noticed facts we can conclude that bilingualism accompanied the Jews even in ancient times, even when they had their own land, and they were not as yet the wanderers they are now. Therefore, language never took on the character of a holy shrine (as is now the case for the Poles). Shortly before the Second Destruction, as well as later, the *form* had already ceased to play first fiddle. The wish to implant deeply certain spiritual treasures was stronger than the desire to confine the people within the framework of a single language. And because that spiritual wish always carried the stamp of what we can boldly call a *modern democracy,* our intellectual leaders made no great fuss about language. Better a bilingual nation than one that has only one language meant for the intellectuals and not for the people.

As a moral-religio-philosophical system, Judaism is not something held in the hands of the few. Its strength comes from its being shared by *all* classes. As early as the Pentateuch we find passages such as the one in which Moses, the lawgiver – arriving as Eldad and Medad are prophesying before the Jewish encampment – says: "If only all Jews were prophets."

Consequently, the intellectual representatives of the people never dealt with the language problem, and, instead, always adapted themselves to the language spoken by the great masses.

Translated by Hana Wirth-Nesher

Editor's Notes [Compiled by translator]

1. This gathering, held in Bukovina in August 1908, was the first international conference to deal with the role of Yiddish in Jewish life. The conference passed a resolution proclaiming Yiddish as a national language, after heated debates between ardent Hebraists, who recognized Hebrew as the only national language of the Jewish people, and committed Yiddishists, who saw Yiddish as the only living language of the Jews in contrast with Hebrew, the language of prayer. This resolution marked a turning point for Yiddish in terms of its cultural prestige. Baal-Makhshoves attended this conference along with other well-known literary figures, among them Abraham Reisen, I. L. Peretz, and Sholem Asch. Mendele and Sholem Aleichem endorsed the conference's resolution, although they were unable to attend due to illness.

2. The initial words of a prayer (literally, "I give thanks"), said immediately upon waking in the morning.

3. *Sifrut* is a Hebrew publication and *Literarishe Monatshriften* is a Yiddish one.

4. One of the most widely read books in Yiddish up to the end of the nineteenth century, *Ze'ena u'Re'ena* is a paraphrase of the Pentateuch, an adaptation aimed at women readers.

5. The Karaites are a Jewish sect that came into being in the eighth century and are characterized primarily by their denial of the Talmudic-rabbinical tradition. Baal-Makhshoves argues here that their lack of a written tradition excludes them from nationhood.

6. The Onkelos is a translation of the Bible into Aramaic from the second century C.E.

ILAN STAVANS (1961–)

"I write in English for Americans about topics they know little about," Ilan Stavans told an interviewer for the *Literary Review*, "and I write in Spanish for Mexicans about topics they are unacquainted with." As essayist, editor, memoirist, and fiction writer, he is prolific in two languages. Born in Mexico City in 1961, Stavans, who moved to the United States in 1985, is a vital intermediary between several cultures – Latin American and North American, Jewish and gentile, academic and popular. The grandson of immigrants from Central Europe and the son of an actor in Yiddish theater, Stavans, whose paternal surname was changed from Stavchansky, wrote his first play in Yiddish, but he published his first novel, *Talia y el cielo* (1979), and many subsequent works in Spanish. Editor of the *Norton Anthology of Latino Literature* and founding editor of *Hopscotch,* a journal of Hispanic culture, Stavans is one of the most visible and vocal commentators on Latin American literature and culture, even, in *The Sounds of Spanglish: An Illustrated Lexicon* (2000), a scholar of its hybrid language.

A sense of exile – geographical, linguistic, cultural – pervades much of Stavans's own writing and accounts for his particular affinity with other marginal figures: not just Latin American Jews like himself, but also other translinguals, authors including Felipe Alfau, Hector Bianciotti, Ariel Dorfman, Rosario Ferré, Franz Kafka, and Fernando Pessoa, who live both in and between languages and whom he has, in *Art and Anger: Essays on Politics and the Imagination* (1996), called "tongue snatchers." Stavans is active as a translator, especially of his own work, from Spanish into English and from English into Spanish. In the autobiographical *On Borrowed Words: A Memoir of Language* (2001), he explicitly defines himself through translingualism. Even after marrying a North American and becoming a citizen of the United States, where he teaches at Amherst College, Stavans embraces his hybrid identity. "I am divided into two hemispheres, two personas," he contends. "The injury between the two will never heal – but that doesn't scare me. I must find happiness in a divided self."

Autobiographical Essay

> My heart is in the East and I am at the edge of the West. Then how can I taste what I eat, how can I enjoy it? How can I fulfill my vows and pledges while Zion is in the domain of Edom, and I am in the bonds of Arabia? – Judah Halevi

> Work of good prose has three steps: a musical stage when it is composed, an architectonic one when it is built, and a textile one when it is woven. – Walter Benjamin

I was born in Mexico City, 7 April 1961, on a cloudy day without major historical events. I am a descendant of Jews from Russia and Poland, businessmen and rabbis, who arrived by sheer chance in Veracruz, on the Atlantic coast next to the Yucatán peninsula. I am a sum of parts and thus lack purity of blood (what proud Renaissance Iberians called *la pureza de sangre*): white Caucasian with a Mediterranean twist, much like the Enlightenment philosopher Moses Mendelssohn and only marginally like the Aztec poet Ollin Yollistli. My idols, not surprisingly, are Spinoza and Kafka, two exiles in their own land who chose to switch languages (Portuguese and Hebrew to Latin, Czech to German) in order to elevate themselves to a higher order, and who, relentlessly, investigated their own spirituality beyond the realm of orthodox religion and routine. Ralph Waldo Emerson, in *Essays: Second Series* (1844), says that the reason we feel one man's presence and not another's is as simple as gravity. I have traveled from Spanish into Yiddish, Hebrew, and English; from my native home south of the Rio Grande far and away – to Europe, the Middle East, the United States, the Bahamas, and South America – always in search of the ultimate clue to the mysteries of my divided identity. What I found is doubt.

I grew up in an intellectually sophisticated middle class, in a secure, self-imposed Jewish ghetto (a treasure island) where gentiles hardly existed. Money and comfort, books, theater and art. Since early on I was sent to Yiddish day school, Colegio Israelita de México in Colonia Narvarte, where the heroes were Sholem Aleichem and Theodor Herzl while people like José Joaquín Fernández de Lizardi, Agustín Yáñez, Juan Rulfo, and Octavio Paz were almost unknown; that is, we lived in an oasis, completely uninvolved with things Mexican. In fact, when it came to knowledge of the outside world, students were far better off talking about U.S. products (Hollywood, TV, junk food, technology) than about matters native – an artificial capsule, our ghetto, much like the magical sphere imagined by Blaise Pascal: its diameter everywhere and its center nowhere.

Mother tongue. The expression crashed into my mind at age twenty, perhaps a bit later. The father tongue, I assumed, was the adopted, alternative and illegitimate language (Henry James preferred the term "wife tongue"), whereas the mother tongue is genuine and authentic – a uterus: the original source. I was educated in (into) four idioms: Spanish, Yiddish, Hebrew, and English. Spanish was the public venue; Hebrew was a channel toward Zionism and not toward the sacredness of the synagogue; Yiddish symbolized the Holocaust and past struggles of the Eastern European labor movement; and English was the entrance door to redemption: the United States. Abba Eban said it better: Jews are like everybody else . . . except a little bit more. A polyglot, of course, has as many loyalties as homes. Spanish is my right eye, English my left; Yiddish my background and Hebrew my conscience. Or better, each of the four represents a different set of spectacles (near-sight, bifocal, night-reading, etc.) through which the universe is seen.

The Abundance of Self

This multifarious (is there such a word?) upbringing often brought me difficulties. Around the neighborhood, I was always *el güerito* and *el ruso*. Annoyingly, my complete name is Ilan Stavchansky Slomianski; nobody, except for Yiddish teachers, knew how to pronounce it. (I get mail addressed to: Ivan Starlominsky, Isvan Estafchansky, and Allen Stevens.) After graduating from high school, most of my friends, members of richer families, were sent abroad, to the United States or Israel, to study. Those that remained, including me, were forced to go to college at home, to face Mexico *tête-à-tête*. The shock was tremendous. Suddenly, I (we) recognized the artificiality of our oasis. What to do? I, for one, rejected my background. I felt Judaism made me a pariah. I wanted to be an authentic Mexican and thus foolishly joined the Communist cause, but the result wasn't pleasing. Among the *camaradas*, I was also "the blondy" and "the Jew." No hope, no escape. So I decided to investigate my ethnic and religious past obsessively and made it my duty to fully understand guys like Maimonides, Arthur Koestler, Mendelssohn, Judah Halevi, Hasdai Crescas, Spinoza, Walter Benjamin, Gershom Scholem, Martin Buber, Franz Rosenzweig, Abraham Joshua Heschel . . . It helped, at least temporarily – nothing lasts forever.

Years later, while teaching medieval philosophy at Universidad Iberoamericana, a Jesuit college in downtown Mexico City, during the 1982 Lebanon invasion, a group of Palestinian sympathizers threw rotten tomatoes at me and my students (99 percent gentiles). Eager to manifest their anger and protest, they had to find an easy target and I was the closest link to Israel around. The whole thing reminded me of a scene that took place at age fourteen, while sitting in Yiddish class at Colegio Israelita. Mr. Lockier, the teacher, was reading from I. J. Singer's *The Family Carnovsky* – the story of three generations in a German-Jewish family enchanted with the nineteenth-century Enlightenment, slowly but surely becoming assimilated into German society until the tragic uprise of Nazism brought unthinkable consequences. The monotonous rhythm of the recitation was boring and nobody was paying much attention. Suddenly, a segment of the story truly captivated me: the moment when Jegor, eldest son of Dr. David Carnovsky's mixed marriage to Teresa Holbeck, is ridiculed in class by Professor Kirchenmeier, a newly appointed principal at the Goethe Gymnasium in Berlin. Singer describes the event meticulously: Nazism is on the rise; the aristocracy, and more specifically the Jews, are anxious to know the overall outcome of the violent acts taking place daily on the city street. Racial theories are being discussed and Aryans glorified. Feverishly anti-Jewish, Kirchenmeier, while delivering a lecture, calls Jegor to the front to use him as a guinea pig in illustrating his theories. With compass and calipers, he measures the length and width of the boy's skull, writing the figures on the board. He then measures the distance from ear to ear, from the top of the head to the chin, and the length of the nose. A packed auditorium is silently watching. Jegor is then asked to undress. He is terrified and hesitates, of course; he is ashamed and feels conspicuous because of his circumcision. Eventually other students, persuaded by Kirchenmeier, help undress the Jew, and the teacher proceeds to show in the "inferior" Jewish strain the marks of the rib structure. He finishes by calling attention to Jegor's genitalia, whose premature development shows "the degenerate sexuality of the Semitic race."

Astonishment. What troubled me most was Jegor's inaction. I suppose it was natural to be petrified in such a situation, but I refused to justify his immobility. So I interrupted Mr. Lockier to ask why didn't the boy escape. A deadly silence invaded the classroom. It was clear I had disturbed the other students' sleep and the teacher's rhythm. "Because . . . he couldn't. He simply couldn't," was the answer I got. "Because that's the way lives are written." I don't know or care what happened next. As years went by I came to understand that concept, the almighty Author of Authors, as intriguing, and the scene in Yiddish class as an allegory of myself and Mexican Jews as an easy and palatable target of animosity. At the Jesuit college almost a decade later, I was the marionette-holder's Jegor Carnovsky – God's joy and toy: the Jew.

Kaleidoscope

Bizarre combination – Mexican Jews: some 50,000 frontier dwellers and hyphen people like Dr. Jekyll and Mr. Hyde, a sum of sums of parts, a multiplicity of multiplicities. Although settlers from Germany began to arrive in "Aztec Country" around 1830, the very first synagogue was not built in the nation's capital until some fifty-five years later. From then on, waves of Jewish immigrants came from Russia, Central and Eastern Europe, Ashkenazim whose goal was to make it big in New York (the Golden Land), but since an immigration quota was imposed in the United States in 1921, a little detour placed them in Cuba, Puerto Rico, or the Gulf of Mexico (the Rotten Land). Most were Yiddish-speaking Bundists: hardworking peasants, businessmen and teachers, nonreligious and entrepreneurial, escaping Church-sponsored pogroms and government persecution, whose primary dream was never Palestine. Hardly anything physical or ideological differentiated them from the relatives that did make it north, to Chicago, Detroit, Pittsburgh and the Lower East Side – except, of course, the fact that they, disoriented immigrants, couldn't settle where they pleased. And this sense of displacement colored our future.

Migration and its discontent. I have often imagined the culture shock, surely not too drastic, my forefathers experienced at their arrival: from *mujik* to *campesino,* similar types in different milieu. Mexico was packed with colonial monasteries where fanatical nuns prayed day and night. Around 1910 Emiliano Zapata and Pancho Villa were making their Socialist Revolution and an anti-Church feeling (known in Mexico as La Cristiada and masterfully examined in Graham Greene's *The Power and the Glory*) was rampant. Aztecs, the legend claimed, once sacrificed daughters to their idols in sky-high pyramids and perhaps were cannibals. Undoubtedly this was to be a transitory stop, it had to be. It was humid and at least in the nation's capital, nature remained in an eternal autumn.

I must confess never to have learned to love Mexico. I was taught to retain a sense of foreignness – as a tourist without a home. The best literature I know about Mexico is by Europeans and U.S. writers: Italo Calvino, André Breton, Jack Kerouac, Greene, Joseph Brodsky, Antonin Artaud, Katherine Anne Porter, Malcolm Lowry, Harriet Doerr . . . I only love my country when I am far and away.

Elsewhere – that's where I belong: the vast diaspora. Nowhere and everywhere. (Am I a name dropper? Me, whose name no one can pronounce?)

Out of the Basement

When the Mexican edition of *Talia in Heaven* (1990) came out, my publisher, Fernando Valdés, at a reception, talked about the merits of this, my first (and so far only) novel. He applauded this and that ingredient, spoke highly of the innovative style, and congratulated the author for his precocious artistic maturity. Memory has deleted most of his comments. I no longer remember what he liked and why. The only sentence that still sticks in my mind, the one capable of overcoming the passing of time, came at the end of his speech, when he said: "For many centuries, Latin America has had Jews living in its basement, great writers creating out of the shadow. And Ilan Stavans is the one I kept hidden until now." A frightening metaphor.

In the past five hundred years, Jews in the Hispanic world have been forced to convert to Christianity or to somehow mask or feel ashamed of their ancestral faith. Their intellectual contribution, notwithstanding, has been enormous. Spanish letters cannot be understood without Fray Luis de León and Ludovicus Vives, without Fernando de Roja's *La Celestina* and the anti-Semitic poetry of Francisco de Quevedo, author of the infamous sonnet "A man stuck to a nose." (*Erase un hombre a una nariz pegado, érase una nariz superlativa, érase una alquitara medio viva, érase un peje espada mal barbado . . .*) In the Americas, a safe haven for refugees from the Inquisition and later on for Eastern Europeans running away from the Nazis, Jewish writers have been active since 1910, when Alberto Gerchunoff, a Russian immigrant, published in Spanish his collection of interrelated vignettes, *The Jewish Gauchos of La Pampa,* to commemorate Argentina's independence. He switched from one language to another to seek individual freedom, to validate his democratic spirit, to embrace a dream of plurality and progress: Yiddish, the tongue of Mendele Mokher Sforim and Sholem Aleichem, was left behind; Spanish, Cervantes's vehicle of communication – Gerchunoff was an admirer of *Don Quixote* – became the new tool, the channel to entertain, educate, and redeem the masses. Like Spinoza, Kafka, Nabokov, and Joseph Brodsky, he was the ultimate translator: a bridge between idiosyncrasies.

The abyss and the bridge. Many decades later, some fifty astonishing writers, from Buenos Aires and Mexico to Lima and Guatemala, including Moacyr Scliar, Clarice Lispector, and Mario Szichman, continue to carry on Gerchunoff's torch . . . but the world knows little about them. The narrative boom that catapulted Gabriel García Márquez, Carlos Fuentes, and others from south of the Rio Grande to international stardom in the sixties managed to sell a monolithic, suffocatingly uniform image of the entire continent as a Banana Republic crowded with clairvoyant prostitutes and forgotten generals, never a multicultural society. To such a degree were ethnic voices left in the margin that readers today know much more about Brazilian and Argentine Jews thanks to Borges's short stories "Emma Zunz" and "The Secret Miracle" and Vargas Llosa's novel *The Storyteller* than to anything written by Gerchunoff and his followers. Sadly and in spite of his anti-Semitic tone, my Mexican publisher was right: in the baroque architecture of Latin American letters, Jews inhabit the basement. And yet, *la pureza de sangre* in the Hispanic world is but an abstraction: native Indians, Jews, Arabs, Africans, Christians . . . the collective identity is always in need of a hyphen. In spite of the "official" image stubbornly promoted by governments from time immemorial, Octavio Paz and Julio Cortázar have convincingly used the salamander, the *axólotl*, as a symbol to describe Latin America's popular soul, always ambiguous and in mutation.

America, America

I honestly never imagined I could one day pick up my suitcases to leave home once and for all. And yet, at twenty-five I moved to New

York. I was awarded a scholarship to study for a master's at the Jewish Theological Seminary and, afterwards, perhaps a doctorate at Columbia University or elsewhere. I fled Mexico (and Spanish) mainly because as a secular Jew – what Freud would have called "a psychological Jew" – I felt marginalized, a stereotype. (Little did I know!) A true chameleon, a bit parochial and nearsighted, a nonconformist with big dreams and few possibilities. Like my globe-trotting Hebraic ancestors, I had been raised to build an ivory tower, an individual ghetto. By choosing to leave, I turned my past into remembrance: I left the basement and ceased to be a pariah. *Talia in Heaven* exemplified that existential dilemma: its message simultaneously encourages Jews to integrate and openly invites them to escape; it alternates between life and memory. Paraphrasing Lionel Trilling, its cast of characters, victims of an obsessive God (much like the Bible's) who enjoys ridiculing them, are at the bloody crossroad where politics, theology, and literature meet.

To be or not: To be. The moment I crossed the border, I became somebody else: a new person. In *Chromos: A Parody of Truth,* Felipe Alfau says: "The moment one learns English, complications set in. Try as one may, one cannot elude this conclusion, one must inevitably come back to it." While hoping to master the English language during sleepless nights, I understood James Baldwin, who, already exiled in Paris and quoting Henry James, claimed it is a complex fate to be an American. "America's history," the black author of *Nobody Knows My Name* wrote, "her aspirations, her peculiar triumphs, her even more peculiar defeats, and her position in the world – yesterday and today – are all so profoundly and stubbornly unique that the very word "America" remains a new, almost completely undefined and extremely controversial proper noun. No one in the world seems to know exactly what it describes." To be honest, the rise of multiculturalism, which perceives the melting pot as a soup of diverse and at times incompatible backgrounds, has made the word "America" even more troublesome, more evasive and abstract: Is America a compact whole, a unity? Is it a sum of ethnic groups unified by a single language and a handful of patriotic symbols? Is it a Quixotic dream where total assimilation is impossible, where multiculturalism is to lead to disintegration? And Baldwin's statement acquires a totally different connotation when one goes one step beyond, realizing that "America" is not only a nation (a state of mind) but also a vast continent. From Alaska to the Argentine pampa, from Rio de Janeiro to East Los Angeles, the geography Christopher Columbus mistakenly encountered in 1492 and Amerigo Vespucci baptized a few years later is also a linguistic and cultural addition: America the nation and America the continent. America, America: I wanted to find a room of my own in the two; or two rooms, perhaps?

On Being a White Hispanic and More

Once settled, I suddenly began to be perceived as Hispanic (i.e., Latino) – an identity totally alien to me before. (My knowledge of spoken Latin is minimal.) To make matters worse, my name (once again?), accent and skin color were exceptions to what gringos had as "the Hispanic prototype." In other words, in Mexico I was perceived as Jewish; and now across the border, I was Mexican. Funny, isn't it? (In fact, according to official papers I qualify as a white Hispanic, an unpleasant term if there was ever one.) Once again, an impostor, en echo. (An impostor, says Ambrose Bierce in *The Devil's Dictionary,* is a rival aspirant to public honors.)

Themselves, myself. Hispanics in the United States – some 22,254,059 according to the 1990 census: white, black, yellow, green, blue, red . . . , twice Americans, once in spite of themselves. They have been in the territories north of the Rio Grande even before the Pilgrims of the Mayflower; and with the Guadalupe Hidalgo Treaty signed in 1848, in which Generalíssimo Antonio López de Santa Anna gave away and subsequently sold half of Mexico to the White House (why only half?), many of them unexpectedly, even unwillingly, became a part of an Anglo-Saxon, English-speaking reality. Today, after decades of neglect and silence, decades of anonymity and ignorance, Latinos are finally receiving the attention they deserve. The second fastest growing ethnic group after the Asians, their diversity of roots – Caribbean, Mexican, Central and South American, Iberian, etc. – makes them a difficult collectivity to describe. Are the Cuban migrations from Holguín, Matanzas, and Havana similar in their idiosyncratic attitude to that of Managua, San Salvador, and Santo Domingo? Is the Spanish they speak their true *lingua franca,* the only unifying factor? Is their immigrant experience in any way different from that of previous minorities – Irish, Italian, Jewish, what have you? How do they understand and assimilate the complexities of what it means to be American? And where do I, a white Hispanic, fit in?

Nowhere and everywhere. In 1985 I was assigned by a Spanish magazine to interview Isaac Goldemberg, a famous Jewish-Peruvian novelist who wrote *The Fragmented Life of Don Jacobo Lerner.* When we met at the Hungarian Pastry Shop at Amsterdam Avenue and 110th Street, he told me, among many things, he had been living in New York for over two decades without mastering the English language because he didn't want his Spanish to suffer and ultimately evaporate. Borges says in his short story "The Life of Tadeo Isidoro Cruz (1829–1874)": Any life, no matter how long or complex it may be, is made up essentially of *a single moment* – the moment in which a man finds out, once and for all, who he is. That summer day I understood my linguistic future lay in the opposite direction from Goldemberg's: I would perfect my English and thus become a New York Jew, an intellectual animal in the proud tradition celebrated by Alfred Kazin . . . and I did. In just a single moment I understood who I could be.

The Double

To write is to make sense of confusion in and around. Didn't somebody already say this? Jean Genet, John Updike? I am a copy, an instant replay, a shadow, an impostor. Everything is an echo. To live is to plagiarize, to imitate, to steal.

I have always had the feeling of living somebody else's life. When

I first read Felipe Alfau's *Locos: A Comedy of Gestures,* I was possessed by the idea that, had I been born in 1902 in Barcelona, as had its author, I would have written his book. The exact same sensation was repeated when discovering Pinhas "Der Nister" Kahanovitch's *The Family Mashber,* a masterpiece of Soviet Jewish fiction by a writer who died in a Russian hospital in 1950 as a result of Stalin's purges. And my mother keeps a yellowish school photograph I once gave her. It was taken when I was eight or nine: although smiling, I really don't look happy; and in the back it has a brief line written: "With love from a non-existent twin brother." Furthermore, I am often sure I am being observed by an omniscient Creature (with capital "C"), who enjoys inflicting pain and laughs at the sorrow of His creatures. I cannot but equate the act of writing to God's impact on Nature: He is simultaneously absent and present in His creation, granting birth and death – the Absolute Novelist, a marionette-holder with a vivid imagination and a bad sense of humor (even if He laughs).

"Total Forgetery"

Acting – my father's trade.

As I was growing up, I remember feeling amazed by his incredible talent. I adored him. Watching his performances, I would be pushed to what Sören Kierkegaard regarded as "an existential vacuum – a mystery." Was he really the man I knew or, instead, a mask-carrier? I was particularly fond of him taking me along on Sunday afternoons. We would leave home alone after lunch. While driving an old Rambler, he would ask me about school and friends, about ideas and books, masturbation and a girl's sexuality. He was a hero, a man of integrity like few others, the only guy I knew who was actually happy, very happy, a few minutes every day: on stage. Then, as my father would park the car, I would begin noticing a slow change of attitude, a metamorphosis, as if a veil, an abyss was now setting us apart. Another self would graciously descend to possess him, to take the man I knew and loved away from me. A few minutes later, I would witness how, without shame, he would undress in front of a mirror, put on a bathrobe, and begin to hide his face in cosmetics. He was becoming somebody else, a stranger, a ghost: today a hotel owner, next season a boxer, a cancer patient, a Jewish prisoner in Germany. His breathtaking masks were infallible: they always hid my dad's true self, deformed it. As a result of that transformation, I felt totally alone.

Alone and lonely. The whole phenomenon inspired in me mixed feelings: I was astonished by the magic and frightened at the same time; I hated the whole thing and yet would literally do anything to return tomorrow and witness it anew. My father would then ask a handyman to seat me behind the stage, next to a curtain, in order for me to watch the show. And that, oh God, was his and my greatest moment on earth, the one we awaited even more eagerly than the facial and physical change he underwent to become a character. With a difference: In front of an audience, he was happy; I, on the other hand, was scared to death – invaded by the kind of fear that simultaneously generates joy and sorrow. What did others think of his "new" self? Could they recognize the true face behind the mask? Was he an impostor?

Alone and lonely and full of envy. I would feel an overwhelming sense of envy, profound and disturbing jealousy toward the audience. They received all his attention, which, in normal circumstances, I would keep for my own, or at most, share with my brother and sister. They would be manipulated, seduced by his talents. Why was he so eager to become other people and take a rest from himself? And hide behind a mask? Even more suspiciously, why did the viewers pay to have him taken away from me? How could people pay for my father to cease being himself? The Author of Authors, the Impostor of Impostors: God as playwright. In my eyes, the entire universe was a vast and mysterious theater in which He (Yahweh, Adonai, Elohim, the Holy Spirit, the Father of Fathers) would capriciously establish what people, the actors, are to do, to say, to think, to hope. My dad's actual stage was a microcosmos that inspired me to philosophize about religion and eschatology, about freedom and determinism. I wondered: while acting, was my father free to refuse pronouncing a certain line of the script?; could he talk to me at least once during the performance (through his real and unimported self)? I also wondered if I, Ilan Stavans (a.k.a., Ilan Stavchansky Slomianski), was free to stop being his son?; could I also become other people – like Shakespeare, be one and many? To answer these many questions, I became a novelist. To write is to make sense of confusion in and around. (It was me who said that.)

To write, perchance to dream. (Or vice versa?) Not long ago an interviewer asked me why didn't I follow his footsteps and enter the stage. My response was short and somewhat condescending. Deep inside, I dislike actors. I find their vulnerability, their trendiness and exhibitionism, disturbing. I would rather live in the shadow than in the spotlight. Besides, I love the theater of the mind and have a terrible fear of dying. It might sound absurd but I see literature as brother to memory and theater as a symbol of the ephemeral present. I write in order to remember and be remembered. Death is the absence of recollection – what Luis G. Rodriguez calls "total forgetery." Theater, on the other hand, is a *performance* art, a transitory game. It is only alive during a night show, afterwards it's gone . . . forever. Nothing remains, nothing. Except perhaps a handful of yellowish photos and (luck permitting) an award or two. And if theater is like a vanishing photograph, writing is signing one's name on concrete: a proof of existence ("I was here. . . ."). By incorporating past and present images, a narrative plays with Time (with a capital "T") in an astonishing fashion: it makes reality eternal. Marcel's desire for his mother's goodnight kiss in Proust's *Remembrance of Things Past* is not a pre–World War I scene alone but, unquestionably, an image for the ages. When death turns me into a ghost, at least something, an ingenious thought or a breath of life, will remain – a written page like those of Virgil, Dante, and Cervantes. Perhaps and perhaps not. The only certainty is that a library is a triumph over nothingness. And yet, the warm human contact my dad encounters while performing is always reinvigorating. Literature, on the other hand, is a secluded activity. Isolation, silence, detachment, escape. You hope someone will read you someday, although nothing (not even the timing of God's laughter) is certain. Thus, decades away of those Sunday afternoons when my father would take me along to his show, I still confess I feel envy: He can be happy, I cannot. I honestly wish I could at times take vacations from myself – like him, have another self. It must be refreshing. Isolation, silence.

Before death and after. Literature, I am perfectly aware, is no paliative to cure a spirit's suffering. The day I die, people will not interrupt their routines, why should they? They will make love, eat, defecate, smoke, and read. They will smile and cry and kiss and hate. It will matter to no one (not even my dearest ones, really) that my life has ceased to be and all is over. The show will go on. Grief – a strange and dishonest feeling. When Calvino and Danilo Kiš, two mentors, died, did I cry? (Albert Camus's protagonist in *The Stranger* is incarcerated for not crying during his mother's funeral.) I did pray for their souls and after that . . . after that, nothing. Only through literature, I feel, can I transcend myself. To write is to overcome the imperfections of nature. I do it every day, every day, every day, every . . . ; otherwise, I sense that a day's 86,400 seconds are meaningless and in vain.

Things to Come

A future encyclopædia, to be published in Brussels in 2087, states that at age thirty-one I wrote a book, *Imagining Columbus,* about the Genoese admiral's fifth and final voyage of discovery, one not across the Atlantic but through the human imagination. It mentions the fact that somewhere after 1995, I published a novel about a Belgian actor of Jewish descent who has trouble distinguishing where reality ends and fantasy begins (poor Konstantin Stanislavski! Or is it Konstantin Stavchansky?) – inspired, obviously, by my dad's trade; translated into numerous languages, the volume was enthusiastically received by critics and readers. Afterwards, I wrote another novel, this one in the style of Vargas Llosa, about the exiled family of a Latin American dictator, after which I won numerous grants and prizes, was internationally applauded and commemorated.

The entry also states that I left an echo, an echo, an echo. Critics prized my oeuvre, comparing it to precursors and successors like Kafka, Spinoza, and Borges. Because of my dual identity, in Mexico I was considered a "bad citizen." My themes always dealt with God as manipulator of human conscience and my existential journey could be reduced to a verse by the Nicaraguan *modernista* poet Rubén Darío: "To be and not to know. . . ." My style was precise and direct, akin to religious insights. Cyril Connolly says in *Enemies of Promise:* "The more books we read, the clearer it becomes that the function of the writer is to produce a masterpiece and that no other task is of any consequence." The encyclopædia claims that toward the end of life, I wrote extraordinarily lasting short stories, as if everything that preceded them was a prophecy. Finally, it states that I died on 18 August 2033, with some twenty-two original books to my credit. After a consuming sickness, I contemplated suicide but a sudden heart attack impeded me from arriving at a nearby New York hospital and nothingness took over. That was also a rainy day without major historical events. God witnessed my death and pretended to suffer, although His was of course an actor's gesture. In fact, He laughed: I was (am) His joy and toy.

ESMERALDA SANTIAGO (1948–)

The eldest of eleven children, Esmeralda Santiago was born in rural Puerto Rico in 1948. In 1961, at the age of thirteen, she moved with her family to Brooklyn, New York. She received a B.A. from Harvard College and an M.F.A. from Sarah Lawrence College. *When I Was Puerto Rican,* the memoir Santiago published in 1993, recounts her childhood in Puerto Rico and the difficult transition to urban life in the United States. A sequel, *Almost a Woman,* appeared in 1998. In writing *When I Was Puerto Rican,* Santiago found herself unable to render into English such distinctive Puerto Rican concepts as *dignidad* and *jíbaro* and instead kept them in Spanish, with a glossary in the back of the book for the benefit of Anglophones who do not know the other language. In 1994, while producing a Spanish version of *When I Was Puerto Rican,* she added a preface unique to that edition that discusses her own linguistic predicament: how she is torn between two tongues, Spanish and English, and can express certain feelings only in her native Spanish.

Introduction to *Cuando era puertorriqueña*

The life recounted in this book was lived in Spanish, but was at first written down in English. Many times, while writing, I was surprised to hear myself speak Spanish while my fingers typed out the same phrase in English. Then the language began to be stammered, and the meaning of what was being said and written was lost, as if observing that I was translating from one language to another caused me to lose both.

I would like to say that this situation occurs only when I am writing, but the truth is that many times, in conversation with friends or relatives, I have found myself in limbo between Spanish and English, wanting to say something that I, caught up in a frustrating linguistic void, could not express. In order to extricate myself, I have to decide in which language, whether Spanish or English, I will formulate my words and trust they will have meaning and that the person I am speaking to will understand me.

The language that I speak most is English. I live in the United States, surrounded by people who speak only English, so that I am the one who has to make herself understood. In my role as a mother, I communicate with teachers, doctors, school bus drivers, the mothers of my children's playmates. As a wife, I make an effort to be understood by my husband, who does not speak Spanish, his relatives, his friends, and his colleagues. As a professional, my essays, stories, and fictions are all written in English for a public, whether Latino or North American, for whom reading is much easier in this language.

But at night, when I am on the threshold of sleep, the thoughts that fill my mind are in Spanish. The songs that murmur to me in dreams are in Spanish. My dreams are a mixture of Spanish and English that is understandable to everyone, that expresses what I want to say, who I am, what I feel. In that shadowy world, language does not matter. What does matter is that I have something to say and can say it without having to tailor it to my listeners.

But obviously, this is in my dreams. Daily life is something else.

When editor Merloyd Lawrence offered me the opportunity to write my memoirs, I never imagined that the process would force me to confront not only my monolingual past, but also my bilingual present. While transcribing the scenes of my childhood, I had to find North American words to express a Puerto Rican experience. How, for example, does one say *cohitre* in English? Or *alcapurrias?* Or *pitittre?* How can I explain what a *jíbaro* is? What North American word has the same meaning as our Puerto Ricanism *cocotazo?*

Sometimes I found a word in English that approximates one in Spanish. But other times I had to conform to Spanish usage of a word, and I had to include a glossary in the book by which people who needed it could find more information about what appeared in the text.

When editor Robin Desser offered me the opportunity to translate my memoirs into Spanish for [the Spanish] edition, I never imagined that the process would force me to realize how much Spanish I have forgotten. In the North American edition, specific words indicate how certain people express themselves. Some people *"smile,"* but others *"grin,"* or *"chuckle,"* or *"guffaw."* In Spanish they smile or laugh in one way or another; but there is no single word that expresses their way of doing it, and two, three, or four descriptive words were needed.

The process of translating from English into Spanish forced me to learn anew the language of my childhood. But it also demonstrated to me that the language I now speak, which I had thought to be Spanish, is a dialect compounded of words from both Spanish and English, joining them to colloquial Puerto Rican expressions and altering them in such a way as to create new words. In my home, for example, we wash the floor with a *mapo,* we buy a *tique* to the movies, we read *panfletos,* we give *el* OK, and we call *pa' atrás* when we are too *bisi* to speak on the telephone.

A few years ago, if someone had pointed out to me all the Spanish idioms in my vocabulary, I would have been embarrassed at evidence of my sloppiness. Today I have come to accept the fact that those idioms that I had to create are what permit me to express myself in my own manner. When I write in English, I have to translate from the Spanish that stores my memories. When I speak in Spanish, I have to translate from the English that defines my present. And when I write in Spanish, I find myself in the middle of three languages – the Spanish of my childhood, the English of my adulthood, and the Spanglish that crosses from one world to the other just as we crossed from our barrio in Puerto Rico to the neighborhoods of Brooklyn.

The title of this book is in the past tense: *When I Was Puerto Rican.* That does not mean that I have ceased being it, but the book describes that stage of my life as defined by the Puerto Rican countryside. When we made the leap of moving to the United States, it changed. I ceased, superficially, being a Puerto Rican country girl by turning into a hybrid between one world and another: a Puerto Rican who lives in the United States, speaks English almost all day, and is part of North American culture day and night.

Here I am considered Latina or Hispanic, in capital letters. In truth, I do not know what that means. I identify myself thus when it is necessary – when I have to fill out forms that offer no alternative, or when I have to support our leaders in their efforts to advance our economic and social situation in the United States. But I do know what it means, for me, to be Puerto Rican. My Puerto Ricanness includes my North American life, my Spanglish, the *sofrito* that enhances my rice with beans, the sauce made of tomatoes, and the salsa made of music. One culture enriches the other, and I have been enriched by both.

Yet I often regret having left my island, my people, my language.

And this regret at times takes the form of anger, resentment over the fact that I did not choose to come to the United States. They carried me off against my will. However, it is this childish anger that nourishes my writing. It makes me face the empty page and fill it with words that try to understand and explain to others what it is to live in two worlds, one North American and the other Puerto Rican. It is this anger that engages my soul and guides my fingers, pointing their way among the smiles and laughs that are so specific in English and that in Spanish are two words that require support by expressing, at times, not the pleasure but the sadness behind them. Doleful smile. Anguished laugh. Words between teeth. And it is that anger that makes it possible for me to pardon who I am. When I was a child, I wanted to be a country girl, and as an adolescent I wanted to be North American. A woman now, I am both, a North American country girl, and I carry my banana stain with pride and dignity.

Translated by Steven G. Kellman

ROSARIO FERRÉ (1938–)

The daughter of Luis A. Ferré, former governor-general of Puerto Rico, Rosario Ferré was born in Ponce, Puerto Rico, in 1938. She received a B.A. in both English and Spanish from Manhattanville College, an M.A. in Latin American literature from the University of Puerto Rico, and a Ph.D. in the same subject from the University of Maryland. Through her criticism, poetry, and fiction, Ferré, a professor at the University of Puerto Rico and a contributing editor of the *San Juan Star,* has become a leading figure in Puerto Rican letters. Her literary career has been ambilingual, alternating between works in Spanish and in English. She has also translated her own fiction from Spanish into English. Ferré's writings in Spanish include the story collection *Papeles de Pandora* (The youngest doll, 1976); the novella *Maldita amor* (Sweet diamond dust, 1987); and the novel *La batalia de las vírgenes* (The battle of the virgins, 1993), as well as poetry and a biography of her father. She has published three novels – *The House on the Lagoon* (1995), *Eccentric Neighborhoods* (1998), and *Flight of the Swan* (2001) – in English. In this brief statement, Ferré reflects on the differences that writing in each of her two languages makes for her.

Bilingual in Puerto Rico

I didn't learn how to speak English until I was seven, and I learned most of it by reading books. By the time I was ten, sneaking into my father's library, I had read *Wuthering Heights, Jane Eyre, The Three Musketeers,* and *The Thousand and One Nights.* I still speak English with a Spanish accent: "canary" and "cannery," "sheet" and "shit" make me tremble when I have to say them, and I often get myself into serious trouble. But Spanish still makes me suck faster at life's breast.

I write Spanish the same way I speak it, fast. Spanish is for me *la lengua escrita,* English is *the written word.* That's why it's impossible for me to write in English the way I write in Spanish. English makes me slow down. I have to think over what I'm going to say twice, maybe three times – which is often healthy because I can't put my foot, or rather my pen, in my mouth so easily. I can't be trigger-happy in English because words take too much effort.

Spanish literature has an oral quality to it, and Caribbean literature especially, since it comes directly from oral tradition. Perhaps that is why it does not translate well. Caribbean stories can be like incantations that lead to alternate realities; their meaning often cannot be discerned until they are read out loud. *The written word* for me has Milton, Shakespeare, and the King James Bible standing behind it, swords drawn. Spanish, *the written tongue,* doesn't have to be taken so seriously; there's more room for *bachata* and *relajo,* for wordplay.

To say it in plain English, I love to write in Spanish. Spanish is like an exuberant jungle I get lost in, meandering down paths of words that may only lead to the rustle of their own foliage. Like

Don Quixote's horse, Rocinante, I can roll on the ground and frolic in Spanish because I don't have to worry about anything; words always mean what they say. I love to make love in Spanish; I've never been able to make love in English. In English, I get puritanical. I could never do a belly dance, dance a flamenco, or do a *zapateo* in English.

Writing in English is like looking at the world through a different pair of binoculars: It imposes a different mind-set. When I write in Spanish, my sentences are often as convoluted as a Baroque *retablo.* When I write in English, I make my sentences straight and simple, because I want to be precise as well as practical. I feel like Emily Dickinson with a loaded gun in my hand: If I shoot, I must bring down my target. Otherwise, I know I'm going to get shot at.

And yet, beneath my Puerto Rican English, a Latino passion throbs, a salsa rhythm swings. I'm always coming and going from English to Spanish, between the conga drums and the violins. Language has become *la guaga aérea;* it keeps me flying between Puerto Rico and New York.

To be a bilingual writer doesn't mean just to be bilingual. A bilingual writer is really two *different* writers, has two very different voices, writes in two different styles, and, most important, looks at the world through two different sets of glasses. This takes a splitting of the self that doesn't come easily and can be dangerous. A specific smell, a sound, or a taste can bring with it a whole universe of reminiscences, as Proust well knew. But sensory experiences are related to words, and while in one language a word can bring a dead person to life, in another that person will remain forever defunct. In traversing linguistic borders, there is a real danger of finding yourself stranded in the connecting labyrinths of words, of losing contact with the springs of the unconscious from which ideas flow.

I see bilingualism as a tremendous advantage. I see no reason to give up one language if I can help it. Having two different views of the world is profoundly enriching. I feel proud that 65 percent of Puerto Rico's population is bilingual, and I am convinced bilingualism should be promoted in the United States. Freedom of speech was, after all, one of the reasons our country was founded.

LUC SANTE (1954–)

Luc Sante was born in 1954 in Verviers, Belgium. When the foundry that employed his father went bankrupt, in 1959, the family emigrated to New Jersey. Nine months later, they returned to Belgium but came back to the United States a few months later.

Pondering his background in a small European country divided between Flemish and Walloon, rural and urban, Catholic and anticlerical, Sante writes: "To have been born Belgian is to have been cast, as if by the zodiac, under the sign of ambivalence." Yet he also feels torn between Europe and America, between French and English, "unassimilable in two cultures, waging a solo war on both fronts."

Sante, who lives in New York City and writes in English, is the author of *Low Life: Lures and Snares of Old New York* (1991) and *Evidence* (1992). He is a frequent contributor to *New York, Slate,* the *New York Review of Books,* and *Granta.* In the following excerpt from his 1998 memoir, *The Factory of Facts,* Sante analyzes the distinct identities that French and English have created for him.

Dummy

In order to speak of my childhood I have to translate. It is as if I were writing about someone else. The words don't fit, because they are in English, and languages are not equivalent one to another. If I say, "I am a boy; I am lying in my bed; I am sitting in my room; I am lonely and afraid," attributing these thoughts to my eight-year-old self, I am being literally correct but emotionally untrue. Even if I submit the thoughts to indirect citation and the past tense I am engaging in a sort of falsehood. I am playing ventriloquist, and that eight-year-old, now made of wood and with a hinged jaw, is sitting on my knee, mouthing the phrases I am fashioning for him. It's not that the boy couldn't understand those phrases. It is that in order to do so, he would have to translate, and that would mean engaging an electrical circuit in his brain, bypassing his heart.

If the boy thought the phrase "I am a boy," he would picture Dick or Zeke from the schoolbooks, or maybe his friends Mike or Joe. The word "boy" could not refer to him; he is *un garçon.* You may think this is trivial, that *"garçon"* simply means "boy," but that is missing the point. Similarly, *maman* and *papa* are people; "mother" and "father" are notions. *La nuit* is dark and filled with fear, while "the night" is a pretty picture of a starry field. The boy lives in *une maison,* with "a house" on either side. His *coeur* is where his feelings dwell, and his "heart" is a blood-pumping muscle. For that matter, his name is Luc, pronounced *lük;* everybody around, though, calls him "Luke," which is an alias, a mask.

He regards the English language with a curiosity bordering on the entomological. Watching the *Amerloques* moving around in their tongue is like seeing lines of ants parading through tunnels bearing sections of leaves. He finds it funny, often enough. In school, for instance, when nutrition is discussed, the elements of a meal are called "servings," a word that always conjures up images of footmen in clawhammer coats bearing covered dishes. Since he knows that his classmates, however prosperous their parents might be, aren't likely to have servants, he substitutes the familiar advertising icon of Mother entering the room with a trussed turkey on a platter, which is no less alien or ridiculous. He gathers that this scene has some material basis in the lives of Americans, although it appears to him contrived beyond belief. American life, like the English language, is endlessly fascinating and hopelessly phony.

His vantage point is convenient, like a hunter's blind. He has some struggles with the new language – it will be years, for example, before his tongue and teeth can approximate the *th* sound, and in the meantime he will have to tolerate laughter every time he pronounces "third" as "turd" – but at the same time he is protected. No one will ever break his heart with English words, he thinks. It is at home that he is naked. If the world outside the door is a vast and apparently arbitrary game, inside lies the familiar, which can easily bruise or cut him. No, his parents aren't monsters, nothing like that, although they may not appreciate their own power. Anyway, he has raised and nurtured enough monsters by himself to inflict pain without need of assistance. The French language is a part of his body and his soul, and it has a latent capacity for violence. No wonder he has trouble navigating between the languages at first: they are absurdly different, doors to separate and unequal universes. Books might allege they are the same kind of item, like a pig and a goat, but that is absurd on the face of it. One is tissue and the other is plastic. One is a wound and the other is a prosthesis.

Of course, the French language would not be so intimate, wrenching, and potentially dangerous to him if he had remained in a French-speaking world. There he would be bombarded by French of all temperatures, flavors, connotations. His friends, his enemies, his teachers, his neighbors, the newspaper, the radio, the billboards, people on the street, pop songs, movies, assembly instructions, lists of ingredients, shouting drunks, mumbling lunatics, indifferent officials, all would transmit in French. Pretty girls would speak French. He would pick up slang, poesy, academese, boilerplate, specialized jargon, cant, nonsense. He would not only hear French everywhere but absorb it unconsciously all the time. He would learn the kinds of things no dictionary will tell you: for example that apparent synonyms are in reality miles apart, each with its own calluses of association. By and by, *je* would become more than his private self, would find itself shoulder to shoulder with the *je* of a million others. There would be traffic and commerce between inner life and outer world. A great many things would go without saying, be taken for granted. It would seem as though language had arisen from the ground, had always been and would always be.

Instead French festers. It is kept in darkness and fed meagerly by spoonfuls. It isn't purposely neglected, of course; there is nothing intentionally punitive about the way it is sequestered and undernourished. On the contrary: it is cherished, cosseted, rewarded for just being, like an animal in a zoo. But like that animal it can only enact a semblance of its natural existence. Its memory of the native habitat grows sparser all the time, and its attempts at normality become playacting, become parody, become rote. Its growth has been stunted, and it correspondingly retains many infantine characteristics. Even as the boy grows gradually tougher and more worldly in English, he carries around a French internal life whose clock has stopped. He is unnaturally fragile, exaggeratedly sensitive in his French core. Not surprisingly, he resents it, wants to expunge it, destroy it, pour salt on its traces to prevent regeneration.

What does this say about the boy's view of his family circumstances? That is a complicated matter. French is his soul, and it is also a prison, and the same terms could be applied to his family. At home he is alone with his parents; no one else exists. It is stifling and comforting in equal measure. Out in the world he is entirely alone. He is terrified but he is free. Or potentially free, anyway; he's too young to know. But one of the things that sustains him in the world is the knowledge of his French innards. He can feel superior about it (his peers don't possess anything equivalent, and they'll never have any idea what it feels like), but it is simultaneously a source of shame. At home he may be alone with his parents, but while they have an awesome power over his infant core, his growing English self is something they don't know and can't touch. You can take all these propositions as mathematical equations. Work them out, forwards or backwards, and you will always arrive at the same reduction, the same answer: he is alone.

My attempt to put any sort of words in the boy's mouth is foredoomed. He doesn't yet have a language. He has two tongues: one is all quivering, unmediated, primal sensation, and the other is detached, deliberate, artificial. To give a full accounting he would have to split himself in two. But I don't know whether I might not have to do the same myself, here and now. To speak of my family, for example, I can hardly employ English without omitting an emotional essence that remains locked in French, although I can't use French, either, unless I am willing to sacrifice my critical intelligence. But there is an advantage hidden in this predicament: French is an archeological site of emotions, a pipeline to my infant self. It preserves the very rawest, deepest, least guarded feelings.

If I stub my toe, I may profanely exclaim, in English, "Jesus!" But in agony, such as when I am passing a kidney stone, I might cry, *"Petit Jésus!"* with all the reverence of nursery religion. Others have told me that when I babble in feverish delirium or talk aloud in my sleep, I do so in French. Preserved, too, in French, is a world of lost pleasures and familial comforts. If someone says, in English, "Let's go visit Mr. and Mrs. x," the concept is neutral, my reaction determined by what I think of Mr. and Mrs. x. On the other hand, if the suggestion is broached in French, *"Allons dire bonjour,"* the phrasing affects me more powerfully than the specifics. *"Dire bonjour"* calls up a train of associations: for some reason I see my great-uncle Jules Stelmes, dead more than thirty years, with his fedora and his enormous white mustache and his soft dark eyes. I smell coffee and the raisin bread called *cramique,* hear the muffled bong of a parlor clock and the repetitive commonplaces of chitchat in the drawling accent of the Ardennes, people rolling their *r*'s and leaning hard on their initial *h*'s. I feel a rush-caned chair under me, see white curtains and a starched tablecloth, can almost tap my feet on the cold ceramic tiles, maybe the trompe l'oeil pattern that covered the entire floor surface of my great-uncle Albert Remacle's farmhouse in Viville. I am sated, sleepy, bored out of my mind.

The triggers that operate this mechanism are the simplest, humblest expressions. They are things that might be said to a child or said often within a child's hearing. There are common comestibles: *une tasse de café, une tartine, du chocolat.* There are interjections and verbal place-markers: *sais-tu, figure-toi, je t'assure, mon Dieu.* And, naturally, there are terms of endearment. In my family, the use of someone's first name was nearly always an indication of anger or a prelude to bad news. My parents addressed me as *fifi, chou* (cabbage), *lapin* (rabbit), *vî tchèt* (Walloon: old cat), *petit coeur.* If I'd done something mischievous, my father would laugh and call me *cûrêye* (Walloon for "carcass" or "spavined horse" – like saying, "you're rotten"); if I'd made myself especially comfortable, such as by taking up most of the couch, he'd shake his head and grin and call me *macrale* (Walloon for "witch"). I regularly got called *tièsse èl aîr* (Walloon: head in the clouds). If my mother was teasing me in mock anger, she'd call me a *petit chenapan* (little scamp); if it was my father, he'd be likely to say *"t'es ô tièssetou"* ("you're a stubborn one," in Walloon). My father's real anger was rare and grave; my mother's boiled over quickly even if it faded just as fast. She might call me a *vaurien* (good-for-nothing) or a *sâle gosse* (dirty kid), an *èstèné* (Walloon for "idiot," literally "bewildered") or a *singlé* (simpleton) or a *nolu* (Walloon: nullity). If I'd really stung her, though, she'd yell *chameau!* (camel), and I liked that, because she was acknowledging I had some kind of power. There are worse words, which still have the capacity to make me cringe: *cochon* (pig), *crapuleux* (vile, vicious), *crotté* (filthy), *mâssî* (ditto: Walloon). Those words are woven through the fabric of my early adolescence.

A few years ago, early in the morning, I was waiting to cross a street in Liège. I wasn't quite awake yet, and was lost in thought, so that when I heard someone shout *"Fais attention! Regarde!"* I immediately stiffened. All of a sudden I was back at the age of eight or nine, being reproved by my parents. As it happened, there was a small boy standing next to me, holding a tray of empty coffee cups which he was returning to the café opposite; his father, manning a flea-market booth behind us, had observed the kid putting a toe into the street unmindful of oncoming traffic. It can easily happen to me, when faced with some officious Francophone creep, shopkeeper or librarian or customs agent, that I lose thirty years and two feet off my height. If I haven't briefed myself beforehand, I crumple. This can happen even though I've kept my French alive internally through reading, and more recently have acquired friends with whom I engage in adult conversation in that language. But even in such circumstances I can find myself tripped up, suddenly sprawled. I can be reading something truly scabrous, something by Georges Bataille, say, turning the pages as an imperturbable adult, and then a phrase will shock me, not some description of outlandish vice but rather a perfectly innocent locution lying in the midst of the smut. It will throw everything else into a new relief. Suddenly it is as if one of my aunts had looked up from her coffee and started spewing obscenities.

Since I live almost entirely in English now, I can regard French with some of the same detachment and sense of the ridiculous with which I once regarded my adopted tongue. If I walk into an American discount store and the loudspeaker starts braying, "Attention shoppers!" I will consign the noise to the realm of static, switch off its ability to reach me except as an irritant. On the other hand, if I am in a Belgian supermarket and the loudspeaker begins its recital, nearly always in a polished female murmur rather than the American male bark: *"Monsieur, madame, nous vous conseillons . . ."* I am bemused, imagining the rapport between the voice and its sleek, well-dressed target, someone so exquisitely put together that he or she can purchase low-fat frozen entrees with a withering superiority, as if picking out a *grand cru classé.* I am never the "you" of American advertising because I consciously slam the door, but in French I am never given the opportunity to spurn the come-on. I am excluded at the gate. Naturally, there is a class factor involved – in French I revert to proletarian status as easily as to childhood – but the exclusion is also due to my status as a counterfeit Belgian, an American pretender.

In Belgium I am an oddity. Having been raised abroad in a bubble of the old culture, I've retained curious verbal archaisms; I may unconsciously say *auto* instead of *voiture* to mean "car," for instance, or *illustré* instead of *revue* to mean "magazine," expressions redolent of the 1930s or '40s, if not earlier. Mingled with a distinct American flavor in my speech is a strong dose of the old Verviers Walloon accent, and the combination confuses anyone who perceives it. One day in Liège I shared the elevator with a neighbor I hadn't previously met. He asked me for the time, and when I told him he suddenly said, "How can it be that you're an American Verviétois?" (He was an actor, with a particularly fine ear.) Sometimes I just pass for a foreigner, and sometimes for a local who's a bit simple, uncertain of what bus to take or what to do with the ticket once on board. Whenever I arrive in the country my speech is halting, awkwardly translated from the American, ill-equipped for anything the slightest bit complex or abstract or for that matter adult. Conversely, terms that were not present in my parents' speech, often because they did not enter ordinary spoken language until after our emigration, can seem absurd, pretentious, empty. They seem that way, that is, until I have spent a few days in the company of French-speaking friends, and so have recovered the language, having effected an internal conversion to its rhythm, from which the idiom follows organically. By the third day I might surprise myself employing one of those brittle new phrases, as if it were the most natural thing in the world.

I can cross the border between English and French, although I can't straddle it. Years ago, when I worked behind the cash register in a store, I resented the demands of the customers and sometimes went out of my way to be rude to them, to put them in their place. After work, though, I might go to some other shop, and there, trying to find out whether the shirt came in a larger size or a darker color, would find myself resenting the arrogance and apathy of the clerks. I had jumped from one side of the fence to the other. I could no more simultaneously occupy the mentality of clerk and client than I could bat a ball to myself in the outfield. Each claim effaced the other. It was useless to try and apportion blame; customers and clerks were both rude and both justified, were in fact interchangeable. This insight is perhaps the closest I've ever gotten to understanding the psychology that lies behind nationalism. The situation is a bit like one of the famous optical illusions: you can see the vase, and then you can see the two profiles, but you can't see both images at once.

Belgium is an ill-fitting suit of a country. It is stitched together from odds and ends, represents a purely strategic decision on the part of the larger powers, has no identity as a nation, and so on. And it unnaturally couples two language groups who are both right and both wrong (actually three language groups if you add the relatively untroubled German-speaking minority – no more than seventy thousand souls in any case). And both principal language groups have ambiguous ongoing relationships with the majority stockholders of their languages, that is, the Dutch and the French. The Flemish and the Dutch in recent years have been forming cultural and trade partnerships, and apparently enjoying themselves at it. Their mutual history is somewhat more vexed, with the Dutch regarding the Flemings with a certain benign hauteur, and the Flemish viewing the Dutch as worldly, as apostates, as lacking in seriousness, not to mention virtue. But they read each other's literatures, and just as the Flemings have adopted the grammar and usage of their cousins, so the Dutch appreciate the particular flavor of Flemish expressions, and have helped themselves to dashes of the idiom. Between the Walloons and the French the situation is less comfortable. Essentially, the French feel superior and the Walloons oblige them by feeling embarrassed. There has long been a Francophile segment of the Walloon population, and as the national tension has risen, so has the noise emitted by a certain minority that favors the detachment of Wallonia from Belgium and its adherence to France. The French have shown no corresponding interest in acquiring five impoverished and déclassé eastern provinces.

The linguistic situation is symptomatic. Popular manuals for the identification and eradication of *belgicismes* were published at least as far back as the eighteenth century and continue to be today. *Le Soir,* out of Brussels, has a weekly feature that reiterates the very same cautions as, for example, the writer who called himself "*un ancien professeur*" uttered in 1806: don't say *tartine,* say instead *beurrée,* and so forth. That example should serve to indicate that the wish to eliminate native expressions has nothing to do with grammatical rigor or the rectification of ambiguities, but is merely the expression of a class-bound shame. Visitors always note that Belgians say *septante* for seventy and *nonante* for ninety, whereas the French say *soixante-dix* and *quatre-vingt-dix,* respectively. I have no idea why Belgians do not also say *octante* for eighty, the three simpler expressions having been used by French-speaking proletarians of both lands for centuries; the arithmetical rebuses are owed entirely to class pretension. Similarly, the city of Liège was known to one and all as Liége until around the time of World War I, when the accent mark was switched in accordance with the lowercase *liège,* which means cork-tree and has no etymological rapport with the city's name. There was even a law passed; the old spelling only survived for a while in the name of the now-defunct *Gazette de Liége,* which was grandfathered. (Among my inheritances from the traditional working class is the old pronunciation of the word, which has caused auditors to look at me funny and even to correct me.) A more recent example of this tendency is what happened across the country to the name of the establishments that make and sell fried potatoes. For untold decades and throughout my childhood they were known as *fritures,* until at some point in the 1970s a humorless functionary decreed the name incorrect, since *friture* is the word for the fat in which the potatoes are fried. Now only establishments older than twenty-five or so years can continue to name themselves that way; the more recent shops must be called *friteries.*

The French, particularly through the agency of their Academy, have long policed their language in such petty ways. Neologisms and loanwords are forbidden, shifts in grammar and usage swiftly curtailed. French was once a major force in the world, among other things the international language of diplomacy. Those who wonder why it has ceded so much of its power to English need look no further than this wish to preserve a seventeenth-century cadaver. Belgians who submit their language to French rules concede twice over. But the submission is by now traditional; after all, the Walloons have done a fairly effective job of killing off their own tongue.

Walloon, the native patois of southern Belgium, is usually identified as a dialect of French, whereas it derived on its own from the Latin of the Roman legions, and is just as old as the patois of Île-de-France, which became the official language. The eleventh edition of the *Encyclopædia Britannica* in fact identifies it as the northernmost Romance language. I once posed the question to a linguist-translator: What is the line separating a language from a dialect? He replied that the situation could be summed up in a phrase: History is written by the victors. The dialect of Île-de-France was the patois of the French kings; it subjugated Walloon as well as Provençal, Norman, Lorrain, Gascon, Picard, Occitan, and so on, and reduced them from languages to dialects. The effect of linguistic imperialism is well described by the great Verviétois philologist Jules Feller (1859–1940), in his *Notes de philologie wallonne* (1912):

> Political necessity, material interest, constraint, and the moral superiority of the conqueror and his language can create within a single century the troubling phenomenon of a tongue being entirely forgotten by its nation. The first generation does its best to gabble the idiom of the foreign invaders. The second generation, if it be to its advantage, already knows the new language better than the old. The third generation for all practical purposes knows and employs only the new.

Feller uses this model to describe the impact of Latin on the Celto-Germanic population of Gallia Belgica, but it applies just as well to the effect of French upon Walloon over the last century (and, incidentally, it is likewise true of the linguistic process that accompanies immigration). Feller goes on to characterize French as "a brilliant soldier of fortune in the army of Romance dialects who has become a general," while Walloon is "a little corps of soldiers, consigned to the fringe of the battalion, who have never gotten the chance to distinguish themselves."

There are texts going back to around the year 1000 that employ Walloon words and phrases within a stew of various strains of French. These do not reflect the true state of the language, because Walloon was the tongue of the general illiterate population, from which authors of texts, mostly members of the clergy, were perforce removed. Walloon literature was inaugurated toward the end of the twelfth or the beginning of the thirteenth century by an anonymous *Moral* of some two thousand verses, and jerked its way forward for another three centuries until French began smothering its neighbors. But Walloon sprang back to life in the seventeenth century, Matthias Navaeus's 1620 *Ode* to the city of Liège being the first distinguished item in its literature. A further flowering occurred in the late eighteenth century, when the opening of a popular theater in Liège inspired the writing of a number of comic plays, some of which are still occasionally performed. Edmund Gosse, in his entry on Walloon literature in the eleventh *Britannica,* notes that in these works "the Walloon humor is displayed with great crudity; anything like sentiment or elevated feeling is unknown."

This state of affairs was to persist. As Feller implies in his metaphor, Walloon had developed far from courts or centers of power; even the prince-bishops of Liège were primarily Germans, and the dukes of Burgundy were educated in French territory. Walloon remained a language of the poor, and consequently its compass was limited to matters of the hearth, the market, the tavern, the soil. You can see this in the Walloon words that made their way into the French language during the late Middle Ages, such as *"estaminet,"* for example, which means a saloon or grog-shop; for that matter many French words that pertain to mining and to the textile trade derive from the Walloon-Picard complex. Walloon never darkened the doors of the centers of learning, even during the great transition to the vulgate that occurred around the time of the Reformation. As a result, it is a language almost entirely free of abstract concepts. An essayist writing in a Parisian review at the beginning of this century asserted that in Walloon "there are a hundred ways to say 'ginever,' but no words for 'idealism' or 'dialectic.' "

It might yet have had a chance to develop in the nineteenth century, had the Belgian educational establishment seized the opportunity afforded by independence to teach Walloon in schools. Instead the opposite occurred: steps were taken to suppress the language, and teachers took it as their mission to "cure" pupils of their native tongue. Belgians today might argue that the institutionalization of Walloon could not have been undertaken, given the friction between Flemish and French speakers, but let us recall that the attempt to erase Flemish reached its peak during the same period. One tangible result of the suppression is that Walloon has remained divided into clusters, separated by differences in vocabulary, grammar, and pronunciation. There are four principal strains: the eastern, centered in Liège; the middle, in Namur; the western, in Charleroi; and the southern, roughly centralized among the towns of Bastogne, Neufchâteau, and Marche-en-Famenne. Not only are the differences among these strains sufficiently great that speakers of the eastern and western varieties can barely understand one another, but variations, sometimes significant ones, can separate the Walloon of one town from that of its neighbor. The closest thing to a unified dictionary that exists is the mammoth *Atlas linguistique de la Wallonie,* a project that began after World War II and was still in progress forty years later. In it each word is accorded two pages, one for the variations and the other for the map on which to locate them. Anyway, the language today is scorned by the middle class, just as it was spoken almost clandestinely by their peasant ancestors a century ago. Feller reports that when he went on word-collecting expeditions in rural villages, most of the people he addressed in Walloon answered him in French, since they were certain he was out to mock them.

But Walloon did have its golden age. It was brief, lasting from the mid-1880s until just before World War I. That period saw an efflorescence of Walloon literature, plays and poems primarily, and the founding of many theaters and periodicals. The New York Public Library possesses a surprisingly large collection of literary works in Walloon, quite possibly the largest outside Belgium, and its holdings are statistically representative of the output. Out of nearly a thousand plays in the collection, only twenty-six were published before 1880. Thereafter the numbers rise gradually year by year, reaching a peak of sixty-nine in 1903, and then they fall again, down to eleven in 1913. Only twenty-one of them were published after World War I. The reasons for this decline remain a mystery; it was not occasioned by the war itself. The statistics presented by the library's holdings are backed up by others: the major era of Walloon comic weeklies, for example, seems to have taken place between 1895 and 1905, after which more periodicals folded than were begun. Literary production occurred at different paces in different cities, but Liège, Verviers, Namur, and Charleroi led the pack, approximately in that order.

In *Fré Cougnou,* one of several Walloon weeklies published in Verviers around the turn of the century, not only were the poems, stories, and jokes in Walloon but nearly all the advertisements as well. One ad features a studio photograph of a man wearing a peasant's smock over his suit, a slouch hat on his head, and a large curved pipe in his mouth; slung over an arm is a wicker basket. The caption reads: "Jules Le Ruth, good Walloon writer, dealer in good cheeses." There were all sizes of talents and all sorts of people (all of them men, though) in the movement. That the movement was (otherwise) genuinely democratic can be seen in Oscar Colson's bibliography of published works covering the prime years 1905 and 1906. The professions of the authors are cited, and besides one university professor, two priests, and a sizable number of teachers and printers, they also include a butcher, a tinsmith, two traveling salesmen, a coal miner, a housepainter, a cordwainer, a bartender, a plumber, an electrician, several accountants, a coppersmith, a bailiff, a crystal engraver, a watchmaker, an insurance adjuster, a glassblower, a mailman, and a number of ordinary factory workers. At its peak, Walloon literature was like a massive exhalation of breath long held in. It approached – as in Lautréamont's exhortation – poetry made by all.

There was, however, perhaps more enthusiasm than substance. Boulevard comedy was the template for theatrical works; the poems were primarily burlesques or sentimental love lyrics. The movement was culturally and socially conservative: the Verviétois poet Alphonse Ramet, who wrote an ode to Spartacus – which alarmed his colleagues, who heard it as a call to revolution – stands out as an exception. The movement was literally provincial, although literature of other languages was translated into Walloon, including fables by La Fontaine, letters by Rousseau, tales by Hans Christian Andersen, plays by Goldoni and Chekhov. The movement had its stars, its innovators, its hacks, its students. In Verviers, Henri Hurard was as great as Scribe; his many plays were hailed in a vigorous critical press, continually revived and reprinted, translated into Picard and the dialect of Charleroi. A street was named after him. To come upon the traces of all this ferment is like finding a city buried under volcanic ash, its people frozen while shopping or bathing or giving speeches – an entire self-contained world is on view, but its glories and standards and shibboleths are now completely forgotten. Among the holdings of the New York Public Library are presentation copies of works inscribed by one then-famous name to another, which were perhaps acquired by Americans in the ruins of World War I and since then have barely been consulted by anyone. In my excitement at encountering this literature I searched long and hard for works to translate into English. I failed. The material is frequently weak if not evanescent; it possesses real merits, but they are entirely bound up with the flavor of the language itself, which does not travel.

The texture of Walloon is hard to convey in another tongue. It resembles French in many ways – if you are conversant with French you can make out the rudiments of Walloon, on the page by sounding it out from hearing someone speak it slowly – but it incorporates elements of Old Low German in its vocabulary, and it also differs in such structural matters as the placement of the adjective before the noun (in French it nearly always comes after). Proper French is said to be *pincé* (pinched); Walloon is the opposite, broadly drawled. Indeed, like the French slang called *argot* it derives a great deal of its force from the ways in which it reverses the conventional French values of decorum, reserve, gestural economy, and elegant style. Walloon is anything but elegant. It roars and bawls and guffaws. It is a great vehicle for the mock-lament, the histrionic complaint, the self-consuming boast, the tender homely croon of reassurance. Its essential medium is the apothegm, of which there are so many that Joseph Dejardin's compilation (1891–1892) comes in two large volumes of small type. It is loud, good-humored, long-suffering, self-mocking, wry, and often psychologically acute. It shares something with Yiddish in these characteristics, as well as in the unbuttoned, elbows-out roominess of its sound. The only translation of it I have ever come across consists of a few Walloon phrases in Apollinaire's *The Poet Assassinated;* the translator, Ron Padgett, had the inspired idea of rendering them into Scottish – "Y'arr a boonie lassie" gives a fair accounting of *"Vs'estez one belle crapeaute di nom di Dio."* Taken on its own terms, Walloon is rich in shadings and subtleties, but those terms are inseparably tied to the ground of a lost world.

Walloon was the household tongue of all the relatives of my grandparents' generation. Their parents in turn might have spoken nothing else; that no one bothered to establish rules for the writing of Walloon until Jules Feller did so at the very beginning of this century, just in time for its decline in currency, partly accounts for the fact that nearly everyone in the family tree before my grandparents' era was illiterate. When I hear Walloon spoken, which is not often, I hear the table talk of countless generations of workers and farmers and their wives, not that I particularly wish to subscribe to notions of collective ethnic memory, but the sound of the language conveys the mentality of its speakers so vividly that it is dense with imprints, like fossils. Hearing old men greet each other – *"Bôdjou, Djôsef," "Bôdjou, Françwès"* – can move me nearly to tears. It is the keenest tangible manifestation of what I've lost, even if it is now pretty much lost to everyone. In my childhood it was already a ghost, if a lively one. My mother's parents ceded to the tenor of their times; they spoke Walloon between themselves but did not teach it to their children and discouraged their bringing bits of it home. My father, on the other hand, grew up in a Walloon-speaking household in a city with a rich Walloon tradition.

If Verviers has an official legend, it is that of the *tchèt volant,* the flying cat, commemorated in a long if not actually endless set of Walloon verses written down in 1641: some local savant wished to test the proposition that a cat could be made to fly, after it had been purged with a laxative, by attaching a helium balloon to each of its limbs. Accordingly the cat was launched from the steeple of St. Remacle, but it did nothing more than flip over several times in midair, land on its feet, and run off. This episode became the founding myth of a tradition of self-satire, which informed the local Walloon literature, notably less lugubriously sentimental than that of certain other cities. Files at the Bibliothèque des Chiroux in Liège list more than seventy-five Walloon societies – amateur or semi-pro theater companies, poetry clubs, singing groups, and friendship leagues – in Verviers at the beginning of the century. My grandfather belonged to at least one of these (I don't know which) and did some acting. My father remembers appearances by him in *Lès Sî Cint Franchimontwès* (1895) by Nicolas Depresseux and *Li Fis dè Gârchampète* (1889), an operetta by Victor Carpentier, two warhorses from the Liégeois repertory.* The latter went through at least four editions between 1889 and 1919, the spellings changing with every one; the preface to the third edition, of 1903, proclaims

* The Six Hundred Franchimontois were a volunteer army who in 1368 unsuccessfully defended Liège's revolt against Charles the Bold. The second title means "the son of the rural constable."

that "it is annually performed by all the societies in Wallonia, and every time is met with calls for an encore."

Following in his footsteps, my father in 1946 joined Amon nos autes, the leading theater company in Verviers at that time. His contract stipulated that he would be paid one hundred francs (two dollars, but in postwar money) for each performance, enjoined him to exclusivity, and posted a fine of one thousand francs should the terms be forfeited. The company was founded in 1932, with all the surviving major figures of the prewar Walloon scene included in its board of advisers, and endured until the 1970s. By 1934, though, its programs already bore the motto *Nos péres djâsît Walon* (our fathers spoke Walloon), an indication that nostalgia was now uppermost. By 1959 things had come to such a pass that the company got in trouble for having two sets in a single scene – theaters of the second rank were only allowed one, and the director was fined 520 francs by the court.

A few years ago I went to see Walloon theater for myself, at the major such establishment in Liège, the Théâtre Communal du Trianon. The spectacle was Nicolas Trockart's operetta *La Bohémiène,* a standard marrying-off-the-daughter period farce. Aside from a handful of very young grandchildren, I was clearly the only person in the audience under sixty. Things began promisingly: the six-piece orchestra played café-concert music passably well, and the stage was set in classic bare-bones style. Unfortunately, the effect was marred as soon as the actors came on, at least the ones younger than their audience; they spoke Walloon with drama-school French accents, and looked like soap-opera stars of the 1970s. The actors seemed to have picked out their own costumes – it quickly became clear that you could judge the merits of the performers by appearance alone the minute they walked onstage. Only the older actors spoke convincing Walloon, could pull off the requisite slapstick, and had bothered to dress appropriately for their roles. What I had taken for ineptitude might well have been contempt. I left, downcast, after the first act.

Walloon today is the province of the elderly, at least those of the working class or in rural communities, along with a few younger diehards and hobbyists in the cities. Most people regard it with a certain embarrassment, like the memory of a bastard grandsire who ate with his hands. The young, who are media fixated and thus Parisianized or Americanized, couldn't care less. To me, growing up, it was both familiar and strange. Sometimes my parents reached for an English phrase and came up with a Walloon one instead – the confusion was understandable given the Germanic strain running among Walloon's Latin roots. (An often-told story in my family related how Lucy Dosquet, when her G.I. suitor arrived looking like a slob, angrily ordered him in Walloon, *"Louke-tu el mireu!"* He understood perfectly, and studied his reflection.) Sometimes my parents said things to each other in Walloon they didn't want me to understand – pertaining to Christmas presents, maybe. I was never taught Walloon, but I had a fair-sized vocabulary anyway (there were concepts I could only express in Walloon; growing pains, for example, were always *crèhioûles*), and I simply absorbed its structure from hearing bits of it from my parents and from hearing my grandparents and great-aunts and great-uncles speak it. I can read it with ease; other applications don't present themselves. Like the lives of my ancestors, Walloon appears humble and yet mighty, elemental and at the same time complex, remote but a part of my fiber. I use what I have of it only internally. It is that sad paradox, a silent tongue.

One of the great stalwarts of Verviétois Walloon in this century was Jean Wisimus (1866–1953), who managed to combine the tasks of textile dealer, newspaper columnist, lexicographer (he compiled the only dictionary of the Verviers tongue that exists), historian, author (of *Dès Rôses èt dès spènes* – Roses and Thorns – a volume of rather affecting reminiscences of the old Verviers), and founder and longtime president of Lu Vî Tchène (The Old Oak), the last major Walloon organization in the city. His first book, however, published in 1921, was *L'Anglais langue auxiliaire internationale* (English, the international second language). Its publication may have been delayed by the war; in any case he begins by addressing concerns that have a distinctly pre-1914 air about them. Universal languages were all the rage then. Dr. Zamenhof's *Esperanto,* Monsignor Schleyer's *Volapük,* Sudre's *Solresol,* Dyer's *Lingualumina,* Bauer's *Spelin,* Dornoy's *Balta,* Marchand's *Dilpok,* the Marquis de Beaufort's *Ido* – all were supposed to bring about international harmony by tearing down the tower of Babel and making the crooked ways straight, and all of them smell like the sort of decorous, idealistic Edwardian science fiction that was about to be buried in the trenches of Verdun. Wisimus has no patience at all with such nonsense: "An artificial language is like canned food; it's a product without flavor or aroma." By contrast, there is English, which has the simplest and most analytical grammar, and furthermore has already invaded every domain ("you visit the *world's fair,* buy a *ticket,* go to the *bar,* watch out for *pickpockets* . . . see the *cakewalk,* the *looping-the-loop, cow-boys* from the *far-west*"). Although some people will always grumble about its errant spelling (*"Der Engländer schreibt 'Jerusalem' und lieszt 'Konstaninopel' "),* its destiny is clear, and anyway, *"Un beau désordre est un effet de l'art"* (a beautiful mess is an artistic effect: Boileau). English, he predicts, will become a worldwide medium of convenience, like the telephone and the telegraph. Unless, that is, Japan conquers the planet. . . .

Somehow, like some sort of Jules Vernian astronaut, I wound up making the journey from Wisimus's Place Verte into the very heart of the linguistic future. For my first communion I was presented with a dictionary whose jacket copy promised it to be "as up-to-date as Telstar!" Two years later I decided I wanted to be a writer, and having made that decision never thought of writing in any language but English. It was at hand, it was all new, it was not the language of my parents, it *was* the language of Robert Louis Stevenson and Rod Serling and the Beatles, it contained a ready-made incentive to competition, and besides, Mrs. Gibbs in the fourth grade at St. Teresa's School in Summit told me I had talent, and that clinched it. Gradually, I successfully passed myself off as another being. I was thirteen or fourteen the last time anyone complimented me on my charming accent. English became my rod and my staff, my tool and my weapon, at length my means of making a living. My mask merged with my skin. My internal monologue ever so gradually shifted from French into English; I even began to talk to cats and dogs (who understand all languages) in English. My most intimate conversations came to be conducted in English. Today, when someone addresses me as "Luke" I respond without a second thought; when I hear *"lük"* I jump as if I'd gotten an electric shock. Even though I know better, I feel as if someone had just looked down into my naked soul.

I tend to avoid speaking French unless I'm in Europe. In America I can't get my French hat on fast enough, and as a result I tend to keep French speakers at a respectful distance, and have often (undoubtedly) appeared rude. I still speak French with my parents, of course, although "French" is perhaps a misleading word there, since over the years we've developed a family dialect, a Franglais that is a lot like Spanglish: *"Nous sommes allés chez les séniores citizeunnes,"* my mother will tell me, describing a visit to the local old-folks club, *"et nous avons mangé du cornebif et du cabbage."* I am almost physically unable to talk to my parents in English, even when they are using the language out of politeness because there is an English speaker present. It would feel as if we were surrounded by the Gestapo, exchanging nonsensical pleasantries studded with code words. Or maybe it would be as if I had invited them to a wild party I was throwing for my friends.

I suppose I am never completely present in any given moment, since different aspects of myself are contained in different rooms of language, and a complicated apparatus of air locks prevents the doors from being flung open all at once. Still, there are subterranean correspondences between the linguistic domains that keep them from stagnating. The classical order of French, the Latin-Germanic high-low dialectic of English, and the onomatopoeic peasant lucidity of Walloon work on one another critically, help enhance precision and reduce cant. They are all operative, potentially. Given desire and purpose, I could make my home in any of them. I don't have a house, only this succession of rented rooms. That sometimes makes me feel as though I have no language at all, but it also gives me the advantage of mobility. I can leave, anytime, and not be found.

Controversies

Africa

NGÙGĨ WA THIONG'O (1938–)

Born in Kenya in 1938, Ngũgĩ wa Thiong'o is the most prominent novelist of East Africa. He studied at the University of Leeds and has taught at the University of Makere, Northwestern University, and the University of Nairobi. A persistent critic of both colonialism and native neocolonialists, Ngũgĩ is a leading advocate of African cultural and linguistic self-determination. He was imprisoned for a year without trial after the production of *Ngaahika Ndeenda* (I will marry when I want, 1977), a play (cowritten with Ngũgĩ wa Mirii) that attacked hypocrisy and corruption in the Kenyan government.

He began his career writing in English and under the Anglicized name James Ngugi. His first novel, *Weep Not, Child* (1964), chronicles the effects of the Mau Mau Rebellion on one Kikuyu family, and his second, *The River Between* (1965), is built around tensions between Christianity and traditional beliefs. *A Grain of Wheat* (1967) is set during the Kenyan struggle for liberation and its immediate aftermath, while *Petals of Blood* (1977) focuses on problems in East Africa following independence. *Caitaani mũtharaba-inĩ* (Devil on the cross, 1982), which Ngugi wrote in Gikũyũ, attacks Kenyan leaders for betraying and exploiting the poor. So, too, does *Matigari ma Njiruungi* (Matigari, 1986).

Ngũgĩ's essays and lectures on literature, culture, and politics have been collected in *Homecoming* (1972), *Writers in Politics* (1981), and *Barrel of a Pen: Resistance to Repression in Neo-colonial Kenya* (1983). In *Decolonising the Mind: The Politics of Language in African Literature* (1986) and *Moving the Centre: The Struggle for Cultural Freedoms* (1993), in which the following (translated) excerpt appeared, he explains why he dropped the name James Ngugi and abandoned the English language for his native Gikũyũ and why other African authors, too, ought not to write in a European language.

Imperialism of Language

English, a Language for the World?

Everyone in the world has a language, either the language of his or her parents or one adopted at birth or at a later stage in life. So when we consider English as a possible language for the world, we are all drawing from the languages and cultures in which we are rooted. The topic also brings up the question of choosing one language from among many languages. What we are therefore discussing is the relationship between English and the various languages of the world. In short, we are really talking about the meeting of languages.

Every language has two aspects. One aspect is its role as an agent that enables us to communicate with one another in our struggle to find the means for survival. The other is its role as a carrier of the history and the culture built into the process of that communication over time. In my book, *Decolonising the Mind* I have described language as the collective memory bank of a people. The two aspects are inseparable; they form a dialectical unity.

However, either of these two aspects can become more pronounced than the other, depending on the circumstances surrounding the use of a language, and particularly those surrounding an encounter between languages. For instance, are the two languages meeting on terms of equality and independence? The quality of the encounter between languages both in the past and in the world today, and hence the dominance of one aspect over the other at a given time, has been determined by the presence or absence of independence and quality between the nations involved.

Let me give one or two examples. Scandinavians know English.

But they do not learn English in order for it to become the means of communication among themselves in their own countries, or for it to become the carrier of their own national cultures, or for it to become the means by which foreign culture is imposed on them. They learn English to help them in their interactions with English people, or with speakers of English, to facilitate commerce, trade, tourism, and other links with foreign nations. For them English is only a means of communication with the outside world. The Japanese, the West Germans, and a good number of other peoples fall in the same category as the Scandinavians: English is not a substitute for their own languages.

When nations meet on terms of independence and equality, they tend to stress the need for communication in the language of the other. They choose the language of the other merely to ease communication in their dealings with one another. But when they meet as oppressor and oppressed, as for instance under imperialism, then their languages cannot experience a genuinely democratic encounter. The oppressor nation uses language as a means of entrenching itself in the oppressed nation. The weapon of language is added to that of the Bible and the sword in pursuit of what David Livingstone, in the case of nineteenth-century imperialism, called "Christianity plus 5 percent." Today he would have probably described the same process as Christianity, debt, plus 40 percent in debt servicing. In such a situation, what is at stake is language as more than a simple means of communication.

Needless to say, the encounter between English and most so-called Third World languages did not occur under conditions of independence and equality. English, French, and Portuguese came to the Third World to announce the arrival of the Bible and the sword. They came clamoring for gold, black gold in chains, or gold that shines as sweat in factories and plantations. If it was the gun which made possible the mining of this gold and which effected the political captivity of their owners, it was language which held captive their cultures, their values, and hence their minds. The latter was attempted in two ways, both of which are part of the same process.

The first was to suppress the languages of the captive nations. The culture and the history carried by these languages were thereby thrown onto the rubbish heap and left there to perish. These languages were experienced as incomprehensible noise from the dark Tower of Babel. In the secondary school that I went to in Kenya, one of the hymns we were taught to sing was a desperate cry for deliverance from that darkness. Every morning, after we paraded our physical cleanliness for inspection in front of the Union Jack, the whole school would troop down to the chapel to sing: "Lead kindly light amidst the encircling gloom, lead thou me on." Our languages were part of that gloom. Our languages were suppressed so that we, the captives, would not have our own mirrors in which to observe ourselves and our enemies.

The second mode of captivation was that of elevating the language of the conqueror. It became the language of the elect. Those inducted into the school system, after having been sifted from the masses of the people, were furnished with new mirrors in which to see themselves and their people as well as those who had provided the new mirrors. In short, they were given a language called English or French or Portuguese. Thus equipped with the linguistic means of escape from the dark Tower of Babel, the newly ordained, or those ready to be ordained as servants of the new order, had their minds systematically removed from the world and the history carried by their original languages. They looked, or were made to look, to a distant neon light on a faraway hill flashing out the word EUROPE. Henceforth Europe and its languages would be the center of the universe.

The French, faithful to the philosophical and aesthetic traditions of their culture, had given the whole process a name: *assimilation.* The English, less aesthetically and philosophically inclined, simply called it *education.* But Lugard, a soldier-turned-administrator who nonetheless retained the bluntness of a military man, had provided the key to understanding what lay behind this pragmatic education program, one that was often formulated in bits and pieces: *indirect rule.* He had coined the phrase to refer to the practice of coopting chiefs to facilitate British rule in Africa. In fact, subsequent educational practice produced more faithful "chiefs" for the system as a whole than those who had been appointed earlier by Lugard. The point, however, is that the mastery of the English language was the measure of one's readiness for election into the band of the elect.

In *Decolonising the Mind* I have described how the process of alienation from our own languages with the acquisition of a new one actually worked. I have told of instances of children being punished if they were caught speaking their African languages. We were often caned or made to carry plaques inscribed with the words "I am stupid" or "I am an ass." In some cases, our mouths were stuffed with pieces of paper picked from the wastepaper basket, which were then passed from one mouth to that of the latest offender. Humiliation in relation to our languages was the key. "Look up unto the hills" was the constant call: that was where the light from Europe shone, and the gateway to it was English. The English language was the bearer of all knowledge in the arts and sciences. According to Greek tradition, Archimedes could have moved the world had he had a firm ground on which to stand. In twentieth-century Africa he would have been advised to stand on the firm ground of the English language in order to move the world. Indeed for some of us, English was made to look as if it was the language spoken by God.

One of our English teachers, ironically a Scotsman, used to urge us to follow the footsteps of Christ in the use of the English language. As you know, when young people learn a new language, they tend to favor the heaviest and longest of words because such words sound more learned. The teacher would tell us that Jesus Christ used the simplest English. The Bible contained the greatest sentence in English literature which happened also to be the shortest. It was left to a student to remind him that Jesus probably spoke

Hebrew, and that the Bible from which the King James Version had been translated was more likely to have been written in Hebrew.*

You may think that I am talking about some attitudes to the English language that prevailed thirty years ago. Well, you are very wrong. Recently, on my way to Berlin with my mind very much on this seminar, I chanced to open the London *Evening Standard* of 7 October 1988, and came across an article concerning the British education secretary Kenneth Baker's visit to the Soviet Union. The paper told us how Baker had been amazed to find English being spoken in a certain part of the Soviet Union: "Just think of it. There I was in Novosibirsk. Two thousand miles from anywhere, and yet the people could speak English perfectly. They've never been to England or America. But they read our classics." That is well and good. Any group learning the language of another group is a positive thing. But why were these citizens of Novosibirsk putting so much work into perfecting their English? According to Kenneth Baker, as quoted by the same issue of the *Standard,* there was a deeper motive: "The Russians associate England with progress, so they work thoroughly and very hard at their English. They want to get away from the old-fashioned totalitarian state-controlled society." You have heard it for yourselves. Socialism, which is only seventy years old, is already old-fashioned. Capitalism, which is four hundred years old, is modern. But the point to note for our argument is that even today English is the means of taking people away from the "gloom" of socialism into the "light" of modern capitalism.

Let me now relate to you very briefly how some of us were taken by English from the dark Babelic towers of nineteenth-century Africa to the modernity of twentieth-century colonial Africa. In my primary school we were taught English from a text under the general series "Oxford Readers for Africa." We used to read the

*I note that Christ spoke Aramaic and not Hebrew and that the New Testament was written in Greek. To correct the child's misconception is hardly to weaken his point, which retains its polemical truth with respect to the teacher's assumptions.

story of a boy called John and a girl called Joan. And it thus came to pass that, while still in my village and before I knew the names of any other towns in Kenya, I already knew about a town called Oxford, where the two children were born, and another called Reading, where John and Joan went to school. We, the new readers, followed them wherever they went. One day we went to visit another town called London; we went to a zoo and walked along the banks of the river Thames. It was a summer holiday. Oh, how many times did the river Thames and the British Houses of Parliament beckon to us from the pages of our English language text books! Even today, when I hear the name of the river Thames or travel in its vicinity, I still remember Joan and John. And Oxford represents to me less the great seat of exclusive scholarship that it is supposed to be than the exclusive home of the fictitious John and Joan of my primary school textbook.

Don't get me wrong. I do not think it a bad thing for a language to be taught in the geographical, cultural, or historical setting of the land which produces it. After all, even the communicative aspect of a language cannot be divorced from its cultural emblems – the Thames for the English language, the Eiffel Tower for the French, the Leaning Tower of Pisa for the Italian, the Great Wall of China for the Chinese, Mecca for the Arabic, Mombasa for the Kiswahili. To know a language in the context of its culture is a tribute to the people to whom it belongs, and that is good. What has, for us from the former colonies, twisted the natural relation to languages, both our own and those of other peoples, is that the languages of Europe – here, English – were taught as if they were our own languages, as if Africa had no tongues except those brought there by imperialism, bearing the label MADE IN EUROPE.

Thus English and the African languages never met as equals, under conditions of equality, independence, and democracy, and this is the root of all subsequent distortions. They met with English as the language of the conquering nation, and ours as the language of the vanquished. An oppressor language inevitably carries racist and negative images of the conquered nation, particularly in its literature, and English is no exception. I do not want to go into this aspect of the language here. Many studies in this area have already been done. Suffice it to say that some works bearing these offensive images, like those of Elspeth Huxley, Karen Blixen, Rider Haggard, Robert Ruark, Nicholas Monsarrat, to name just a few, found their way into the school English curriculum. Imagine it: if the African languages had all died, African people would have had to define themselves in a language that had such a negative conception of Africa as its legacy.

What prevented our languages from being completely swallowed up by English and other oppressor languages was that the rural and urban masses, who had refused to surrender completely in the political and economic spheres, also continued to breathe life into our languages and thus helped to keep alive the histories and cultures they carried. The masses of Africa would often derive the strength needed in their economic and political struggles from those very languages. Thus the peoples of the Third World had refused to surrender their souls to English, French, or Portuguese.

But the Third World was not the only place where English tried to grow on the graveyard of other peoples' languages. Even in Britain I have heard similar complaints from regions whose original languages had been swallowed up by English or in regions where they are putting up a last ditch struggle to prevent their languages from being killed and buried forever.

Once again, I am not only talking about complaints that I heard many years ago. When I returned from West Berlin, I happened to open a newspaper, the *Morning Star* of 21 October 1988, only to find an article by Lyn Marierid of the Welsh Language Society protesting the continuing decline of the Welsh language:

> In recent years, rural areas, which have for decades been considered strongholds of the language, have become completely Anglicised as ordinary working-class people have been systematically priced out of their native areas.
>
> Perhaps some readers are asking at this point why it should be so important to retain such a language as Welsh.

> If we consider it important for a people to be aware of their past in order to be able to shape their future, then it is pointedly relevant. For generations, the Welsh working class was utterly dependent on the Welsh language and culture.
>
> Now it appears that the Welsh language in Wales is under threat of death. That, indeed, is the cost of "yuppiefication" in this particular part of Britain. Should it die, then the history of a whole people would be a closed book for many people.
>
> As socialists we know that capitalist culture seeks to deny working people their rightful place in their own history so that it may not be a source of inspiration for their continued struggle in the present.
>
> Language too is denied them for similar reasons.
>
> Languages do not grow, age and die. They do not become irrelevant to the "modern age" due to some intrinsic fault in their composition.
>
> They are lost when the predominant class in society has no use for them.

The decline of the Welsh language has roots in the inequality prevailing between the nationalities that inhabited the two linguistic regions. Even Kenneth Baker, when talking about the spread of English in Russia, did not say, from what one gathers in reading the report in the *Evening Standard,* that the Soviets looked up to Britain for progress. They looked to England, the original home of the English language.

Today, the West European languages and African languages are where they are in relation to one another, not because they are inherently progressive or backward but because of the history of oppression on one hand, and the resistance to that oppression on the other. That history of oppression dates back a long time, but it is best symbolized by the Berlin Conference of 1884 at which Africa, for example, was carved up into various "spheres of influence" of the European powers. Today we can see that English, outside its home base in Britain and the United States, has firmly taken root in all respects only in those areas of the globe – and these are quite considerable – which have been within the Anglo-American economic and political empire stretching from Queen

Victoria to Ronald Reagan. These are also the areas in which neocolonialism has taken firm root. The rulers of these neocolonies feel that they share the same outlook as the rulers of the United States and Britain because, quite apart from many other things they have in common, they speak the same tongue and share the value systems of the English-speaking ruling classes the world over.

The consequences of that history of inequality and oppression can be seen in each of the affected countries in Africa, particularly in the internal relations between the various classes and in the external relations with other countries. In these countries, English, French, and Portuguese occupy the center stage. They are the official languages of instruction, of administration, of commerce, trade, justice, and foreign communications. In short, they are the languages of power. But they are still spoken only by a minority within each of the nationalities that make up these countries. The majority of the working people in Africa retain our African languages. Therefore the majority of the people are excluded from center stage since they do not have mastery of the language of power. They are also excluded from any meaningful participation in modern discoveries. English, French, and Portuguese are the languages in which the African people have been educated; for this reason the results of our research into science, technology and of our achievements in the creative arts are stored in those languages. Thus a large portion of this vast knowledge is locked up in the linguistic prison of English, French, and Portuguese. Even the libraries are really English (or indeed French or Portuguese) language fortresses inaccessible to the majority. So the cultivation of these languages makes for more effective communication only between the elite and the international English-speaking bourgeoisie. In short the elite in Africa is, in linguistic terms, completely uprooted from the peoples of Africa and tied to the West.

As for external relations between Africa and the world, African languages hardly occupy any place of honor. Once again their place has been occupied by English, French, or Portuguese. Among the official languages at the United Nations there is not a single language of African origin. In fact it is interesting that of the five continents, the only one not represented linguistically at the United Nations is Africa. It is surely time that Kiswahili, or Hausa, Wolof, Shona, Amharic, or Somali be made one of the official languages of the United Nations Organization and all its organs; but that is a matter for another seminar. At present we are discussing English as a possible language for the world.

I have so far discussed or pointed out only the racist tradition of the English language. As a language of imperialism, it could not but be marked by the very disease it carried. But as the language of the people of Britain and America, it also has a democratic tradition, reflecting the democratic struggles and heritage of the British and American people. In its democratic tradition it has added to the common pool of human creativity; in the arts, for instance, with such great names as Shakespeare, Milton, Blake, Shelley, Dickens, Conrad, Bernard Shaw, Graham Greene, to name only a few. I am not surprised that Kenneth Baker found Soviet children in Siberia reading some of these classics of the English language. If he had also gone to even the remotest village in Africa he might very well have found more children struggling with Dickens, alongside Brecht, Balzac, Sholokhov, and of course Sembene Ousmane, Alex la Guma, Vieira, and other African writers. A lot of this material would be available in English translation. That side of the English language is important, and it is part of the common heritage of humankind along with what has been contributed by other languages, including those from Africa. But English as a language for the world is another matter.

English, a language for the world? It would certainly be good for each country in the world to have a language in which all nationalities inhabiting its boundaries could participate. It would be equally good if the world had a language in which all the nations of the earth could communicate. A common language of communication within a country, a common language of communication for the world: that is the ideal, and we have to struggle for it.

But that language, whichever it would be, should not be planted in the graveyard of other languages within one country or in the world. We must avoid the destruction that English has wrought on other languages and cultures in its march to the position it now occupies in the world. The death of many languages should never be the condition for the life of a few. On the contrary, the lives of many languages should add life to whichever language emerges as the transnational or universal language of communication between people. We, the present generation, must distance ourselves from the false and bloody logic of development theory handed to us by imperialism: the claim that the cleanliness of one person must depend on pouring dirt onto others; that the health of a few must depend on their passing their leprosy onto others; that the wealth of a few people or a few nations must be rooted in the poverty of the masses of people and nations.

So, what would be the proper foundation for the emergence and the universal acceptance of a language for the world?

First, the absolute independence and equality of all nations in the economic, political, and cultural spheres. Such an equality would of course be reflected in the equality of languages. We live in one world. All the languages in the world are real products of human history.

They are our common heritage. A world of many languages should be like a field of flowers of different colors. There is no flower which becomes more of a flower on account of its color or its shape. All such flowers express their common "floralness" in their diverse colors and shapes. In the same way our different languages can, should, and must express our common being. So we should let all our languages sing of the unity of the people of the earth, of our common humanity, and above all of the people's love for peace, equality, independence, and social justice. All our languages should join in the demand for a new international economic, political, and cultural order.

Then the different languages should be encouraged to talk to one another through the medium of interpretation and translation. Each country should encourage the teaching of languages from the five continents of the earth. There is no reason why each child should not master at least three languages as a matter of course. The art of translation and interpretation should be an integral subject in schools, but it is sad to note that in the English education system and in English culture generally, the art of translation does not enjoy the same status as the other arts. Through translations, the different languages of the world can speak to one another. European languages have always communicated with one another such that today it is possible to read nearly all the classics of Russian, French, or German literature and philosophy in any of those languages, thanks to the art of translation. But there is very little mutual translation between African languages and, say, English and French. And the colonial dominance of English and French in African lives has made African languages so suspicious of one another that there is hardly any inter-African communication. In any case, very few resources, if any, nationally or internationally, have been put into the development of African languages. The best minds among lettered Africans have been channeled into the developing of English, French, and Portuguese. But, difficult as the case may be, interlanguage communication through translation is crucial. If on top of all of this there were one common language, then the different languages of the world could further communicate with one another via the international common language. In that way, we could build a real foundation for a common world culture that is firmly rooted in, and draws its real sustenance from, all the peoples of the world with their distinct experiences and languages. Our internationalism would be truly rooted in all the peoples of the world.

When there is real economic, political, and cultural equality among nations and there is *democracy,* there will be no reason for any nation, nationality, or people to fear the emergence of a common language, be it Kiswahili, Chinese, Maori, Spanish, or English, as the language of the world. A language for the world? A world of languages! The two concepts are not mutually exclusive provided there is independence, equality, democracy, and peace among nations.

In such a world, English, like all the other languages, can put in an application, and despite its history of imperialist aggression against other languages and peoples, English would make a credible candidate. Such applicants must in the meantime work hard to remove such negative qualities as racism, sexism, national chauvinism, and negative images of other nationalities and races so as to meet the criteria of acceptance as a language for the world. In this respect Kiswahili would make an excellent candidate for the world language. It already has the advantage of never having grown in the graveyard of other languages. Kiswahili has created space for itself in Africa and the world without displaying any national chauvinism. The power of Kiswahili has not depended on its economic, political, or cultural aggrandizement. It has no history of oppression or domination of other cultures. And yet Kiswahili is now spoken as a major language in Eastern, Central, and Southern Africa as well as in many other parts of the world.

I have nothing against English, French, Portuguese, or any other language for that matter. They are all valid in as far as they are languages and in as far as they do not seek to oppress other nations, nationalities, and languages. But if Kiswahili or any other African language were to become the language for the world, this would symbolize the dawn of a new era in human relations between the nations and peoples of Africa and those of other continents. For these reasons I for one would like to propose Kiswahili as the language for the world.

Translated from the Gikũyũ by
Wangũi wa Goro and Ngũgĩ wa Thiong'o

GABRIEL OKARA (1921–)

Born in Bumodi, Nigeria, in 1921, Gabriel (Imomotimi Gbaingbain) Okara writes his poetry and fiction in English. Largely self-taught, he has attempted to explore and embody African ideas and folklore in his work while using a European language. In his first novel, *The Voice* (1964), Okara experiments with reconfiguring English to echo the syntax, rhythms, and mind-set of his native Ijaw language. His poetry collection *The Fisherman's Invocation* (1978) won the Commonwealth Prize in 1979. In the following remarks, written while he was still working on *The Voice,* Okara argues that English can and must be redesigned to express African experiences.

African Speech . . . English Words

Trying to express ideas even in one's own language is difficult because what is said or written often is not exactly what one had in mind. Between the birth of the idea and its translation into words, something is lost. The process of expression is even more difficult in the second language of one's own cultural group. I speak not of merely expressing general ideas, but of communicating an idea to the reader in the absolute or near absolute state in which it was conceived. Here, you see I am already groping for words to make you understand what I really mean as an African.

"Once an African, always an African; it will show in whatever you write," says one school of thought. This implies that there is no need for an African writer to exert a conscious effort to make his writing African through the use of words or the construction of sentences. Equally it seems to say that the turns of phrase, the nuances and the imagery which abound in African languages, thinking, and culture are not worth letting the world know about.

As a writer who believes in the utilization of African ideas, African philosophy, and African folklore and imagery to the fullest extent possible, I am of the opinion the only way to use them effectively is to translate them almost literally from the African language native to the writer into whatever European language he is using as his medium of expression. I have endeavored in my words to keep as close as possible to the vernacular expressions. For, from a word, a group of words, a sentence and even a name in any African language, one can glean the social norms, attitudes and values of a people.

In order to capture the vivid images of African speech, I had to eschew the habit of expressing my thoughts first in English. It was difficult at first, but I had to learn. I had to study each Ijaw expression I used and to discover the probable situation in which it was used in order to bring out the nearest meaning in English. I found it a fascinating exercise.

Some words and expressions are still relevant to the present-day life of the world, while others are rooted in the legends and tales of a far-gone day. Take the expression "he is timid," for example. The equivalent in Ijaw is "he has no chest" or "he has no shadow." Now a person without a chest in the physical sense can only mean a human that does not exist. The idea becomes clearer in the second translation. A person who does not cast a shadow of course does not exist. All this means is that a timid person is not fit to live. Here, perhaps, we are hearing the echoes of the battles in those days when the strong and the brave lived. But is this not true of the world today?

In parting with a friend at night a true Ijaw would say, "May we live to see ourselves tomorrow." This again is reminiscent of the days when one went about with the danger of death from wild beasts or hostile animals dogging one's steps. But has the world we live in changed so much? On the other hand, how could an Ijaw born and bred in England, France or the United States write, "May we live to see ourselves tomorrow" instead of "Goodnight"? And if he wrote "Goodnight," would he be expressing an Ijaw thought? Is it only the color of one's skin that makes one an African?

In the Ibo language they say something like, "May dawn come," or "May it dawn." Once again it is a wish or a prayer. Isn't the grave sometimes likened to an endless night and is it not only the dead that go to the grave? The Ibos sometimes lighten this somber thought with the expression, "You sleep like a rat while I sleep like a lizard." Because it is thought that rats never sleep, while lizards are heavy sleepers, this never fails to produce peals of laughter.

Why should I not use the poetic and beautiful, "May we live to see ourselves tomorrow" or, "May it dawn," instead of "Goodnight"? If I were writing a dialogue between two friends, one about to leave after visiting the other at night, I would do it this way:

"Are you getting up now?" said Otutu as he saw his friend heaving himself up with his two hands gripping the arms of the chair he was sitting on.

"Yes I am about walking now. The night has gone far," Beni, his friend, said, for he was a very fat man.

"May we live to see ourselves tomorrow," Otutu said after seeing his friend to the door.

"May we live to see ourselves tomorrow," his friend also said and walked panting into the night.

What emerges from the examples I have given is that a writer can use the idioms of his own language in a way that is understandable in English. If he uses their English equivalents, he would not be expressing African ideas and thoughts, but English ones.

Some may regard this way of writing in English as a desecration of the language. This is of course not true. Living languages grow like living things, and English is far from a dead language. There are American, West Indian, Australian, Canadian and New Zealand versions of English. All of them add life and vigor to the language while reflecting their own respective cultures. Why shouldn't there be a Nigerian or West African English which we can use to express our own ideas, thinking and philosophy in our own way?

CHINUA ACHEBE (1930–)

Chinua Achebe was christened Albert, after the husband of Britain's Queen Victoria, when he was born in 1930 in the Igbo region of southeastern Nigeria. His father was a teacher for the Church Missionary Society, and he attended Christian schools in which instruction was conducted in English. He began using the indigenous name Chinua, an abbreviation for Chinualumogu, which translates as "My spirit, come fight for me," when he entered University College in Ibadan. After graduation in 1953, Achebe began working for the Nigerian Broadcasting Service, eventually becoming its first director of external broadcasting. His first book, *Things Fall Apart* (1958), set in rural Nigeria at the time of the initial contacts between the British and the Igbo, became the most widely read and respected novel produced in Africa.

Achebe continued to depict Nigerian society through the colonial and postcolonial eras in the novels *No Longer at Ease* (1960), *Arrow of God* (1964), *A Man of the People* (1966), and *Anthills of the Savannah* (1987). *Beware Soul Brother* (1971) is a volume of poems, *Girls at War and Other Stories* (1972), a collection of short fiction. Achebe was active in the unsuccessful attempt of eastern Nigeria to secede as the independent nation of Biafra, which precipitated a devastating civil war from 1967 to 1970. An outspoken opponent of Nigerian military dictatorships, he has spent many years in exile, teaching since 1991 at Bard College in New York State.

The African Writer and the English Language

In June 1952, there was a writers' gathering at Makerere, impressively styled "A Conference of African Writers of English Expression." Despite this sonorous and rather solemn title, it turned out to be a very lively affair and a very exciting and useful experience for many of us. But there was something which we tried to do and failed – that was to define "African literature" satisfactorily.

Was it literature produced *in* Africa or *about* Africa? Could African literature be on any subject, or must it have an African theme? Should it embrace the whole continent or south of the Sahara, or just *black* Africa? And then the question of language. Should it be in indigenous African languages or should it include Arabic, English, French, Portuguese, Afrikaans, et cetera?

In the end we gave up trying to find an answer, partly – I should admit – on my own instigation. Perhaps we should not have given up so easily. It seems to me from some of the things I have since heard and read that we may have given the impression of not knowing what we were doing, or worse, not daring to look too closely at it.

A Nigerian critic, Obi Wali, writing in *Transition 10* said: "Perhaps the most important achievement of the conference . . . is that African literature as now defined and understood leads nowhere."

I am sure that Obi Wali must have felt triumphantly vindicated when he saw the report of a different kind of conference held later at Fourah Bay to discuss African literature and the university curriculum. This conference produced a tentative definition of African literature as follows: "Creative writing in which an African setting is authentically handled or to which experiences originating in Africa are integral." We are told specifically that Conrad's *Heart of Darkness* qualifies as African literature while Graham Greene's *Heart of the Matter* fails because it could have been set anywhere outside Africa.

A number of interesting speculations issue from this definition, which admittedly is only an interim formulation designed to produced an indisputably desirable end, namely, to introduce African students to literature set in their environment. But I could not help being amused by the curious circumstance in which Conrad, a Pole writing in English, could produce African literature while Peter Abrahams would be ineligible should he write a novel based on his experiences in the West Indies.

What all this suggests to me is that you cannot cram African literature into a small, neat definition. I do not see African literature as one unit but as a group of associated units – in fact the sum total of all the *national* and *ethnic* literatures of Africa.

A national literature is one that takes the whole nation for its province and has a realized or potential audience throughout its territory. In other words a literature that is written in the *national* language. An ethnic literature is one which is available only to one ethnic group within the nation. If you take Nigeria as an example, the national literature, as I see it, is the literature written in English; and the ethnic literatures are in Hausa, Ibo, Yoruba, Efik, Edo, Ijaw, etc.

Any attempt to define African literature in terms which overlook the complexities of the African scene at the material time is doomed to failure. After the elimination of white rule shall have been completed, the single most important fact in Africa in the second half of the twentieth century will appear to be the rise of individual nation-states. I believe that African literature will follow the same pattern.

What we tend to do today is to think of African literature as a newborn infant. But in fact what we have is a whole generation of newborn infants. Of course, if you only look cursorily, one infant is pretty much like another; but in reality each is already set on its own separate journey. Of course, you may group them together on the basis of anything you choose – the color of their hair, for instance. Or you may group them together on the basis of the language they will speak or the religion of their fathers. Those would all be valid distinctions; but they could not begin to account fully for each individual person carrying, as it were, his own little, unique lodestar of genes.

Those who in talking about African literature want to exclude North Africa because it belongs to a different tradition surely do not suggest that black Africa is anything like homogeneous. What does Shabaan Robert have in common with Christopher Okigbo or Awoonor-Williams? Or Mongo Beti of Cameroon and Paris with Nzekwu of Nigeria? What does the champagne-drinking upper-class Creole society described by Easmon of Sierra Leone have in common with the rural folk and fishermen of J.P. Clark's plays? Of course, some of these differences could be accounted for on individual rather than national grounds, but a good deal of it is also environmental.

I have indicated somewhat offhandedly that the national literature of Nigeria and of many other countries of Africa is, or will be, written in English. This may sound like a controversial statement, but it isn't. All I have done has been to look at the reality of present-day Africa. This "reality" may change as a result of deliberate, e.g., political, action. If it does, an entirely new situation will arise, and there will be plenty of time to examine it. At present it may be more profitable to look at the scene as it is.

What are the factors which have conspired to place English in the position of national languages in many parts of Africa? Quite simply the reason is that these nations were created in the first place by the intervention of the British, which, I hasten to add, is not saying that the peoples comprising these nations were invented by the British.

The country which we know as Nigeria today began not so very long ago as the arbitrary creation of the British. It is true, as William Fagg says in his excellent new book, *Nigerian Images,* that this arbitrary action has proved as lucky in terms of African art history as any enterprise of the fortunate Princess of Serendip. And I believe that in political and economic terms too this arbitrary creation called Nigeria holds out great prospects. Yet the fact remains that Nigeria was created by the British – for their own ends. Let us give the devil his due: colonialism in Africa disrupted many things, but it did create big political units where there were small, scattered ones before. Nigeria had hundreds of autonomous communities, ranging in size from the vast Fulani Empire founded by Usman dan Fodio in the north to tiny village entities in the east. Today it is one country.

Of course there are areas of Africa where colonialism divided up a single ethnic group among two or even three powers. But on the whole it did bring together many peoples that had hitherto gone their several ways. And it gave them a language with which to talk to one another. If it failed to give them a song, it at least gave them a tongue, for sighing. There are not many countries in Africa today where you could abolish the language of the erstwhile colonial powers and still retain the facility for mutual communication. Therefore those African writers who have chosen to write in English or French are not unpatriotic smart alecks with an eye on the main chance – outside their own countries. They are by-products of the same process that made the new nation-states of Africa.

You can take this argument a stage further to include other countries of Africa. The only reason why we can even talk about African unity is that when we get together we can have a manageable number of languages to talk in – English, French, Arabic.

The other day I had a visit from Joseph Kariuki of Kenya. Although I had read some of his poems and he had read my novels, we had not met before. But it didn't seem to matter. In fact I had met him through his poems, especially through his love poem, "Come Away My Love," in which he captures in so few words the trials and tensions of an African in love with a white girl in Britain:

> Come away, my love, from streets
> Where unkind eyes divide
> And shop windows reflect our difference.

By contrast, when in 1960 I was traveling in East Africa and went to the home of the late Shabaan Robert, the Swahili poet of Tanganyika, things had been different. We spent some time talking about writing, but there was no real contact. I knew from all accounts that I was talking to an important writer, but of the nature of his work I had no idea. He gave me two books of his poems which I treasure but cannot read – until I have learned Swahili.

And there are scores of languages I would want to learn if it were possible. Where am I to find the time to learn the half dozen or so Nigerian languages, each of which can sustain a literature? I am afraid it cannot be done. These languages will just have to develop as tributaries to feed the one central language enjoying nationwide currency. Today, for good or ill, that language is English. Tomorrow it may be something else, although I very much doubt it.

Those of us who have inherited the English language may not be in a position to appreciate the value of the inheritance. Or we may go on resenting it because it came as part of a package deal which included many other items of doubtful value and the positive atrocity of racial arrogance and prejudice which may yet set the world on fire. But let us not in rejecting the evil throw out the good with it.

Some time last year I was traveling in Brazil, meeting Brazilian writers and artists. A number of the writers I spoke to were concerned about the restrictions imposed on them by their use of the Portuguese language. I remember a woman poet saying she had given serious thought to writing in French! And yet their problem is not half as difficult as ours. Portuguese may not have the universal currency of English or French, but at least it is the national language of Brazil with her 80 million or so people, to say nothing of the people of Portugal, Angola, Mozambique, etc.

Of Brazilian authors I have only read, in translation, one novel by Jorge Amado, who is not only Brazil's leading novelist but one of the most important writers in the world. From that one novel, *Gabriela,* I was able to glimpse something of the exciting Afro-Latin culture which is the pride of Brazil and is quite unlike any other culture. Jorge Amado is only one of the many writers Brazil has produced. At their national writers' festival there were literally hundreds of them. But the work of the vast majority will be closed to the rest of the world forever, including no doubt the work of some excellent writers. There is certainly a great advantage to writing in a world language.

I think I have said enough to give an indication of my thinking on the importance of the world language which history has forced down our throats. Now let us look at some of the most serious handicaps. And let me say straightaway that one of the most serious handicaps is *not* the one people talk about most often, namely, that it is impossible for anyone ever to use a second language as effectively as his first. This assertion is compounded of half truth and half bogus mystique. Of course, it is true that the vast majority of people are happier with their first language than with any other. But then the majority of people are not writers. We do have enough examples of writers who have performed the feat of writing effectively in a second language. And I am not thinking of the obvious names like Conrad. It would be more germane to our subject to choose African examples.

The first name that comes to my mind is Olauda Equiano, better known as Gustavus Vassa, the African. Equiano was an Ibo, I believe from the village of Iseke in the Orlu division of Eastern Nigeria. He was sold as a slave at a very early age and transported to America. Later he bought his freedom and lived in England. In 1789 he published his life story, a beautifully written document which, among other things, set down for the Europe of his time something of the life and habit of his people in Africa, in an attempt to counteract the lies and slander invented by some Europeans to justify the slave trade.

Coming nearer to our times, we may recall the attempts in the first quarter of this century by West African nationalists to come together and press for a greater say in the management of their own affairs. One of the most eloquent of that band was the Honorable Casely Hayford of the Gold Coast. His presidential address to the National Congress of British West Africa in 1925 was memorable not only for its sound common sense but as a fine example of elegant prose. The governor of Nigeria at the time was compelled to take notice and he did so in characteristic style: he called Hayford's Congress "a self-selected and self-appointed congregation of educated African gentlemen." We may derive some amusement from the fact that British colonial administrators learned very little in the following quarter of a century. But at least they *did* learn in the end – which is more than one can say for some others.

It is when we come to what is commonly called creative literature that most doubt seems to arise. Obi Wali, whose article "Dead End of African Literature" I referred to, has this to say:

> Until these writers and their Western midwives accept the fact that any true African literature must be written in African languages, they would be merely pursuing a dead end, which can only lead to sterility, uncreativity and frustration.

But far from leading to sterility, the work of many new African writers is full of the most exciting possibilities. Take this from Christopher Okigbo's *Limits:*

> Suddenly becoming talkative
>   like weaverbird
> Summoned at offside of
>   dream remembered
> Between sleep and waking
> I hand up my egg-shells
> To you of palm grove,
> Upon whose bamboo towers hang
> Dripping with yesterupwine
> A tiger mask and nude spear. . . .
>
> Queen of the damp half light,
>   I have had my cleansing.
> Emigrant with air-borne nose,
>   The he-goat-on-heat.

Or take the poem, *Night Rain,* in which J. P. Clark captures so well the fear and wonder felt by a child as rain clamors on the thatch roof at night and his mother, walking about in the dark, moves her simple belongings:

> Out of the run of water
> That like ants filing out of the wood
> Will scatter and gain possession
> Of the floor. . . .

I think that the picture of water spreading on the floor "like ants filing out of the wood" is beautiful. Of course if you had never made fire with faggots, you may miss it. But Clark's inspiration derives from the same source which gave birth to the saying that a man who brings home ant-ridden faggots must be ready for the visit of lizards.

I do not see any signs of sterility anywhere here. What I do see is a new voice coming out of Africa, speaking of African experience in a worldwide language. So my answer to the question *Can an African ever learn English well enough to be able to use it effectively in creative writing?* is certainly yes. If on the other hand you ask: *Can he ever learn to use it like a native speaker?* I should say, I hope not. It is neither necessary nor desirable for him to be able to do so. The price a world language must be prepared to pay is submission to many different kinds of use. The African writer should aim to use English in a way that brings out his message best without altering the language to the extent that its value as a medium of international exchange will be lost. He should aim at fashioning out an English which is at once universal and able to carry his peculiar experience. I have in mind here the writer who has something new, something different to say. The nondescript writer has little to tell us, anyway, so he might as well tell it in conventional language and get it over with. If I may use an extravagant simile, he is like a man offering a small, nondescript routine sacrifice for which a chick, or less, will do. A serious writer must look for an animal whose blood can match the power of his offering.

In this respect Amos Tutuola is a natural. A good instinct has turned his apparent limitation in language into a weapon of great strength – a half-strange dialect that serves him perfectly in the evocation of his bizarre world. His last book, and to my mind, his finest, is proof enough that one can make even an imperfectly learned second language do amazing things. In this book, *The Feather Woman of the Jungle,* Tutuola's superb storytelling is at last cast in the episodic form which he handles best instead of being painfully stretched on the rack of the novel.

From a natural to a conscious artist: myself, in fact. Allow me to quote a small example from *Arrow of God,* which may give some idea of how I approach the use of English. The Chief Priest in the story is telling one of his sons why it is necessary to send him to church:

> I want one of my sons to join these people and be my eyes there. If there is nothing in it you will come back. But if there is something there you will bring home my share. The world is like a Mask, dancing. If you want to see it well you do not stand in one place. My spirit tells me that those who do not befriend the white man today will be saying *had we known* tomorrow.

Now supposing I had put it another way. Like this for instance:

> I am sending you as my representative among these people – just to be on the safe side in case the new religion develops. One has to move with the times or else one is left behind. I have a hunch that those who fail to come to terms with the white man may well regret their lack of foresight.

The material is the same. But the form of the one is *in character* and the other is not. It is largely a matter of instinct, but judgment comes into it too.

You read quite often nowadays of the problems of the African writer having first to think in his mother tongue and then to translate what he has thought into English. If it were such a simple, mechanical process, I would agree that it was pointless – the kind of eccentric pursuit you might expect to see in a modern Academy of Lagado; and such a process could not possibly produce some of the exciting poetry and prose which is already appearing.

One final point remains for me to make. The real question is not whether Africans *could* write in English but whether they *ought to.* Is it right that a man should abandon his mother tongue for someone else's? It looks like a dreadful betrayal and produces a guilty feeling.

But for me there is no other choice. I have been given this language and I intend to use it. I hope, though, that there always will be men, like the late Chief Fagunwa, who will choose to write in their native tongue and ensure that our ethnic literature will flourish side by side with the national ones. For those of us who opt for English, there is much work ahead and much excitement.

Writing in the London *Observer* recently, James Baldwin said:

> My quarrel with the English language has been that the language reflected none of my experience. But now I began to see the matter another way. . . . Perhaps the language was not my own because I had never attempted to use it, had only learned to imitate it. If this were so, then it might be made to bear the burden of my experience if I could find the stamina to challenge it, and me, to such a test.

I recognize, of course, that Baldwin's problem is not exactly mine, but I feel that the English language will be able to carry the weight of my African experience. But it will have to be a new English, still in full communion with its ancestral home but altered to suit its new African surroundings.

ANDRÉ BRINK (1935–)

Born in Vrede, South Africa, to an Afrikaner family, André Brink first attracted attention as a member of the Sestigers, a movement of young writers attempting to transform Afrikaans literature during the 1960s. His earliest writings were in his native language, but, opposing apartheid, he found it easier to evade censorship if he published in English rather than Afrikaans. Brink translated some of his own novels – including *'n Cove wit seison* (A dry white season, 1979) and *Houd-den-bek* (A chain of voices, 1982) – into English, and he has translated Lewis Carroll, William Shakespeare, Henry James, and others into Afrikaans. He wrote the novels *States of Emergency* (1988), *An Act of Terror* (1991), and *Imaginings of Sand* (1996) and the nonfiction books *Writing in a State of Siege: Essays on Politics and Literature* (1983) and *Reinventing a Continent* (1996) directly in English. The CNA Prize, South Africa's most prestigious literary honor, is awarded each year to one book in English and one book in Afrikaans, and Brink is the only author to have won it in each of the two categories. He has served as a professor of Afrikaans and Dutch at South Africa's Rhodes University, but he has since 1991 been Professor of English at the University of Cape Town. "English and the Afrikaans Writer," an essay from *Writing in a State of Siege,* examines the situation of many Afrikaner writers who, like Brink, are ambilingual.

English and the Afrikaans Writer

> It is as if the aspiring young writer, including the Afrikaans writer, were told: "If you have something to say, my boy, then write in English! And if you don't know English well enough, then learn it like Joseph Conrad: but write in English and save your soul!"
> – N. P. Van Wyk Louw

1

English has always played an important role in the world of the Afrikaans writer, ever since some of the earliest forms of written Afrikaans made their appearance in the work of English writers (cf. Andrew Geddes Bain's *Kaatje Kekkelbek* in 1846). At the time of the First Language Movement, from 1875 onwards, English was experienced as the language of the oppressor (C. P. Hoogenhout: " 'Tis English, English, nought but English; English that one sees and hears. / In our schools and in our churches 'tis the slaughter of our tongue"), but the real struggle at that stage was with Dutch. The fight with English was a form of open, conventional warfare involving two different groups, two separate cultural identities; the fight with Dutch was more intimate and obscure, a fierce civil war with guerrilla tactics. English was a material and political threat, but Dutch jeopardized the very *raison d'être* of Afrikaans by humiliating it as a "kitchen language," an inferior and largely unwritten patois.

Many of the pioneers of Afrikaans literature were prepared to write in English when it suited them; but not in Dutch. In a very real sense Dutch had become an utterly foreign language within the Cape context (in the Transvaal it was kept alive, artificially, through the wiles and stubbornness of President Kruger). And after nearly a century of British rule, English, however much resented as the language of the oppressor, had become a window on the world – whereas Dutch, except in Church circles maintaining strong ties with Holland, was almost irrelevant.

This may account, to some extent, for the special love-hate relationship between Afrikaans and English once the battle against Dutch had been won: English, as a great and established world language, was experienced as a threat to the survival of the small new language which had so precariously taken root locally; but at the same time it provided a means of communication with the entire outside world. And it is significant that the staunchest chauvinist in the struggle for Afrikaans and one of the most untiring pioneers in the establishment of literary tradition, C. J. Langenhoven, had for many years championed the cause of English as the sole official language of the country, before taking up the cudgels for Afrikaans.

Several poets from the first generations of Afrikaans writers in the twentieth century wrote much of their work in English. Eugène Marais made his debut as a poet in English before publishing, in 1905, what is now generally acknowledged to be the first wholly successful Afrikaans lyric; and several of his major contributions to nonfiction during his more mature years were also in English (including *The Soul of the Ape*).

Louis Leipoldt, who, like Marais, spent several years of study and research in Britain, often claimed that all his poetry was originally written in English and then translated – a dubious claim he is alleged to have maintained until someone once challenged him actually to quote a couple of lines from one of his lyrics in English.

Even early writers who wrote exclusively in Afrikaans revealed the influence of English on their work: there is more than a dash of Scott in J. H. H. de Waal, even though his primary inspiration must have been the Dutch novelist Van Lennep; and much of Jan Celliers's *Die Vlakte* derives from Shelley's *Cloud*, via Jacques Perk. And this, really, became indicative of the relationship between Afrikaans writing and English literature for many years: if English was practically never employed in the writing of Afrikaans authors during the decades between the two world wars it remained a stimulus, often a source of inspiration. Even when that inspiration was derived from works in other languages, like French, English often served as the vehicle to convey the original. Let it be said, however, that the Afrikaans writer has traditionally been a rather formidable linguist, exploring a variety of other literatures, from Greek and Latin to Italian and German, in the original. One of the results of this activity has been the veritable epidemic of translations from other languages to appear in Afrikaans – a phenomenon which seems to be characteristic of other more or less geographically restricted languages like Finnish, Icelandic, Swedish, Danish and Norwegian. If there have been comparatively fewer works translated from English into Afrikaans than from languages like French or German, this must be ascribed to the obvious fact that English is already accessible to most Afrikaans readers.

2

Two extreme tendencies emerged in the course of the 1930s. On the one hand there was an increasing sense of linguistic purism, degenerating into puritanism: an exaggerated and often ridiculous fear of English influences on Afrikaans, resulting in a witch hunt to eradicate all anglicisms from the language – an activity prompted by very real fears at the outset, but persisting much longer than was necessary, eventually threatening the Afrikaans language itself with impoverishment and undernourishment. Today this attitude survives mainly as a symptom of political (extreme right) conviction, but originally the aims were laudable and positive enough – namely to avoid the "easy way out" in trying to cope linguistically with new challenges; and, instead of simply borrowing solutions from English, the syntactic, semantic and morphological possibilities of Afrikaans itself were explored. But even then the results were often curiously negative. The works of Sangiro (a noted writer of animal and nature stories), for example, were widely praised – and as widely prescribed in schools – because they were found to be "wholly free of anglicisms." That they abounded in germanisms, and that major portions were in fact plagiarized from German, did not seem to bother anyone.

At the other extreme, it happened for the first time that an Afrikaans writer started writing, with equal facility and equal felicity, in both Afrikaans and English, as a matter of free choice, and not as a result of background (as in the case of Leipoldt and Marais) or politics (as in the case of Langenhoven). The writer in question is, of course, Uys Krige. There is something of a consistent procedure in Krige's writing of poetry and drama, which usually is done first in Afrikaans and translated subsequently, sometimes with an interval of decades; but his choice of a language medium for prose seems arbitrary. Some of his best work has been written in English first (*The Way Out*, "Death of a Zulu"), but at least an equal amount in Afrikaans. What is of particular significance is that, with Krige, the Afrikaans and English texts are never absolutely identical. There is very little evidence of "translation" in the ordinary sense of the word: in every instance the "translation" becomes a rethinking, a recasting of the original in terms of the medium of the new language.

And where languages differ as radically, especially syntactically, as Afrikaans and English, this leads to variations worthy of closer analysis. In Krige's short stories, or nonfiction narratives, especially, the difference between Afrikaans and English narrative tenses creates notable and often exciting temporal shifts. In his poetry the translated version is invariably longer than the original (whether the poem in question is one of his own or one of, say, Lorca's; even his magnificent rendering of *Twelfth Night* contains the characteristic and brilliant "Krige cadenzas"); in his plays the translated version is – surprisingly! – often drastically shortened. In every case there is, obviously, a thematic resemblance; but the rendering in the new language bears witness of a thorough re-experience of the basic material. And it often happens that, after translating a given text, the original is also revised – amounting, effectively, to a retranslation from the first translated form. This is especially notable in Krige's one-act plays, first written in Afrikaans, then rewritten in English, and finally recomposed in Afrikaans.

In the course of the 1930s Uys Krige was unique in this respect, and in many ways he remains unique within the context of the whole of Afrikaans literature. But it is significant that at least one of his contemporaries, Elisabeth Eybers, has also developed into a skillful and highly sensitive translator of her own poems into English. In addition, she occasionally produces a poem exclusively in English – all the more remarkable for a poet living, for the past decade and more, in voluntary exile in Holland.

3

Since the Second World War it has been happening increasingly – although it is by no means a common phenomenon yet – that works by Afrikaans writers become available in English: either in translations by others (Chris Barnard, Etienne Leroux), or in their own translations (Jan Rabie, W. A. De Klerk). An author like De Klerk, who spent several years in Britain immediately after the war, has also started publishing directly in English (his *Puritans in Africa*), but only nonfiction, and for all too obvious reasons of a mainly political nature. Among the younger poets there appear to be several who write equally well (or, in some cases, equally badly) in Afrikaans and English. And there are others, among whom Wopko Jensma is the most notable, who use the vernacular of the black townships in a hotchpotch of Africanized Afrikaans and English in which, in its most inspired moments, one seems to recognize the stirrings of an altogether new poetic language. This is evident also in recent poetry by black poets like Sipho Sepamla.

4

Historically, then, the importance of English for the Afrikaans writer, not only as a source of inspiration but also as a form of expression, can be established without any problem. More important, when surveying the contemporary scene, is the emergence of a climate anticipated in a certain sense by Van Wyk Louw's famous anticensorship letter to *Die Burger* in 1963, a portion of which was quoted as a motto for this article:

> At a recent prize-giving ceremony I happened to find myself in the proximity (spiritually at least) of a compatriot who writes in English. She publishes her books abroad and apparently earns good money with them; no South African censorship can touch her (it may even be to her advantage!); she can bring her royalties into South Africa from all over the world and the government will welcome this "influx of capital." It occurred to me: She can ignore our censorship. But what about me and my Afrikaans colleagues? We shall have to try and bow under this yoke. Or . . . ?
>
> I doubt whether even Lord Milner could have devised a more effective way of hamstringing Afrikaans and allowing English a free rein. It is as if the aspiring young writer (including the Afrikaans writer) were told: "If you have something to say, my boy, then write in English! And if you don't know English well enough, then learn it like Joseph Conrad: but write in English and save your soul!"
>
> Truly, as an Afrikaner who has never made a secret of his Afrikaner nationalism, either here or abroad, I find it impossible to grasp the motive which could have seduced a Nationalist government into formulating a Bill of such dubious "morality" and so utterly anti-Afrikaans.

It seems to me that two sets of factors operate in the present situation. One of them, censorship, as viewed by Louw, is negative: using English as a form of survival. But the other is positive: turning to English to complement the experience lived in Afrikaans, and vice versa. It becomes a dual exploration, a bifocal vision, of a single experience – that of living in (South) Africa.

In order to appreciate this, more is required than a simple historical survey. For in order to find an answer to the question: *Why should an Afrikaans writer write in English?* it is first necessary to ask: *Why write in Afrikaans?*

5

At first sight, of course, it seems a question so obvious as to be slightly ridiculous. After all, any writer uses the language which comes most naturally to him. In the majority of cases this is the language with, and within, which he grew up. When his environment, including his linguistic environment, changes it often provides a stimulus to explore the sound-memories of his mother tongue even more acutely than before: Breyten Breytenbach or Lawrence Durrell did not start writing in French after they had given up the countries of their birth. But in some cases writers did have to start writing in the language of their new environment, usually when they had no hope of communicating with their previous societies any more, or no interest in doing so. And so a Joseph Conrad or a Vladimir Nabokov would emerge. Within the context of Afrikaans literature we have Jan van Melle, who wrote his best work in Afrikaans, not in his native Dutch; and, especially, the flamboyant Peter Blum, who left behind his German-French-Italian background to become one of the most brilliant, if short-lived, comets to streak through our poetic skies.

In countries where two or more languages are spoken, social, political or other conditions may prompt a writer from one language group to write in another language also accessible and more or less natural to him: both Maeterlinck and De Ghelderode were Flemish by birth and upbringing, yet both chose to write in French. Especially where the mother tongue is restricted, geographically or otherwise, there may be a strong tendency to use a world language for literary communication (most of the leading French or English writers from Africa would fall in this category), although, of course, the same situation may be a stimulus to promote the local language: after all, that was one of the central motives behind the emergence of national literatures in the Renaissance, or even as late as the nineteenth century (what Mistral did for Provençal is exactly what leading local writers have been trying to do for Afrikaans).

Within a society with a particularly strong and active group mystique, like the Afrikaner, the use of the mother tongue for literary expression would be even more obvious, even if it meant severely restricting one's readership. In return, there was – certainly until as late as the Second World War – the compensation of being held in especially high esteem by one's society. In Afrikaans circles the writer used to fulfill the time-honored function of the *vates* – probably because, in the very beginning of the language struggle, the writers were also political or national leaders. Even writers decidedly "different" in their political or moral or religious outlook (like Marais, who insulted Paul Kruger and became a morphine addict in a puritanical society; or the enigmatic Leipoldt with his highly unorthodox views on anything from wine to religion; or Toon van den Heever with his *mania blasphematoria*) were not only tolerated but widely accepted and occasionally revered.

The clash of Van Wyk Louw with Verwoerd in the early 1960s, and the advent of the Sestigers at more or less the same time, brought a drastic change. Louw, always obscure and elitist in the eyes of the masses, had nevertheless acquired sufficient prestige as sage and soothsayer to remain "acceptable," certainly in cultural circles. But the iconoclast Sestigers caused bewilderment, confusion and incredible hostility – all the more so for being supported by the majority of Afrikaans newspapers, the very organs which had traditionally been the champions of the national, or the Establishment's, "cause."

It had often happened in the past that Afrikaans writers castigated their people. Marais and Leipoldt did it, so did Van Wyk Louw. And they never hesitated to attack the Establishment: Van Wyk Louw wrote vicious poems against the "oppressor" of the 1930s; W. E. G. Louw published a series of ranting sonnets against the "renegade" General Hertzog (poems which, if written by a supporter of the [black] South African Students' Organization today, might earn the writer a term in jail). But somehow it was "all right" – either because the "oppressor" was someone else, or, more likely, because everything was kept "in the family." The Sestigers were different. Most of them had gone through the crucible of longer or shorter sojourns in a society totally alien to their own, namely Paris. This experience had become the main common denominator among them: essentially an experience of existentialist agony; of being forced to reexamine everything previously taken for granted, including one's own identity, one's history, one's links with one's community. Where the physical alienation from South Africa coincided with upheavals like that caused by Sharpeville, the experience became even more acute. And when these young writers returned to "their own people" it resulted in violent clashes and misunderstandings. The more desperately they wanted to "belong," in a traditional sense, the more rejected they were made to feel because of their "difference" – but this in turn proved intensely stimulating and creative. Essentially they were torn between different sets of forces: Europe (through the existential nature of their experience and their self-discovery) and Africa (through the nature of their language); the local and the universal; the group and the individual.

The important thing was that they all wanted to write in Afrikaans. Which was not as easy as it might sound, for by then their spiritual environment had changed so radically as to become almost "uncontainable" in Afrikaans. On the most basic level, Afrikaans simply lacked an adequate vocabulary to express the essential existential experiences; to say nothing of a vocabulary for the expression of (sexual) love. It had to be invented, remade, adapted. In an effort to explain the great efficacy of his translation of *Twelfth Night* Uys Krige suggested that Afrikaans, today, found itself at the same stage of development as Elizabethan English. And certainly this experience of the youth and virility, the malleability of this young language has been one of the most exhilarating aspects about writing in Afrikaans. Every sentence, to us, became a journey of exploration. Every page we wrote was also a mapping of wild and new territories: not only in terms of the experience expressed, but primarily in terms of *language.*

And this, I think, provides the most important clue toward an answer to our question: *Why write in Afrikaans?*

It is an answer which lies in the intrinsic "genius" of the language itself. The Dutch came to Africa with a variety of dialects at a crucial stage of development and were forced into the melting pot of a wholly new environment, subject to all sorts of extraneous and internal influences – and gradually a new language emerged, adapted to the needs of this new, African situation. A view held by more and more linguists today is that, in fact, the Afrikaans language emerged from the efforts of non-Dutch speakers to speak Dutch in an African environment. Hence the very development of the language implied a dimension of the exploration of the African experience, a process intrinsic to the language itself.

In the suprematist terms of his age Langenhoven praised Afrikaans as "the only white-man's language to be made in this country and not imported, ready-made, from overseas." Of course, this also suggests an inherent restriction: Afrikaans, when it was consciously promoted as a language, was essentially African by nature (in the sense of being shaped in, for, and out of Africa), but it was not African in the same way as, say, Zulu or Xhosa or Swahili. It was a "white" language (even though this appellation ignores the incalculable contribution especially of the coloreds toward its shaping and its growth). It was, in other words, a political instrument. And *at the time* that was an integral part of its very strength, and one of the main reasons why it eventually established itself as an officially recognized language.

The early writers in Afrikaans experienced the joy and wonder of exploring and expressing themselves, their time and their land in a language not yet formalized but in all respects adaptable to the requirements of their experience. Inasmuch as many of them were not (yet) good craftsmen, many or most of their efforts turned out to be literary failures. But as their craftsmanship improved – and as their tools were shaped and honed – a literature evolved which proved an exciting and wholly satisfying blend of the European and the African experience.

That is why most Afrikaans writers have found it impossible to write in anything but Afrikaans. English still proved too "European," often as remote from the realities of the African experience as Dutch or German, whereas wholly indigenous languages like Zulu or Xhosa lacked the European dimension which, for white writers, continued to form a vital part of their experience.

Now it should also become evident why certain Afrikaans writers did manage to use English as a medium of expression parallel to Afrikaans: Uys Krige, for so many years a wanderer, a "migratory bird," emotionally tied to his people yet temperamentally a loner, explored all the musical possibilities of Afrikaans – but also found it quite natural to switch to English when writing about experiences abroad, or about experiences with a broader human content. Elisabeth Eybers began to experiment with English after she left South Africa; De Klerk did so when he felt ostracized by his "people" and welcomed by English speakers. Much of this last situation would seem to apply to the Sestigers too; surely, the liberating effect of their Parisian ecstasies and agonies made world languages more accessible to them.

Yet their first impulse was to turn to Afrikaans. (Even Jan Rabie, who, during his seven years in Paris, had almost all the short fictions that were collectively entitled *21* published in English first. Breytenbach, on the other hand, during fifteen years of voluntary exile in Paris, did not write a single word in any language but Afrikaans.) For them to turn to English, something else had to happen: something had to occur within South Africa, and English itself had to be revealed in a new light.

6

The English language that arrived at the Cape at whatever date one might care to choose – 1875, 1803 or 1820 – was altogether different from the conglomeration of Dutch dialects in 1652. Naturally all languages continue to change and develop; but the English transplanted to the Cape was undeniably a language already largely formalized and structured: whatever changes may have occurred since then have made little difference to the basic semantic, morphological and syntactic systems and processes of the language, and (apart from minor problems with accent) the Londoner of today has very little trouble in understanding English as it is spoke in South Africa. (Whereas Dutch literary reviews, with a highly erudite readership, are reluctant to publish any material in Afrikaans unless accompanied by a Dutch translation.)

Moreover, while the majority of the British settlers of 1820 were from the lower classes the very nature of the South African economic situation soon established English as a *bourgeois* language on the continent. (Afrikaans, on the other hand, retained its working-class connections until at least the Second World War.) It was, in fact, as difficult for the English language to adapt to Africa in the nineteenth century as it would have been for a gentleman in top hat and tails to adjust to life in the bush. Adapt and adjust it did, let there be no doubt about that – and the current renaissance of English literature in South Africa provides splendid confirmation of the fact – but for a very long time, it seems to me, the nature of the language itself acted as a deterrent in the evolution of a significant indigenous literature. It seems almost incredible, in retrospect, that *The Story of an African Farm* could evoke, in 1883, so convincingly the essential Africanness of Olive Schreiner's experience; and her achievement is all the more remarkable if compared with what followed during the next half-century or so – a period when, with a handful of notable exceptions, English writers in South Africa seemed interested in the land only for what color it could provide, with a number of misspelled *kopjes, sjamboks, veldtschoens* or *Vrouw Grobbelaars* thrown in for good measure. And it was the language as such which stood in the way – at least until the triumvirate of the magazine *Voorslag* (Whiplash), Roy Campbell, William Plomer and Laurens Van der Post, effected an emancipation of South African English from its colonial bonds.

During the 1930s a remarkable reconnaissance of the country started, expressed in a language more fully shaped to the needs of the situation. And out of that venture, via the great contribution of Herman Charles Bosman (himself, like Van der Post, an Afrikaner writing exclusively in English), Alan Paton and others, emerged a vital and viable new literature bearing the paradoxical stamp of art in being both utterly local and utterly universal in its exploration of man in space and time.

Today, it appears to me – and I can as yet attempt only a tentative statement about it – a most interesting situation has come about. In the past, most Afrikaans works seemed more or less untranslatable into English (and an anthology like *Afrikaans Poems with English Translations* proved the point), and vice versa. I know from experience that it is easier to translate from French or Spanish or German into Afrikaans than from English. Yet I have, with sweat and close to tears, attempted translations from the works of Graham Greene, Henry James, and even Lewis Carroll and Shakespeare. But I would hesitate to attempt Nadine Gordimer in Afrikaans, just as I would be reluctant to translate Van Wyk Louw into English: in dealing with the experience of living-in-Africa, the one is so quintessentially "English," the other so "Afrikaans" (which is intended as a compliment to both) that their remoteness from one another is increased by their contingency. And this goes for much of the best work written in Afrikaans and in South African English until quite recently.

But this situation appears to be changing, at least in the work of certain authors. If I read Stephen Gray's *Local Colour* or J. M. Coetzee's *Dusklands* the fact that both are written in English seems almost coincidental. If I were stopped in the middle of a passage and asked whether I was reading a book in English or Afrikaans I might have to check the text before I could be quite sure. The same goes for, say, an Afrikaans novel by John Miles. And I find it even more obvious in much of the poetry written in either language in the country today. The change must, at least to some extent, lie in the language itself. Yet there is nothing "English" about John Miles's Afrikaans and nothing "Afrikaans" about Coetzee's English. (And I am deliberately *not* choosing examples like Van der Post, Athol Fugard or Bosman, where the syntactic patterns of Afrikaans are evident just below the surface; or some passages of Etienne Leroux which are obviously "English" in inspiration.) So the major change must have occurred in what *surrounds* the language, in its framework of reference, its patterns of possibilities, semantic or otherwise. And this would imply that both languages have reached a point where they are now fully geared to the realities of Africa: both have become sufficiently Africanized to cope with

Africa. Both have roots in Europe, but both have chosen Southern Africa as their "operational area." If this is so – and at this stage I can offer it only as conjecture – it would explain why Afrikaans authors may find it more "natural" at this stage than before to communicate not only in Afrikaans but in English as well.

7

What makes it particularly interesting is that this should occur at the very stage when at least some Afrikaans writers are forced seriously to consider the possibility of switching languages anyway.

This is caused partly – but only partly – by censorship. Van Wyk Louw's somber predictions about the disastrous effects of the 1963 Publications and Entertainments Act were not quite realized, perhaps for the very reason that he voiced them in time. During the decade following the introduction of censorship Afrikaans literature certainly lost some of its verve and boldness. The decade which had started with so much promise and excitement ended with something of a whimper. Yet the factual situation was that, initially, censorship did not hit Afrikaans literature as hard as English. (Political considerations probably decided the issue: however recalcitrant, the Afrikaans writer was still regarded by the authorities as "one of us.")

The turning point came with the 1974 banning of *Kennis van die Aand* (Looking on darkness). At last, it seemed, Afrikaans writers had overstepped the limit; the old taboos against ostracizing "one's own" no longer operated; and once that had happened, it became easier to repeat the destructive action. Within a year four more Afrikaans works were banned. Under the new Publications Act (1974) it has become abundantly clear that Afrikaans films are allowed much less scope than imported products: even innocuous swear words can lead to bans. And it would appear that the same is becoming true of literature. I have the impression that the position of ten years ago has now been reversed and that English writers (always provided they are not black!) are allowed somewhat more freedom than their Afrikaans colleagues.

But censorship is only a symptom of a much larger evil. What, in the language movement of the nineteenth century, proved to be the forte of Afrikaans (the fact that it was a political instrument) has now developed into an Achilles' heel. For as the Afrikaner became politically dominant his language also began to bear the stamp of exclusiveness – namely of White Afrikaner Nationalist Calvinist exclusiveness.

At least two extreme reactions to this alarming and saddening situation are possible, with a whole spectrum of intermediary ones. The one is denial and escape: refusing to write in Afrikaans any longer, and turning to English as the only way out. This attitude seems to be exemplified by Adam Small, who, after a brilliant beginning as an Afrikaans poet and dramatist, seems finally to have turned his back on the language. His latest work includes a volume of poetry in English, and an anthology of translations from Van Wyk Louw – both of which are atrocious. And yet: "if you don't know English well enough, then learn it like Joseph Conrad!" If one's work is consistently threatened by banning, it might well become necessary for more writers than just Adam Small to turn to English. On the other hand, it would be sad – and unforgivably defeatist – to do so unless it became totally impossible to write or publish in Afrikaans. And that day has not yet come. In fact, I am convinced that if Afrikaans writers would act with enough conviction and resourcefulness, trying to stay at least one step ahead of censorship all the time, it may not become necessary to escape into English at all. After all, that would sign a final death sentence for the language.

The other extreme reaction to the threat of Afrikaans becoming an exclusive political language is the one adopted by most younger writers so far: and that is deliberately to expand the scope of the language to reveal and to prove that it *is* more than the shibboleth of a faction. It becomes a creative effort to substantiate what Van Wyk Louw rather ambitiously claimed in the 1930s, namely that there should be nothing, but nothing, which cannot be said in Afrikaans.

If in *such* a situation Afrikaans writers turn to English, in addition to their own language, it would not imply escape but a positive and creative act of exploration.

After all, the experience of the Sestigers (as of their predecessors in the poetry of the 1930s) did contribute much toward the "opening up" of the language. If they did direct techniques and influences acquired elsewhere toward their journey of discovery inward – into themselves, into the land, into the language itself – they also brought about a measure of sophistication, of "internationalization" in Afrikaans literature. Consequently it is only natural to look outward toward other reading publics and markets as well: if only, initially at least, to obtain a greater measure of objectivity in one's evaluation of the local scene.

8

For myself, English has offered, above all, the challenge of a new medium: a challenge to myself, to try and convey to a public remote from Africa something of my African experience; but also a test of and a challenge to the language. It started with *Kennis van die Aand,* where intrinsic motives (the urge to attempt "saying" the novel in a new language medium) as well as extraneous ones (censorship) combined to create the challenge. It became, purely on the level of the creative process itself, one of the most revealing experiences of my life: not "translating" the work, but rethinking it in the framework of a new language; even more important, perhaps, refeeling it. It even underwent a change of title, to *Looking on Darkness,* indicative of the process involved. It helped me discover a lot about my own language – more than any translation I had attempted previously. It is remarkable, for example, what difference there exists between the "loads" of emotional content the two languages can carry. Afrikaans, like French, appears to offer a much higher resistance to overstatement; it is much more at ease with superlatives and emotions. In English the threshold of overstatement is reached much more readily; "valid" emotionalism in Afrikaans soon becomes unbearable in English. And this is but one, obvious, illustration of how one is forced to "refeel" a novel in a new medium.

The experiment was carried a step further in my next novel, *An Instant in the Wind.* Making notes during the year which preceded the actual writing of the book, I found that more than half of these preliminary thoughts came to me, quite spontaneously, in English. (This was probably influenced by the fact that I was working on *Looking on Darkness* during some of this time.) Since the novel deals, essentially, with two modes of experiencing Africa (expressed in terms of a journey undertaken, in 1750, by a white woman and a black man from the wilderness of the Cape hinterland back to civilization), it was interesting to see how far the planning of the book could be influenced by thinking in English when dealing with the white character and in Afrikaans when imagining the black slave. It was quite impossible to adhere to a completely mechanical procedure, of course; rigorous application of the rule might have killed the book in the bud. Yet it was remarkable to see to what extent the two languages spontaneously associated themselves with the two spheres of experience represented by the main characters.

The few preliminary passages written to get the "feel" of the book, after sorting the notes, were all in English. But, probably conditioned by previous writing, when I actually sat down to write, it happened in Afrikaans. That was only the beginning, though. Using the first draft as a guide, the whole book was then reworked in English. In the process some episodes contained in the Afrikaans draft simply fell away; a couple of new ones emerged quite spontaneously. After completion of this draft I spent some time working on both: some of the new "English" episodes were incorporated in the Afrikaans text, but one or two – including what I regard as a most vital one – simply didn't "work" in Afrikaans. (The opposite was also true in a few cases.) The novel was then completed in English – and from that text a final Afrikaans version was prepared. There are still differences between them, and to my mind there is nothing to be done about that: the novel exists in two languages, but each language imposed its own demands on the final shape of the work.

The same might conceivably happen if a painter were to produce a work in a range of reds and then repeat it in, say, shades of blue: I can well imagine that the different colors would impose their separate "logics" on the respective works, even to the extent of demanding a variation in shapes and textures. And returning from that dual experience the painter will probably know more about red and blue than before: discovering much about the red through working in blue, and the other way round.

I write in English, but I can never be an English writer: I can never use English like Nadine Gordimer or Dan Jacobson or Alan Paton. Not only because they have lived in the language from birth, but because their use of it embodies a peculiar form of being, of being-in-Africa, being-in-English. The English I use must bear the weight of my Afrikaans, of my Afrikaansness, because only in that way can I be true to my experience of the world as it takes shape, and assumes or produces meaning, in the act of verbalization.

HEIN WILLEMSE (1957–)

During most of the last half of the twentieth century, apartheid, a system of legalized racial segregation, was imposed by the white minority on the black majority of South Africa. Under apartheid, Afrikaans, which evolved from the interaction of Dutch, the language of the Boer settlers, with indigenous African languages, as well as English, French, and German, became the medium of instruction in schools for nonwhite students. On 16 June 1976, a mass rally was held in the Soweto township to protest the compulsory use of Afrikaans. Police responded violently, killing about one hundred of the protestors, making them martyrs and inspirations to a movement that eventually, in 1992, led to the end of minority rule. The new South African constitution granted eleven languages – Afrikaans, but also English, Ndebele, Pedi, Sotho, Swati, Tsonga, Tswana, Xhosa, Venda, and Zulu – official status. The word "apartheid" comes from Afrikaans, and it is notable that the Soweto Uprising, the event that most galvanized resistance to racial oppression in South Africa, was a declaration of linguistic independence.

A native speaker of Afrikaans, Hein Willemse is a poet, academic, and activist. His poetry collections include *Angsland* (Land of anguish, 1981) and *Die Lê van die Land* (The lie of the land, 1987). In this essay, written, in English, before the end of apartheid, Willemse, who was himself classified "colored," notes the bizarre consequence of compulsory instruction in Afrikaans – the fact that people of mixed race outnumber Afrikaners as speakers of the language. Like Caliban, enslaved by the European exile Prospero in Shakespeare's play *The Tempest,* many of them appropriated the tyrant's tongue in order to curse him.

The Black Afrikaans Writer

A Continuing Dichotomy

1

Language is usually a highly charged issue.[1] It is axiomatic that "the linguistic is always at base the *politico*-linguistic, a sphere within which the struggles of imperial conqueror with subjugated state, nation-state with nation-state, region with region, class with class, are fought out."[2] The case of Afrikaans is not dissimilar. Afrikaans is so embedded in the political arena of present-day South Africa that any final projection as to its ultimate position should really be suspended until we have won our political emancipation (and/or until the last Afrikaans speaker has died). For many South Africans Afrikaans is anathema; for other South Africans Afrikaans is the language of their bread and butter; for many other South Africans Afrikaans is the language of their most intimate experiences. And many of these South Africans are black.[3]

This paper represents a personal account. Hence the often personal tone and style. And may I dedicate it to three fellow South Africans who have struggled and striven toward the realization of the whole South African nation:

1. Dikobe wa Mogale – poet, jailed in 1984 to ten years' imprisonment for alleged terrorist activities; and to the memory of:
2. Alex la Guma – novelist, veteran exile who died in Havana, Cuba, on 13 October 1985.
3. Benjamin Moloise – poet, executed on 19 October 1985 for the alleged slaying of a policeman.

Their case histories exemplify the position of the creative personality in South Africa more powerfully than any paper or treatise.

This is an indication of the extreme anger, anguish, determination and resolve of the South African oppressed. The fact that they wrote in English is peripheral. What is relevant, however, is that their lives, their writing, were completely intertwined with that of the South African freedom struggle. Let no one underestimate the extent of their example on future generations of writers.

Afrikaans is known primarily as the language of the Afrikaner. The language of the oppressor. Many people still recall the numerous placards in Soweto, June 1976: "No Afrikaans," "Away with Afrikaans," "Afrikaans stinks." The motorial cause for that extensive period of unrest, it is generally accepted, was the enforced teaching of science subjects in Afrikaans:

> To an educational system already subject to severe strains was added the doctrinaire ruling on the use of Afrikaans mathematics and social studies. This was objectionable on several grounds: few teachers were qualified to use the language, proficiency in English was popularly regarded as a prerequisite for clerical employment, and Afrikaans was unacceptable for ideological reasons.[4]

Ideologically, Afrikaans equals Afrikaner rule. It was (and *is*) an identifiable element of the everyday repression and inconveniences of black South Africans' lives. To scorn Afrikaans is to symbolically declare your abhorrence of the present political dispensation.

The events of 16 June 1976 sparked nationwide protests, acts of subversion and deaths. Black Afrikaans-speaking students like myself were drawn into various political activities: the layout, printing and distribution of pamphlets; organizing of political meetings; and the arrangement of cultural forms of protests. And frequently I read my poems. In Afrikaans. That year many deaths occurred across the country. In the Western Cape, black working-class areas like Guguletu, Nyanga, Elsie's River, Ravensmead and Heideveld bore the brunt of the police fire. Ironically, in a series of upheavals that started out as a reaction against Afrikaans, many Afrikaans-speaking people (primarily those in the three last-mentioned areas) were killed. This juxtaposition may appear to be melodramatic but it represents rather graphically the dilemma of the black Afrikaans writer.

So many atrocities are perpetrated in the name of "Law and Order," many of these *in* official Afrikaans. Given the generally high level of bilingualism in South Africa, some black Afrikaans writers may expediently opt out and write in English, in the process avoiding the suspicion of being less committed and literarily in cahoots with Afrikaner rule. Personally, however, this would have meant the premature death of my creative endeavors, and the beginning of an unbearable language schizophrenia. The task now is to continue writing in Afrikaans and to be constantly aware of this dichotomy: the oppressed writing in the language of the oppressor. One also has to accept as fact that Afrikaans is at once the language of the conqueror and the language of the oppressed. This, furthermore, implies that the black Afrikaans writer must constantly be in pursuit of a literary commitment *in Afrikaans* which is overtly counter-hegemonic.

2

I propose to address the following: a short overview of the debate on the origins of Afrikaans; Afrikaans as language of Afrikaner nationalism; Afrikaans as language of the oppressor; Afrikaans as language in the current insurrection.

Afrikaans has a very short history. As a written language it is less than two hundred years old. As a spoken language it probably developed during the ensuing years of frequent contact between the European colonizers and the aboriginal Khoikhoi and San people:

> The Khoi . . . were among the first to change the Dutch language by adapting it to their own tongue and pronunciation. They consequently altered the grammatical structure of Dutch and progressively developed the Afrikaans language. The Dutch colonists, caught up in this creolization process, consciously and unconsciously adapted the simplified Dutch.[5]

With the importation and indenture of slaves from Angola, Java, Madagascar and Malaysia, the creolization of Cape Dutch or proto-Afrikaans received further impetus.[6]

The genesis of this new pidgin, Afrikaans (literally: from Africa, Africa's), has for years been the terrain of exhausting ideological battles.[7] Opposed to the above almost logical, linguistic interaction theory, van der Merwe, from a diachronic purist position, concludes:

> It is clear [that] no non-whites as a group or as individuals influenced Dutch to such an extent that it changed to Afrikaans. . . . We recognise non-white influence with regard to our vocabulary, nothing more.[8]

According to van der Merwe, these loanwords are negligible, not affecting the grammatical and syntactical core of Cape Dutch. He asserts that Afrikaans "has its origins in and from the spoken language of the Whites" who "spontaneously" developed latent tendencies of their Western Germanic dialects.[9]

Afrikaans has, since the rise of Afrikanerdom around the turn of the century, been closely identified with the Afrikaner. Afrikaans, vulgarized Dutch, became the valued possession of the Afrikaner. Afrikaans has been usurped and used as a prominent ideological vehicle in the Afrikaner's ensuing battle for political hegemony (c. 1890–1948). The close affinity between Afrikaans and the post-1948 South Africa became more pronounced. Consider the renowned Afrikaner writer André Brink's evaluation of the relationship Afrikaans/Afrikaner-rule:

> More and more, the Afrikaans language of apartheid became eroded by newspeak, by the necessary distortions imposed by the adherence to an ideology which has to shape the world to its own image. In simplistic terms, the language of apartheid, colonized by the imperialistic activities of politicians, has now become the Language of the Lie. . . . Because of the power it wields . . . the establishment's voice is the one that resounds in the world. And so Afrikaans has become identified, more and more, in the mind of the world, with the apartheid ideology.[10]

Not only "in the mind of the world," but also in the experience of the majority of South Africans, Afrikaans equals apartheid and repression. Afrikaans is the language of the *baas* (boss):

> Morning Baas,
> Baas,
> Baas Kleinbaas says,
> I must come and tell
> Baas that,
> Baas Ben's Baas says,
> Baas Ben want to see
> Baas Kleinbaas if
> Baas don't use
> Baas Kleinbaas,
> Baas.[11]

Compare also this scene from *Woza Albert!*:

PERCY: En nou! En nou? Who is this? Who is sitting around eating lunch with my kaffirs? That's why you're getting cheeky, hey? Ja, you sit around and have lunch with terrorists!

MBONGENI: Hau! He's not a terrorist, Baas! He's a big man from heaven![12]

Wa Ntodi's poem reveals the suzerainty of the *baas* over the worker. This servility is convincingly illustrated on the level of dialogue:

> Afrikaans (unlike English) marks the distinction between the polite and the familiar second person prenominal form – *u/jy*. But in racist South Africa, in the contact between coloniser and colonised, boss and labourer, even the polite *u* is not sufficiently distanced. The flexibility and economy of the syntactical shifter are lost and nouns and proper names (all Afrikaans in this poem) are retained. The consequence is an enormous clogging up, an enormous redundancy of information. The poem enacts, ironically, at the level of dialogue, the inefficiency, the opaqueness of apartheid colonialism.[13]

Afrikaans is the language of the riot policeman *sjambokking* students. It is the language of the ill-mannered shop attendant. It is the language of the eviction notice. Afrikaans is the language in which a former minister of police, Jimmy Kruger, said on the death of Black Consciousness activist Steve Biko: "Dit laat my koud" [It leaves me cold].[14] Given this proven legacy of callousness, inhumanity and brutality, and then certainly not only at the level of language, is it any wonder that black people demonstrated so forcefully their rejection of apartheid and Afrikaans?

Afrikaans Literature, the Afrikaner's canonized cultural goods, has in essence been a faithful bedfellow of Afrikaner nationalism and Afrikaner identity. Especially during the earlier decades of this century. D. F. Malan, in a speech in 1908, exemplifies the attitude which nurtured this proximity:[15]

> Elevate the Afrikaans language to a written language, make her the bearer of our culture, of our history, our national ideals and with that elevate the *volk* [literally: nation; here it refers exclusively to the Afrikaners], who speak it. . . . The Afrikaans Language Movement is nothing more than an awakening of our *volk* to a feeling of their own value and to the call to take up a more dignified position in the world civilization.[16]

It is against this background of close affinity between Afrikaans, Afrikaans Literature and Afrikaner Nationalism as well as the ideological maneuverability of the language that the position of black Afrikaans writers must be considered. They participate in a literature tightly bound by Afrikaner identity. With these odds it is no surprise that the overall production of black Afrikaans writers is rather scanty. Since 1944 only fourteen black Afrikaans writers, mostly poets, have published their work.

May I overburden you with a note on the use of Afrikaans? Afrikaans, in large parts of the Cape, Transvaal and Orange Free State, has to a significant extent been the language of the impoverished underlings: the farm laborers, the fishermen, the general populace of the barren hinterland. The upwardly mobile and the career-minded consciously chose English. This is material in understanding the political and social insertion of black Afrikaans poets. The majority of them are of rural extraction with late teenage introduction to urban life, usually due to the furtherance of their scholastic careers.[17]

Given the rural extraction of some of the earlier black Afrikaans writers, and the overall political and the structural organization of the essentially colonialist society, some of these writers succumbed to what Frantz Fanon called the processes of assimilation.[18] To illustrate, I will compare the rather interesting cases of Peter Abrahams and S. V. Petersen.

In Abrahams's book of poetry, *A Black Man Speaks of Freedom* (1940), there are some revealing poems: especially on the relationship of the poet vis-à-vis the community. In "Self," the poet sees himself as representative of the people:

I'm a poet
And through hunger
And lust for love and laughter
I have turned myself into a voice,
Shouting the pain of the people
And the sunshine that is to be

In "Laughter," Abrahams's militant and even revolutionary proclivities surface. Stridently he rejects Christianity and the religious acceptance of fate:

I have learned to love
Burningly
With the fiercest fire;
And I have discarded my humility
And the "Will of God"
And the stories of my wise teachers
Arming myself with the wretchedness
In every plain man's life,
And all the tomorrows my soldiers
I battle on behalf of Freedom
That will restore the laughter of man

Petersen wrote at about the same time. His reaction to similar circumstances is self-scorning and, as opposed to Abrahams's strident call for freedom, a curious contradiction manifests itself. In a poem, "By Seweweekspoort," he contemplates:

Versonke in myself,	Lost in myself,
–'n swerweling, oplaas tot rus	–a wanderer, finally chained
geboei, gebind –	to repose, bound –
het ek vrede hier gevind	I have found peace here

In another poem, "Aand op Riversdal," he says:

En so het ek die land aanskou, –	And so I behold the land, –
Self tot rus gebind, geboei . . .	myself bound in repose, chained . . .
Dit was aand,	It was evening,
Aand op Riversdal	Evening in Riversdale

This specific yearning for peacefulness and tranquility – and eventually for broader societal freedom – is contradicted by the imagery, namely that of peacefulness in fetters. Petersen's notion of freedom is limited and the expected representative voice of the oppressed collective does not appear in his work. Petersen's concern is more with the personal outreach of a particular individual. This intense and well-nurtured individuality of Petersen is indeed a salient feature of his poetry. Unlike Abrahams, he never really establishes or attempts to establish a close rapport with the black mass. Petersen's relationship with the dominant cultural order is pronounced, and it influenced his relationship to that of the oppressed. His call is for the recognition of his blood relationship with the Afrikaner, or if you prefer, the oppressor. That's as far as my illustration goes.

It is not uncommon for black Afrikaans writers to go through a phase of denial and questioning their decision to write in Afrikaans.[19] Especially after 1976 no black Afrikaans writer can be spared the intellectual anguish of rationalizing his choice of language. My decision to continue writing in Afrikaans has been profoundly influenced by an incident in Namibia.

As a member of a dramatic troupe, I went on a nationwide

Namibian tour. Lüderitz, a small fishing town on the Atlantic coast, was our first stop. We were to play three or four one-acts – among other things, an English-language play, *Inkululeko.* We arrived at noon, to be met by the president of the local branch of the organizing Students' Organisation. He spoke English – rather haltingly, until he overheard an Afrikaans conversation among some of the players. And then he said something like: "My goeie God, ek't gedink julle praat net Engels. Ek't nie geweet hoe om vir julle te sê dat daai Engelse stuk nie hier gaan werk nie. Almal praat hier net Afrikaans" (Good God, I thought you only spoke English. I didn't know how to tell you that that English performance wouldn't work here. Everyone here speaks only Afrikaans).

And although I knew that Afrikaans was the *lingua franca* in Namibia, it struck me for the first time that we had a very real problem of communication. We realized that *Inkululeko* (the Xhosa for "freedom") could not be performed, whatever its message. After much discussion, it was clear that the political message was too important to cancel our performance. The only viable option was to translate the work into Afrikaans. Five hours later we had – in verse – a tentative Afrikaans equivalent of *Freedom.* For the next week we rehearsed incessantly and polished the Afrikaans translation while traversing the meandering dirt roads in a cramped Volkswagen. For the whole of that tour we never once performed *Inkululeko* in English. There are times when one cannot deny one's experience. That was such a time.

In a country where many writers describe their roles as functionaries engaged in popular struggle, they must consequently demonstrate their affinity with society. They must speak, in more ways than one, the language of their audience:

> Any pupil who spoke Afrikaans was treated with contempt by some teachers and most pupils. So naturally one attempted as far as possible to hide the fact that you were Afrikaans-speaking. On leaving high school I decided never to speak Afrikaans unnecessarily. This was my protest against the Afrikaner government; the

> *volk* and the system in this country. Later in my development I came to realise that workers on the farms speak Afrikaans. Workers on the Cape Flats and elsewhere speak Afrikaans. I became aware of the fact that if I wanted to identify with the struggle of the working class I had to speak, understand and write the language we all know.[20]

This *raison d'être* for writing Afrikaans may be severely criticized by conservative and reactionary critics as utilitarianism at variance with Literariness and Literary Exclusivity. And very little of this literature for/about/by working-class people may be considered acceptable in the Afrikaans canon. I really doubt, however, whether acceptance into the ruling-class culture is at all the objective. It is obvious that we have here a cultural activity created under trying circumstances, the writing of embattled people searching and struggling for a comfortable niche.

In recent political movements the message of liberation, in some areas, is rendered in Afrikaans. The language being consciously part of the message. During the recent and still-continuing struggles in this part of the country, the Western Cape, school children are singing these battle songs:

PW is 'n terroris (x3) Le Grange is 'n murderer, (x3) Ma, ek wil 'n Casspir hê, (x3) Ma, ek wil 'n Buffel hê. (x3)	PW is a terrorist (x3) Le Grange is a murderer (x3)* Ma, I want a Casspir (x3) Ma, I want a Buffel. (x3)

Or:

Die mamams, die pappas, die boeties, die sussies, die uncles, die anties, die hondjies, die katjies, is almal tesame in die struggle.	The mommies, the daddies, the brothers, the sisters, the uncles, the aunties, the doggies, the kitties, are all together in the struggle.

*P. W. Botha was State President of South Africa; Le Grange was Minister of Law and Order.

Or the trade unionists sing:

Klim op die wa (x2)	Climb on board the wagon (x2)**
Klim op Cosatu se wa	Climb on board COSATU's wagon
Almal wat Cosatu lief het,	Everyone who loves COSATU
klim op Cosatu se wa.	Climb on board COSATU's wagon.

These are evidence of a more relaxed attitude toward the use of Afrikaans in practical political activity. Also, in organized political groups there is a sensitivity to prevent the situation where, in oppositional discourses, elements of the upcoming classes are suppressed and marginalized. Profoundly at work is the development of a counter-hegemony. Currently the political organizations are sensitive to working-class demands and value working-class acceptability. This sensitivity also extends to the sphere of language.

For the black writer to write in Afrikaans is an overtly political act. He cannot ignore the Afrikaans literary heritage. Afrikaans literature has in essence always been directed to one particular portion of this country: the Afrikaner. The need of black Afrikaans writers is to take as their audience the whole of the South African nation, "to learn how to speak," in the words of Jeremy Cronin, "with the voices of this land."[21]

The basic historical fact for the black writer is that blacks have not yet attained their political emancipation. The writer finds him-/herself in continuous contestation with the ruling order in South Africa. In this sense it is paramount for the black writer to contribute toward a visible counter-hegemonic literature – a literary voice that continues to be the embodiment of a people engaged in political and social struggle.[22]

The need for a visible counter-hegemonic literature extends into the area of publication. This implies, for example, that all the major Afrikaans publishing houses are off-limits. The political and economic interests of the South African government and these pub-

**The ox wagon is a symbol of the Voortrekkers, the Afrikaans settlers, and therefore of Afrikaans nationalism. Here the symbol is turned against the Afrikaaners.

lishers are decidedly coterminous. To publish with one of these publishing houses would lead to an unavoidable compromise.[23]

The position of the black Afrikaans writer is indeed overburdened with extra-literary issues. For many observers these concerns may appear to be peripheral, not really affecting the essential craft of writing. The materiality of writing, especially language, however, cannot be ignored when it forms such a prominent part of the power struggles in one's society.

Notes

1. This paper was read in its original form by the author at the University of Iowa, Iowa City; the African Studies Association conference (23–27 November 1985), New Orleans; and at a writer's forum at Dora Falck, Muizenberg, May 1986.

2. Terry Eagleton, *Criticism and Ideology* (London: Verso, 1976), pp. 54–55.

3. Although the majority of the Afrikaans-speaking blacks would be classified "colored," i.e., mulatto, in South Africa, I know from personal experience that there are other so-called "African" classified people who have as their first language Afrikaans. See also Elsa Joubert, *Poppie* (Johannesburg: Jonathan Ball, 1981), p. 14: "Everybody spoke Afrikaans, even the Rhodesian Africans and Xhosas and Sothos living there."

4. Tom Lodge, *Black Politics in South Africa since 1945* (Johannesburg: Ravan, 1976), pp. 54–55.

5. Kenneth Jordaan, "The Origins of the Afrikaners and Their Language, 1652–1720: A Study in Miscegenation and Creole," *Race* 15, no. 4 (London, 1974): 462.

6. Marius Valkhoff, *New Light on Afrikaans and "Malayo-Portuguese"* (Louvain: Editions Peeters Imprimerie Orientaliste, 1972), p. 65.

7. For English overviews of these debates see Jordaan and Valkhoff.

8. H. J. J. M. van der Merwe, "Die ontstaan van Afrikaans," in *Afrikaans: sy aard en ontwikkeling,* ed. H. J. J. M. van der Merwe (Pretoria: J. L. van Schaik, 1972), p. 29.

9. Ibid., p. 50.

10. André Brink, "The Future of Afrikaans," *Leadership S.A.* 3, no. 2 (Johannesburg, 1984): 34–35.

11. Motshile wa Ntodi, "South African Dialogue," in *Century of South African Poetry,* ed. Michael Chapman (Johannesburg: Ad. Donker, 1981), p. 347. [This English-language poem uses the Afrikaans word *"baas,"* which means

"boss" but is associated with white Afrikaans dominance, hence the noun "baaskap," "boss-hood" or "boss-ship." In this poem, the worker uses "Baas" to address the middle-aged employer and "Kleinbaas," "little boss," for the employer's son. – *Editor's Note*]

12. Percy Mtwa, Mbongeni Ngema and Barney Simon, *Woza Albert!* (London: Methuen, 1983), pp. 50–51.

13. Jeremy Cronin, "'Laat ons ranks vassa' – African Poets and the Use of Afrikaans," in *Swart Afrikaanse skrywers,* ed. Julian Smith, Alwyn van Gensen and Hein Willemse (Bellville: U.W.C., forthcoming).

14. Oswalk Mbuyseni Mtshali, "The Removal of Our Village – Kwa Bhanya," in *Fire-flames* (Durban: Shuter and Shooter, 1980), p. 43.

15. In 1948 Malan's Nationalist Party came to power on the apartheid election ticket.

16. Quoted in Hermann Giliomee and Heribert Adam, *Afrikaner mag: opkoms en toekoms* (Stellenbosch: Universiteits – uitgewery, 1981), p. 80; translation by Hein Willemse.

17. Hein Willemse, "Die wrange klag, die satire en opstandigheid van die kleurling: Towards a Critical Reconstruction of the Intellectual History of Black Afrikaans Poets," in *The Political Economy of Race I,* ed. Wilmot James (Bellville: U.W.C., 1984).

18. See the following instructive quotation from Richard Rive, *Writing Black* (Cape Town: David Philip, 1981), p. 6: "I grew up in an atmosphere of shabby respectability, in a family chafing against its social confinement to dirty, narrow streets in a beaten-up neighbourhood. Our hankering after respectability became obsessive. We always felt we were intended for better things. The family spoke Afrikaans, as the youngest I was spoken to in English. We were members of the Anglican church."

19. S. V. Petersen and Adam Small, for instance, published respectively *Meditations on the Brink* and *Black, Bronze, Beautiful* (Johannesburg: Ravan, 1975). Small's *The Orange Earth* and an English translation of *Kanna hy kô hystoe* (Kanna, he is coming home) and Peter Snyders's *Violations* have been performed.

20. Beverley Jansen, "Poësiepaneelbespreking," in *Swart Afrikaanse skrywers,* ed. Smith, van Gensen and Willemse.

21. Jeremy Cronin, *Inside* (Johannesburg: Ravan, 1984).

22. For analysis of the influence of apartheid on literature see V. A. February, *Mind Your Colour* (London: Routledge and Kegan Paul, 1981); G. J. Gerwel, *Literatuur en Apartheid* (Bellville: Kampen, 1983); and R. M. Kavanagh, *Theatre and Struggle in South Africa* (London: Zed Press, 1985).

23. This is not a shared or representative opinion. The majority of black Afrikaans writers still publish with the major Afrikaans publishing houses.

India

RAJA RAO (1909–)

A legacy of the British raj, English is one of fifteen languages officially recognized as national or major in India. Though it is spoken regularly by only about 4 percent of the population and can count on fewer native speakers than Hindi, Bengali, Marathi, Telugu, Tamil, Gujarati, or Urdu, English in India is both a lingua franca for the diverse subcontinent and the language of the intelligentsia. Along with Mulk Raj Anand and R. K. Narayan, Raja Rao pioneered the use of English as the medium of Indian fiction.

Born in 1909 in Mysore, Rao left India for France at the age of eighteen in order to study literature and history. *Kanthapura* (1938), his first novel, portrays the movement for independence from Britain, and he spent World War II in India active in the underground resistance. From 1965 to 1983, he taught philosophy at the University of Texas at Austin. Other Rao novels include *The Serpent and the Rope* (1960), *The Cat and Shakespeare: A Tale of India* (1965), *Comrade Kirillov* (1976), and*The Chessmaster and His Moves* (1988). His short stories have been collected in *The Cow of the Barricades and Other Stories* (1947) and *The Policeman and the Rose* (1978).

In his brief foreword to *Kanthapura,* Rao explains the challenge to him of writing the novel in English rather than his native Kannada. Like many African authors who employ English, French, or Portuguese, Rao claims that, in choosing not to use an indigenous language, Indians have appropriated and transformed English into a supple instrument capable of conveying their own experiences and emotions.

From the Author's Foreword to *Kanthapura*

There is no village in India, however mean, that has not a rich *sthala-purana,* or legendary history, of its own. Some god or god-like hero has passed by the village – Rama might have rested under this pipal-tree, Sita might have dried her clothes, after her bath, on this yellow stone, or the Mahatma himself, on one of his many pilgrimages through the country, might have slept in this hut, the low one, by the village gate. In this way the past mingles with the present, and the gods mingle with men to make the repertory of your grandmother always bright. One such story from the contemporary annals of a village I have tried to tell.

The telling has not been easy. One has to convey in a language that is not one's own the spirit that is one's own. One has to convey the various shades and omissions of a certain thought-movement that looks maltreated in an alien language. I use the word "alien," yet English is not really an alien language to us. It is the language of our intellectual makeup – like Sanskrit or Persian was before – but not of our emotional makeup. We are all instinctively bilingual, many of us writing in our own language and in English. We cannot write like the English. We should not. We cannot write only as Indians. We have grown to look at the large world as part of us. Our method of expression therefore has to be a dialect which will some day prove to be as distinctive and colorful as the Irish or the American. Time alone will justify it.

SALMAN RUSHDIE (1947–)

Born in Bombay into a multilingual family that spoke Urdu, Hindi, and English, Salman Rushdie was educated in England at Rugby School and Cambridge University. His second novel, *Midnight's Children* (1981), an allegorical epic that surveys the history of sovereign India through the fates of characters born at the moment of independence, 15 August 1947, gained Rushdie acclaim and Britain's prestigious Booker Prize. But it was *The Satanic Verses* (1988) that transformed the author into a hunted celebrity, after the spiritual leader of Iran, the Ayatollah Ruhollah Khomeini, issued a fatwa condemning Rushdie to death for alleged blasphemy against Islam. Despite being denied entry to his native country during most of a decade spent in hiding, Rushdie, a British subject who eventually moved to New York, was India's most famous author, perhaps even the most famous author in the world.

Other Rushdie novels include *Shame* (1983), *Haroun and the Sea of Stories* (1990), *The Moor's Last Sigh* (1995), *The Ground beneath Her Feet* (1999), and *Fury* (2001). He published a nonfiction book, *Homelands: Essays and Criticism,* in 1991, and coedited, with Elizabeth West, *The Vintage Book of Indian Writing (1947–1997)* in 1997. As an impresario of Indian writing, Rushdie was asked in June 1997 by the editors of the *New Yorker* to select and introduce texts by his contemporaries for inclusion in a special issue of the magazine devoted to literary India. In his introduction, "Damme, This Is the Oriental Scene for You!" he surveys writing in India and concludes that, at least in English, it is enjoying a golden age.

Some critics have attacked Rushdie for presuming to market Indian literature to the West in a package that distorts it. Only a small minority of Indians regularly speaks English, and a sizable percentage does not understand the language at all. Rushdie was faulted for characterizing the subcontinent's culture as largely English-speaking and for his ignorance of important literary work being done in Hindi, Urdu, Bengali, Malayalam, Gujarati, and other indigenous languages. Centuries before the current crop of Indians began exchanging their native tongues for English, authors such as Dadu, Kabir, Meerabai, Namdev, and Raidas were using two, three, or even four of the Indian languages. Yet both Rushdie and his critics must concede that the pioneering fiction of Mulk Raj Anand, R. K. Narayan, and Raj Rao has led in recent years to an extraordinary efflorescence of Anglophonic literary talent, making India one of the world's most dynamic laboratories for literary translingualism.

Damme, This Is the Oriental Scene for You!

I once gave a reading to a gathering of university students in Delhi, and when I'd finished a young woman put up her hand. "Mr. Rushdie, I read through your novel *Midnight's Children,*" she said. "It is a very long book, but never mind, I read it through. And the question I want to ask you is this: Fundamentally, what's your point?" Before I could attempt an answer, she spoke again: "Oh, I know what you're going to say. You're going to say that the whole effort, from cover to cover – that is the point of the exercise. Isn't that what you were going to say?"

"Something like that, perhaps," I got out.

She snorted. "It won't do."

"Please," I begged. "Do I have to have just one point?"

"Fundamentally," she said, with impressive firmness, "yes."

Contemporary Indian literature remains largely unknown in the United States, in spite of its considerable present-day energy and diversity. The few writers who have made an impression (R. K. Narayan, Vikram Seth) are inevitably read in a kind of literary isolation: texts without context. Some writers of Indian descent, such as V. S. Naipaul and Bharati Mukherjee, reject the ethnic label "Indian writers," perhaps in an effort to place themselves in other, better-understood literary contexts. Mukherjee sees herself nowadays as an American writer, while Naipaul would perhaps prefer to be read as an artist from nowhere and everywhere. Indians – and, following the partition of the subcontinent almost fifty years ago, one should also say Pakistanis – have long been migrants, seeking their fortunes in Africa, Australia, Britain, the Caribbean, and America, and this diaspora has produced many writers who lay claim to an excess of roots: writers like the Kashmiri-American poet Agha Shahid Ali, whose verses look toward Srinagar from Amherst, Massachusetts, by way of other catastrophes. He writes:

> what else besides God disappears at the altar?
> O Kashmir, Armenia once vanished. Words are nothing,
> just rumors – like roses – to embellish a slaughter.

How, then, is one to make any simple, summarizing statement – "Fundamentally, what's your point?" – about so multiform a literature, hailing from that huge crowd of a country (close to a billion people at the last count), that vast, metamorphic, continent-size culture, which feels, both to Indians and to visitors, like a nonstop assault on the senses, the emotions, the imagination, and the spirit? Put the Indian subcontinent in the Atlantic Ocean and it would reach from Europe to America; put it together with China and you've got almost half the population of the world.

These days, new Indian writers seem to emerge every few weeks. Their work is as polymorphous as the place. The approaching fiftieth anniversary of Indian independence is a useful pretext for a survey of half a century of postliberation writing. For many months now, I have been reading my way through this literature, and my Delhi interrogator may be pleased to hear that the experience has indeed led me to a single – unexpected and profoundly ironic – conclusion.

This is it: The prose writing – both fiction and nonfiction – created in this period by Indian writers working in English is proving to be a stronger and more important body of work than most of what has been produced in the eighteen "recognized" languages of India, the so-called "vernacular languages," during the same time; and, indeed, this new, and still burgeoning, "Indo-Anglian" literature represents perhaps the most valuable contribution India has yet made to the world of books. The true Indian literature of the first postcolonial half century has been made in the language the British left behind.

It is a large claim, though it may be an easy one for non-Indian readers to accept; if most of India's English-language writers are still largely unknown in the West, the problem is far greater in the case of the vernacular literatures. Of India's non-English-language authors, perhaps only the name of the 1913 Nobel Prize–winning Bengali writer Rabindranath Tagore would be recognized internationally, and even his work, though still popular in Latin America, is now pretty much a closed book in the United States. In any case, it is a claim that runs counter to much of the received critical wisdom within India itself. It is also not a claim that I ever expected to make.

Admittedly, I did my reading only in English, and there has long been a genuine problem of translation in India – not only into English but between the vernacular languages – and it is possible that good writers have been ill served by their translators' inadequacies. Nowadays, however, such bodies as the Indian Academy of the Arts (the Sahitya Akademi), UNESCO, and Indian publishers themselves have been putting substantial resources into the creation of better translations, and the problem, while not eradicated, is certainly much diminished.

Ironically, the century before independence contains many vernacular-language writers who would merit a place in any anthology: besides Rabindranath Tagore, there are Bankim Chandra Chatterjee, Dr. Muhammad Iqbal, Bibhutibhushan Banerjee (the author of *Pather Panchali,* on which Satyajit Ray based his celebrated Apu trilogy of films), and Prem Chand, the prolific (and therefore rather variable) Hindi author of, among many other works, the famous novel of rural life, *Godaan; or, The Gift of a Cow.* Those who wish to seek out their leading present-day successors should try, for example, O. V. Vijayan (Malayalam), Suryakant Tripathi, also known as "Nirala" (Hindi), Nirmal Verma (Hindi), U. R. Ananthamurthy (Kannada), Suresh Joshi (Gujarati), Amrita Pritam (Punjabi)), Qurratulain Hyder (Urdu), and Ismat Chughtai (Urdu), and make their own assessments. English versions exist of at least some of these writers' works; sometimes, as in the case of Vijayan, translated by the author.

To my own considerable astonishment, however, there is only one Indian writer in translation whom I would place on a par with the Indo-Anglian. (Actually, he's better than most of them.) That is Saadat Hasan Manto, an immensely popular Urdu writer of low-life fictions, whom conservative critics sometimes scorn for his choice of characters and milieus, much as Virginia Woolf snobbishly disparaged the fictional universe of James Joyce's *Ulysses.* Manto's masterpiece is the short story "Toba Tek Singh," a parable of the partition of India, in which it is decided that the lunatics, too, must be partitioned – Indian lunatics to India, Pakistani lunatics to the new country of Pakistan. But for the inmates of an asylum in Lahore everything is unclear: the exact site of the frontier, and of the places of origin of the insane persons, too. The lunacies in the asylum become, in this savagely funny story, a perfect metaphor for the greater insanity of history.

The lack of first-rate writing in translation can only be a matter for regret. However, to speak more positively, it is a delight to be able to celebrate the quality of a growing collective English-language oeuvre, whose status has long been argued over, but which has, in the last twenty years or so, begun to merit a place alongside the most flourishing literatures in the world.

For some Indian critics, English-language Indian writing will never be more than a postcolonial anomaly – the bastard child of Empire, sired on India by the departing British. Its continuing use of the old colonial tongue is seen as a fatal flaw that renders it forever inauthentic. Indo-Anglian literature evokes in these critics the kind of prejudiced reaction shown by some Indians toward the country's community of Anglo-Indians – that is, Eurasians.

Fifty years ago, Jawaharlal Nehru delivered, in English, the great "freedom at midnight" speech that marked the moment of independence:

> At the stroke of the midnight hour, when the world sleeps, India will awake to life and freedom. A moment comes, which comes but rarely in history, when we step out from the old to the new, when an age ends, and when the soul of a nation, long suppressed, finds utterance.

Since that indisputably Anglophone oration, the role of English itself has often been disputed in India. Attempts to coin medical, scientific, technological, and everyday neologisms in India's continental shelf of languages to replace the commonly used English words have sometimes succeeded but have more often comically failed. And when the Marxist government of the state of Bengal announced, in the early 1980s, that the supposedly elitist, colonialist teaching of English would be discontinued in government-run primary schools, many on the left denounced the decision itself as elitist, because it would deprive the masses of the many economic and social advantages of speaking the world's language and only the affluent private-school elite would henceforth have that privilege. A well-known Calcutta graffito complained, "My son won't learn English. Your son won't learn English. But Jyoti Basu" – the Chief Minister – "will send his son abroad to learn English." One man's ghetto of privilege is another's road to freedom.

Like the Greek god Dionysius, who was dismembered and afterward reassembled – and who, according to the myths, was one of India's earliest conquerors – Indian writing in English has been called "twice-born" (by the critic Meenakshi Mukherjee) to suggest its double parentage. While I am, I must admit, attracted by the Dionysian resonances of this supposed double birth, it seems to me to rest on the false premise that English, having arrived from outside India, is and must necessarily remain an alien there. But my own mother tongue, Urdu, which was the camp argot of the country's earliest Muslim conquerors, was also an immigrant language, forged from a combination of the conquerors' imported Farsi and the local languages they encountered. However, it became a naturalized subcontinental language long ago; and by now that has happened to English, too. English has become an Indian language.

Its colonial origins mean that, like Urdu and unlike all other Indian languages, it has no regional base; but in all other ways it has emphatically come to stay.

(In many parts of South India, people will prefer to converse with visiting North Indians in English rather than in Hindi, which feels, ironically, more like a colonial language to speakers of Tamil, Kannada, or Malayalam than does English, which has acquired in the South an aura of lingua-franca cultural neutrality. The new Silicon Valley–style boom in computer technology which is transforming the economies of Bangalore and Madras has made English in those cities an even more important language than before.)

Indian English, sometimes unattractively called "Hinglish," is not "English" English, to be sure, any more than Irish or American or Caribbean English is. And part of the achievement of English-language Indian writers is to have found literary voices that are as distinctively Indian, and also as suitable for any and all the purposes of art, as those of other English-language writers in Ireland, Africa, the West Indies, and the United States.

However, Indian critical assaults on this new literature continue to be made from time to time. Its practitioners are denigrated for being too upper-middle-class; for lacking diversity in their choice of themes and techniques; for being less popular in India than outside India; for possessing inflated reputations on account of the international power of the English language, and of the ability of Western critics and publishers to impose their cultural standards on the East; for living, in many cases, outside India; for being deracinated to the point where their work lacks the spiritual dimension essential for a "true" understanding of the soul of India; for being insufficiently grounded in the ancient literary traditions of India; for being the literary equivalent of MTV culture, or of globalizing Coca-Colonization; even, I'm sorry to report, for suffering from a condition that one sprightly recent commentator, Pankaj Mishra, calls "Rushdie-itis . . . a condition that has claimed Rushdie himself in his later works."

It is interesting that so few of these criticisms are literary in the pure sense of the word. For the most part, they do not deal with language, voice, psychological or social insight, imagination, or talent. Rather, they have to do with class, power, and belief. There is a whiff of political correctness about them: the ironic proposition that India's best writing since independence may have been done in the language of the departed imperialists is simply too much for some folks to bear. It ought not to be true, and so must not be permitted to be true. (That many of the attacks on English-language Indian writing are made in English by Indian writers who are themselves members of the college-educated, English-speaking elite is a further irony.)

Let us quickly concede what must be conceded. It is true that most of these writers come from the educated classes of India; but in a country still bedeviled by high illiteracy levels how could the situation be otherwise? It does not follow, however – unless one holds to a rigid, class-war view of the world – that writers with the privilege of a good education will automatically write novels that seek only to portray the lives of the bourgeoisie. It is true that there tends to be a bias toward metropolitan and cosmopolitan fiction, but there has been, during this half century, a genuine attempt to encompass as many Indian realities as possible, rural as well as urban, sacred as well as profane. This is also, let us remember, a young literature. It is still pushing out the frontiers of the possible.

The point about the power of the English language, and of the Western publishing and critical fraternities, also contains some truth. Perhaps it does seem, to some "home" commentators, that a canon is being foisted on them from outside. The perspective from the West is rather different. Here what seems to be the case is that Western publishers and critics have been growing gradually more and more excited by the voices emerging from India; in England, at least, British writers are often chastised by reviewers for their lack of Indian-style ambition and verve. It feels as if the East were imposing itself on the West, rather than the other way around. And, yes, English is the most powerful medium of communication in the world. Should we not, then, rejoice at these artists' mastery of it, and at their growing influence? To criticize writers for their success in "breaking out" is no more than parochialism (and parochialism is perhaps the main vice of the vernacular literatures). One important dimension of literature is that it is a means of holding a conversation with the world. These writers are ensuring that India – or, rather, Indian voices (for they are too good to fall into the trap of writing *nationalistically*) – will henceforth be confident, indispensable participants in that literary conversation.

Granted, many of these writers do have homes outside India. Henry James, James Joyce, Samuel Beckett, Ernest Hemingway, Gertrude Stein, Mavis Gallant, James Baldwin, Graham Greene, Gabriel García Márquez, Mario Vargas Llosa, Jorge Luis Borges, Vladimir Nabokov, and Muriel Spark were or are wanderers, too. Muriel Spark, accepting in March 1997 the British Literature Prize for a lifetime's achievement, went as far as to say that travel to other countries was essential for all writers. Literature has little or nothing to do with a writer's home address.

The question of religious faith, both as a subject and as an approach to a subject, is clearly important when we speak of a country as near to bursting with devotions as India; but it is surely excessive to use it – as does one leading academic, the redoubtable Professor C. D. Narasimhaiah – as a touchstone, so that Mulk Raj Anand is praised for his "daring" merely because, as a leftist writer, he allows a character to be moved by deep faith, while Arun Kolatkar's poetry is denigrated for "throwing away tradition and creating a vacuum" and thereby "losing relevance" because in "Jejuri," a cycle of poems about a visit to a temple town, he skeptically likens the stone gods in the temples to the stones on the hillsides nearby ("and every other stone / is god or his cousin"). In fact, many of the writers I admire have a profound knowledge of the "soul of India"; many have deeply spiritual concerns, while others are radically secular, but the need to engage with – to make a reckoning with – India's religious self is everywhere to be found.

The cheapening of artistic response that the allegations of deracination and Westernization imply is notably absent from the Indo-

Anglian writers' work. As to the claims of excessive Rushdie-itis, I can't deny that on occasion I've felt something of the sort myself. On the whole, however, it seems to be a short-lived virus, and those whom it affects soon shake it off and find their own, true voices.

(An interesting sidelight. After the 1981 publication of my novel *Midnight's Children,* I learned that the idea of a long saga-novel about a child born at the exact moment of independence – midnight, 14–15 August 1947 – had occurred to other writers, too. A Goan poet showed me the first chapter of an abandoned novel in which the "midnight child" was born not in Bombay but in Goa. And as I traveled round India I heard of at least two other aborted projects – one in Bengali, the other in Kannada – with nearly similar themes.)

At any rate, there is not, need not be, and should not be an adversarial relationship between English-language Indian literature and the other literatures of India. In my own case – and I suspect in the case of every Indo-Anglian writer – knowing and loving the Indian languages in which I was raised has remained of vital personal and artistic importance. Hindi-Urdu, the "Hindustani" of North India, remains an essential aspect of my sense of self as an individual, while as a writer I have been partly formed by the presence, in my head, of that other music – the rhythms, patterns, and habits of thought and metaphor of all my Indian tongues.

Whatever language we Indians write in, we drink from the same well. India, that inexhaustible horn of plenty, nourishes us all.

The first Indian novel in English was a dud. *Rajmohan's Wife* (1864), is a poor, melodramatic thing. The writer, Bankim, reverted to Bengali and immediately achieved great renown. For the next seventy years or so, there was no English-language fiction of any quality. It was the generation of independence – "midnight's parents," one might call them – who were the true architects of this new tradition. (Jawaharlal Nehru himself was a fine writer; his autobiography and letters are important, influential works. And his niece Nayantara Sahgal, whose early memoir, *Prison and Chocolate Cake,* contains perhaps the finest evocation of the heady time of independence, went on to become a major novelist.)

In that generation, Mulk Raj Anand was influenced by both Joyce and Marx but most of all, perhaps, by the teachings of Mahatma Gandhi. He is best known for social-realist works like the novels *Untouchable* (1935) and *Coolie* (1936), studies of the life of the poor, which could be compared to postwar Italian neorealist cinema (De Sica's *The Bicycle Thief,* Rossellini's *Rome, Open City*). Raja Rao, a scholarly Sanskritist, wrote of his determination to make an Indian English for himself, but even his much praised portrait of village life, *Kanthapura,* published in 1938, now seems dated, its approach at once grandiloquent and archaic. The centenarian autobiographer Nirad C. Chaudhuri has been, throughout his long life, an erudite, contrary, and mischievous presence. His view, if I may paraphrase and summarize it, is that India has no culture of its own, and that whatever we now call Indian culture was brought in from outside by the successive waves of conquerors. This view, polemically and brilliantly expressed, has not endeared him to many of his fellow Indians. That he has always swum so strongly against the current has not, however, prevented *The Autobiography of an Unknown Indian* from being recognized as a masterpiece.

The most significant writers of this first generation, R. K. Narayan and G. V. Desani, have had opposite careers. Narayan's books fill a good-sized shelf; Desani is the author of a single novel, *All about H. Hatterr,* and that volume is already fifty years old. Desani is almost unknown, while Narayan is, of course, a figure of world stature, for his creation of the imaginary town of Malgudi, so lovingly made that it has become more vividly real to us than most real places. (But Narayan's realism is leavened by touches of legend; the river Sarayu, for instance, on whose shores the town sits, is one of the great rivers of Hindu mythology. It is as if William Faulkner had set his Yoknapatawpha County on the banks of the Styx.)

Narayan shows us, over and over again, the quarrel between traditional, static India, on the one hand, and modernity and progress, on the other, represented, in many of his stories and novels, by a confrontation between a "wimp" and a "bully": *The Painter of*

Signs and his aggressive beloved with her birth-control campaign; *The Vendor of Sweets* and the emancipated American daughter-in-law with the absurd "novel-writing machine"; and the mild-mannered printer and the extrovert taxidermist in *The Man-Eater of Malgudi.* In his gentle, lightly funny art he goes to the heart of the Indian condition and beyond it – into the human condition itself.

The writer I have placed alongside Narayan, G. V. Desani, has fallen so far from favor that the extraordinary *All about H. Hatterr* is at present out of print in India. Milan Kundera once said that all modern literature descends from either Richardson's *Clarissa* or Sterne's *Tristram Shandy,* and if Narayan is India's Richardson, then Desani is his Shandean other. *Hatterr*'s dazzling, puzzling, leaping prose is the first genuine effort to go beyond the Englishness of the English language. Desani's central figure – "fifty-fifty of the species," the half-breed as unabashed antihero – leaps and capers behind the work of many of his successors. Desani writes:

> The earth was blotto with the growth of willow, peach, mango-blossom, and flower. Every ugly thing, and smell, was in incognito, as fragrance and freshness.
>
> Being prone, this typical spring-time dash and activity, played an exulting phantasmagoria-note on the inner-man. Medically speaking, the happy circumstances vibrated my ductless glands, and fused me into a wibble-wobble *Whoa, Jamieson!* filip-and-flair to *live, live!*

Or, again:

> The incidents take place in India.
>
> I was exceedingly hard-up of cash: actually, in debts.
>
> And, it is amazing, how, out in the Orient, the shortage of cash gets mixed up with romance and females somehow!
>
> In this England, they say, if a fellah is broke, females, as a matter of course, forsake.
>
> Stands to reason.
>
> Whereas, out in the East, they attach themselves!
>
> Damme, this is the Oriental scene for you!

This is the "babu-English," the semiliterate, half-learned English of the bazaars, transmuted by erudition, highbrow monkeying around, and the impish magic of Desani's unique phrasing and rhythm into an entirely new kind of literary voice. Hard to imagine I. Allan Sealy's more recent, Eurasian comic epic, *The Trotter-Nama* – an enormous tome swirling with digressions, interpolations, exclamations, resumptions, encomiums, and catastrophes – without Desani. My own writing, too, learned a trick or two from him.

Ved Mehta is a writer known both for his astute commentaries on the Indian scene and for his several distinguished volumes of autobiography. The most moving of these is *Vedi,* a memoir of a blind boyhood that describes cruelties and kindnesses with equal dispassion and great effect. (More recently, Firdaus Kanga, in his autobiographical fiction *Trying to Grow,* has also transcended physical affliction with high style and comic brio.)

Ruth Prawer Jhabvala, the author of the Booker Prize–winning *Heat and Dust* (afterward made into a Merchant-Ivory movie), is a master of the short-story form. As a writer, she is sometimes underrated in India because, I think, the voice of the rootless intellectual (so quintessentially her voice) is such an unfamiliar one in that country, where people's self-definitions are so rooted in their regional identities.

That Jhabvala has a second career as an award-winning screenwriter is well known. But not many people realize that India's greatest film director, the late Satyajit Ray, was also an accomplished author of short stories. His father edited a famous Bengali children's magazine, *Sandesh,* and Ray's biting little fables are made more potent by their childlike charm.

Anita Desai, one of India's major living authors, merits comparison with Jane Austen. In novels such as *Clear Light of Day* – written in a lucid, light English full of subtle atmospherics – she displays both her exceptional skill at social portraiture and an unsparing, Jane-like mordancy of insight into human motivations. *In Custody,* perhaps her best novel to date, makes fine use of English to depict the decay of another language, Urdu, and the high literary culture that lived in it. Here the poet, the last, boozing, decrepit custodian of the dying tradition, is (in a reversal of Narayan) the "bully," and the novel's central character, the poet's young admirer, is the "wimp." The dying past, the old world, Desai tells us, can be as much of a burden as the awkward, sometimes wrongheaded present.

Though V. S. Naipaul approaches India as an outsider, his engagement with it has been so intense that no account of its modern literature would be complete without him. His three nonfiction books on India – *An Area of Darkness, India: A Wounded Civilization,* and *India: A Million Mutinies Now* – are key texts, and not only because of the hackles they have raised. Many Indian critics have taken issue with the harshness of his responses. Some have fair-mindedly conceded that he does attack things worth attacking. "I'm anti-Naipaul when I visit the West," one leading South Indian novelist told me, "but I'm often pro-Naipaul back home."

Some of Naipaul's targets, like (this is from *A Wounded Civilization*) the intermediate-technology institute that invents "reaping shoes" (with blades attached) for Indian peasants to use in harvesting grain, merit the full weight of his scorn. At other times, he appears merely supercilious. India, his migrant ancestors' lost paradise, apparently cannot stop disappointing him. By the third volume of the series, however, which was written in 1990, he seems more cheerful about the country's condition. He speaks approvingly of the emergence of "a central will, a central intellect, a national idea," and disarmingly, even movingly, confesses to the atavistic edginess of mood in which he made his first trip almost thirty years earlier: "The India of my fantasy and heart was something lost and irrecoverable. . . . On that first journey, I was a fearful traveller."

In *An Area of Darkness,* Naipaul's comments on Indian writers elicit from this reader a characteristic mixture of agreement and dissent. He writes:

> The feeling is widespread that, whatever English might have done for Tolstoy, it can never do justice to the Indian "language" writers. This is possible; what little I read of them in translation did not

> encourage me to read more. Premchand . . . turned out to be a minor fabulist. . . . Other writers quickly fatigued me with their assertions that poverty was sad, that death was sad . . . and many of the "modern" short stories were only refurbished folk tales.

Here he is expressing, in his emphatic, unafraid way, what I have also felt (though I think more highly of Premchand than he). He also says:

> The novel is of the West. It is part of that Western concern with the condition of men, a response to the here and now. In India thoughtful men have preferred to turn their backs on the here and now and to satisfy what President Radhakrishnan calls "the basic human hunger for the unseen." It is not a good qualification for the writing or reading of novels.

And here I can accompany him only some of the way. It is true that many learned Indians go in for a sonorously impenetrable form of critico-mysticism. I once heard an Indian writer of some renown, who was much interested in India's ancient wisdoms, expounding his theory of what one might call Motionism. "Consider Water," he advised us. "Water without Motion is – what? Is a lake. Very well. Now, Water plus Motion is – what? Is a river. You see? The Water is still the same Water. Only Motion has been added. By the same token," he continued, making a breathtaking intellectual leap, "Language is Silence, to which Motion has been added."

(A fine Indian poet, who was sitting beside me in the great man's audience, murmured in my ear, "Bowel without Motion is – what? Is constipation! Bowel plus Motion is – what? Is shit!")

So I agree with Naipaul that mysticism is bad for novelists. But, in the India I know, for every obfuscating Motionist there is a debunking Bowelist whispering in one's ear; for every unworldly seeker for the ancient wisdoms of the East there is a clear-eyed witness responding to the here and now in precisely that fashion which Naipaul inaccurately calls uniquely Western. And when Naipaul concludes by saying that in the aftermath of the "abortive" Indo-British encounter India is little more than a (very Naipaulian) community of mimic men – that the country's artistic life has stagnated, that "the creative urge" has "failed," that "Shiva has ceased to dance" – then I fear he and I part company altogether. *An Area of Darkness* was written as long ago as 1964, a mere seventeen years after independence and a little early for an obituary notice. The growing quality of Indian writing in English may yet change his mind.

In the 1980s and '90s, the flow of that good writing has become a flood. Bapsi Sidhwa is technically Pakistani, but literature has no need of partitions, particularly since Sidhwa's novel *Cracking India* is one of the finest responses made to the horror of the division of the subcontinent. Gita Mehta's *A River Sutra* is an important attempt by a thoroughly modern Indian to make her reckoning with the Hindu culture from which she emerged. Padma Perera, Anjana Appachana (whose major new novel, *Listening Now,* will be published next January), and Githa Hariharan, less well known than Sidhwa and Mehta, confirm the quality of contemporary writing by Indian women.

A number of different styles of work are evolving: the Stendhalian realism of a writer like Rohinton Mistry, the author of two acclaimed novels, *Such a Long Journey* and *A Fine Balance,* and of a collection of stories, *Tales from Firozsha Baag;* the equally naturalistic but lighter, more readily charming prose of Vikram Seth (there is, admittedly, a kind of perversity in invoking lightness in the context of a book boasting as much sheer avoirdupois as *A Suitable Boy,* which runs to a thousand three hundred and forty-nine pages); the elegant social observation of Upamanyu Chatterjee (*English August*); and the more flamboyant manner of Vikram Chandra (*Love and Longing in Bombay*). Amitav Ghosh's most impressive achievement to date is the nonfiction study of India and Egypt, *In an Antique Land.* It may be that his greatest strength will turn out to be as an essayist of this sort. Sara Suleri, whose memoir *Meatless Days* is, like Bapsi Sidhwa's *Cracking India,* a visitor from across the Pakistani frontier, is a nonfiction writer of immense originality and grace. And Amit Chaudhuri's languorous, elliptical, beautiful prose is impressively impossible to place in any category at all.

Most encouragingly, yet another talented generation has begun to emerge. The Bengali-Keralan writer Arundhati Roy has arrived to the accompaniment of a loud fanfare. Her novel, *The God of Small Things,* is full of ambition and sparkle, and is written in a highly wrought and utterly personal style. Equally impressive are the debuts of two other first novelists. Ardashir Vakil's *Beach Boy* and Kiran Desai's *Strange Happenings in the Guava Orchard* are, in very unalike ways, highly original books. The Vakil book, a tale of growing up near Juhu Beach, Bombay, is sharp, funny, and fast; the Kiran Desai, a Calvinoesque fable of a misfit boy who climbs a tree and becomes a sort of petty guru, is lush and intensely imagined. Kiran Desai is the daughter of Anita: her arrival establishes the first dynasty of modern Indian fiction. But she is very much her own writer, the newest of all these voices, and welcome proof that India's encounter with the English language, far from proving abortive, continues to give birth to new children, endowed with lavish gifts.

The map of the world in the standard Mercator projection is not kind to India, making it look substantially smaller than, say, Greenland. On the map of world literature, too, India has been undersized for too long. Fifty years after India's independence, however, that age of obscurity is coming to an end. India's writers have torn up the old map and are busily drawing their own.

C. J. S. WALLIA (1945–)

IndiaStar Review of Books (*www.indiastar.com*), an online journal founded in 1995, features original essays, short stories, and poetry as well as reviews of nonfiction, fiction, and film. The publisher and editor of *IndiaStar Review,* C. J. S. Wallia, who was born in the Punjab region of India, received a B.A. from Punjab University and a Ph.D. from Stanford University and teaches editing and publishing courses in the extension program of the University of California at Berkeley. Writing for the *IndiaStar Review* about the June 1997 issue of the *New Yorker* devoted to contemporary Indian authors, Wallia faulted Rushdie's provocative introductory essay for neglecting the wealth and variety of work that is not Anglophone.

Response to Salman Rushdie

This special issue of *The New Yorker* magazine commemorates the fiftieth anniversary of India's independence. Although its cover announces a "fiction issue," the magazine devotes more pages to contributions in nonfiction than fiction. Moreover, the nonfiction pieces are of higher quality – with one exception: the problematic framing essay, "Damme, This Is the Oriental Scene for You," by Salman Rushdie.

Salman Rushdie's essay "Damme, This Is the Oriental Scene For You" is flawed not only in its condescending title but also in its basic premise that the significant writing in India is only in English. The title is the sort of writing that prompted Professor Nair to famously characterize Rushdie's writing as "clever, but silly." Rushdie disdains India's many highly developed literary languages, dubbing them as merely "parochial." Nowhere in the essay does he mention that only 5 percent of the population of India is English-using bilinguals. This is the figure cited by Braj Kachru, author of *The Other Tongue: English across Cultures.* Other linguists have cited comparable figures and some as low as 2 percent. One of my colleagues, a Euro-American professor of English, was incredulous when I quoted the 5 percent figure because, after reading Rushdie's essay, she was under the impression that at least 50 percent of India's population is fluent in English.

A redeeming feature in Rushdie's essay is his finally acknowledging the influence of G. V. Desani on his writing. In 1982, Feroza Jussawalla, in her book *Family Quarrels,* had observed:

> Salman Rushdie's recent novel *Midnight's Children* has been widely acclaimed for its experimental style, often considered sui generis – in a class of its own and generating itself. That it is . . . another imitative work is overlooked. Uma Parameswaran notes that Rushdie sees himself more in the tradition of writers from the empire that struck back, rather than in the tradition of Anand, Narayan or Rao. Among the Indian writers is G. V. Desani, who is Rushdie's avowed master for he "showed how English could be bent and kneaded until it spoke in an authentically Indian voice."

Feroza Jussawalla's and Uma Parameswaran's early assessments of the extent of Desani's influence on Rushdie were right on the mark. In this essay, Rushdie now grudgingly concedes that he "learned a trick or two from him."

I wish Bill Buford, the editor, had sought the framing essay from a literary critic like Harish Trivedi or Meenakshi Mukherjee instead of Rushdie, whose flawed piece has tarnished this sterling magazine's special issue.

Deprivations

GERDA LERNER (1920–)

Born in Vienna in 1920, Gerda Lerner was eighteen when, a Jew endangered by Nazism, she fled her native Austria one week before the massive anti-Semitic violence of Kristallnacht. In 1939, she emigrated to the United States, the only member of her family granted a visa. Embracing her new American identity and the English language, she became a prominent scholar and champion of women's history, a professor at the University of Wisconsin, and a founder of the National Organization for Women. Her books include *Black Women in White America* (1972), *The Female Experience: An American Documentary* (1976), and *The Creation of Patriarchy* (1986). In the following excerpt from her 1997 collection of essays, *Why History Matters: Life and Thought,* Lerner recounts her rediscovery of the German language and a part of her own abandoned identity.

Living in Translation

DEDICATED TO MY SISTER NORA

When I came to the United States in 1939 as a refugee from Hitler fascism, I had, like all refugees, a very problematic relationship with the English language. On the one hand, I wanted desperately to learn English and to speak it well. This was my meal ticket, absolutely essential if I was to get work. On the other hand, I felt a responsibility to uphold, treasure and keep intact the integrity of the German language which fascism had stolen from me, as it had stolen all my worldly possessions. The Nazis spoke a language of their own – first a jargon of slogans and buzz words; later the language of force and tyranny. Words no longer meant what they said; they meant what the Nazis intended them to mean, and so, gradually, they became empty of meaning. Like banners flapping forever in the wind, they flapped around the skeleton of German speech until all that could be heard was the clattering words pretending to meaning they could not encompass. Seen in that light, it was the obligation of every antifascist German-speaking refugee to uphold the old language, so that some day it might be restored.

I had, in the last two years before my emigration, studied English with a private tutor. The results were pathetic. The book from which I studied must have been more than fifty years old. It operated on the assumption that the manners, habits and customs of English gentlemen constituted a universal norm. One learned some vocabulary and, most importantly, a dozen or so phrases which presumably equipped one to enter into polite British society.

"Will you come and have tea at my home?"

"I shall be delighted."

"May I introduce you to my good friend Roger Forsythe?"

To which the proper reply was: "Delighted to make your acquaintance, sir."

If one were seated in front of someone, it was essential to lean back toward the person behind one and say politely: "Please excuse my back." Or, as the occasion warranted, one might make use of the phrase "Please excuse my glove." Unclear was whether what one was apologizing for was having or not having a glove.

The phrase book, carefully memorized, would equip the German-speaker to navigate through the quaint old-fashioned British village, purchase a few choice items at the greengrocer's (the book was heavy on the use of the Saxon genitive), exchange a few polite phrases at the fishmonger's and return to one's hostelry where the crucial question: "Where's the Ladies?" was never to be asked. One was simply to observe where the Ladies was. With the important distinction between "will" and "shall" obsessively fixed in one's mind one was supposed to be able to announce: "I shall be taking the 8:20 train to London" and instruct the ubiquitous servants to "fetch my trunk from my room."

All of which was worse than useless in giving instructions to a New York City cabbie or in understanding his growling response to any question. Fishmongers and greengrocers refused to make an appearance, and servants, such as could be identified, had no intention of fetching anything without a tip which exceeded the immigrant's means and comprehension. One gestured one's way through the first weeks and learned that a firm "no" and "buzz off" were more valuable than any of the learned phrases.

"Please, I desire a job," was a declaration which was certain to land the applicant in a plastic chair in the employment agency, to wait all morning to be called while watching other applicants get their referral slips.

"Excuse please, lady, your newspaper announcement said there was job as 'lady's aide' and I wait all morning why never you call me?"

"There's nothing for you today. Come back tomorrow."

"Please I desire – "

"You got no references. You can't speak English. You got no experience. This ain't the welfare."

Learning English, the kind spoken in New York City with its multiple accents, innumerable slang words, abbreviations, elisions, swallowed syllables and exploding expletives, was a bare-bones necessity.

I listened to the radio for hours a day, especially to the advertisements, which usually had longer sentences than the rest of the show. One could go to the movies for twenty-five cents, and I spent many evenings studying language at the movies. I listened with intense attention to people's speech and I read my way through the Children's Books section of the public library, gradually advancing to Young Adolescents.

English was a simple language, compared with German, French and Latin. The verbs had simple endings, if any; one did not add adjectives and adjectival constructs to nouns in long chains ("The no longer quite youthful, but otherwise still good-looking, pipe smoking general etc."). The beginner learned to rely on the auxiliary verbs – to be, to have, to do. I kept book on the hundreds of meanings of the verb "to do" and learned at least fifty ways of using "to get." Since the finer shadings of syntax and vocabulary eluded me, I thought of the language as blunt and utilitarian, and devoid of subtlety.

Living in translation and lacking both an adequate vocabulary and sense of the rhythm of the language it was as though my adult knowledge had to be transposed into the vocabulary of a six-year-old. It does not take long to learn to get by in English; to master the language takes years.

I began to write poetry in English before I could properly speak or write. Since I wrote free verse in ordinary speech, patterning my style after Bertolt Brecht, and getting effects by sharply contrasting images and striking sound patterns, I could achieve some sort of effect with the most primitive means. Writing poetry was then my way of venturing out into a higher level of language connection, but

I deliberately stayed primitive, fearing to make a fool of myself if I tried to be poetic.

For nearly two years, I managed on that level of crude communication, while my thoughts and dreams went on unperturbed in German. I forced myself to read only in English. Whether I read newspapers, magazines or books, I always had a dictionary nearby. I would look up each word I did not know; for a while I kept a small notebook with words and definitions. I was quite aware of the fact I was living a split life, thinking in one language and speaking in another. I could not find adequate words for the thoughts I wanted to express. I said things, and people rephrased them, translating for themselves. More and more, as I began to move among English-speakers, I lived with an overwhelming sense of inadequacy and frustration.

What made matters worse was that I had aspired to become a linguist in German. I studied Old German and Middle High German in Gymnasium and had done a year's work on my honors thesis, which was a close textual analysis of a dozen German ballads. I was fascinated with languages and had hoped to go to the university to study comparative languages. For at least four years prior to my graduation I had been an acolyte of the writer Karl Kraus, whose every work I had read and reread and whom I considered my foremost teacher.

Karl Kraus was an essayist, satirist, playwright and, in the opinion of many literary critics, the finest poet writing in German in the twentieth century. His monumental drama "for a Martian theatre," *The Last Days of Mankind,* written after World War I, was perhaps the outstanding pacifist work created out of that terrible European cataclysm. As editor of the satirical journal *Die Fackel* (The torch), Kraus held up a mirror to his contemporaries, exposing their follies, cruelties and self-serving hypocrisy in savage, brilliant essays and aphorisms. He regarded himself as the last of the German "Classics" and as the upholder of a humanistic tradition of form, style and language in a world deaf to its own speech and forgetful of its history. Kraus was fanatic about the German language, which he mastered in all its complexities of dialects and intonations. He wrote long essays about two lines of poetry and devoted one celebrated issue of his journal to a two-hundred-page essay on the subject of "The Comma." To read Kraus, study his essays and attend his remarkable "Readings" – performances at which he not only read his own works but put on complete dramas such as *King Lear,* reading all the parts in the play – these were formative experiences for a young person interested in language. Kraus presented a constant challenge – being one of his disciples one learned to watch one's speech and one's writing. Meaning was to be found, as Kraus put it, "by tapping along the guiding rope of language." Young writers coming under Kraus's spell either gave up altogether or attempted to write in his voice, until at last they found their own.

Kraus, a Jew born in Czechoslovakia, then part of the Austro-Hungarian empire, was anti-Semitic, arrogant, elitist and in the last five years of his life, politically reactionary. Earlier, he was a savage critic of bourgeois life, of greed, corruption and exploitation. He had excoriated the military, complacent politicians and shoddy literati and espoused the causes of downtrodden workers, exploited peasants and victimized prostitutes. At the time I came under his influence, he had made his peace with the semifascist totalitarianism of Chancellor Dollfuss's government, which he defended out of disgust with the failings of weak liberalism and corrupt democracy. I was totally opposed to Dollfuss and his government and my politics were more radically left than Kraus's had ever been, yet I managed to disregard his turn to conservatism, even his betrayal of his own beliefs, because of his impact on my artistic and linguistic sensibilities. I attended each of his Readings and his many lectures, read his work and every work he recommended, honed my own writings on his demanding essays on language and worshipped at his feet. In 1936 I attended his funeral and cried bitterly, as though he had been a personal friend. In all my life, no single writer has ever influenced me as profoundly as did Karl Kraus.

One of his incredible accomplishments was to "translate" Shakespeare without knowing English. He had read the several current German Shakespeare translations, the chief one by Tieck, representing a German Romanticist rewrite of Shakespeare, and found them wanting. Having read all the French translations and putting these beside the German versions and then, word for word, comparing them with the English version, he had sensed what was missing: the Anglo-Saxon structure and bluntness of Shakespeare's speech and his poetry, which could not be rendered adequately in the words and rhythms of German Romantic poetry. Kraus undertook his own "translation" – one might better call it an intuitive adaptation in German and it was these versions he used in his Shakespeare readings. I think I have never read Shakespeare in better German than in these free adaptations. Kraus got Shakespeare right. Thinking about his accomplishment and the way he went about it gave me new insights into the art of translation. A translator might get the literal meaning, and yet miss the other layers of meanings, all the resonances conveyed to hearer and reader in the original. She might miss the richness of ambiguity, the force that stretches a word's meaning beyond its formal definition, the pulse and vibrations of tone that resonate over and above mere content. It seemed to me then and it does now, after I have worked for years on translations and lived for decades in translation, that the overtones and resonances are more significant than the literal meaning. If a choice has to be made, I would choose texture over mere information.

To come from the speech of Karl Kraus to the imbecile stammerings of an immigrant American was a fall, indeed, symbolic of all the rest of it—the loss of economic security, of status, of potential, of opportunity. All refugees experienced that fall, and many, perhaps most, never got over it. They lived their lives in the new land either as temporary exiles or constantly in denial. The world they had lost became more attractive, more worthy, the longer they were away from it. In New York City's Washington Heights they created a small Mittel-Europa of familiar shops, coffeehouses and organizations. Their cynical stance toward the United States gave them a sense of continuity; they were and would remain Europeans transplanted against their will into an alien environment.

When I made the decision, in my second year here, to become an American writer, I made the decision to abandon such attitudes, to become, in fact, a voluntary emigrant from Europe. I embraced America with gratitude and fascination, as I embraced its primary language. If that meant suppressing and denying some of my European habits in thought and attitude, so be it. I was young enough to start anew. There are many gains in such an enterprise, not the least of it, citizenship and familiarity in a formerly alien culture. But there is a cost to it, greater than I ever wanted to admit to myself. I am trying to reckon up that cost, at last, after fifty years and more.

*

In an irony of fate, the very first paid "job" I had in the United States was as a translator of a rather esoteric sort. I had nearly gone under in the first eight months as an immigrant, unable to find work, due mostly to the fact that employers of casual labor and domestic work found me "overqualified," and I was too afraid of getting in trouble with the Immigration Service to seek even private assistance. Then, an orthopedist I had met through one of my refugee friends required the services of someone able to translate from Latin to English. I volunteered and, for five dollars an hour, translated a medical treatise on the hip joint from Latin into English. I earned enough to support myself for two weeks and to regain some sense of self-respect. My fancy classical education, might, after all, equip me for self-support. In fact, it did not, not for another twenty years, when it was finally useful in allowing me to continue my academic education.

If you are forced to give up your mother tongue, what is lost? In a way, losing one's mother tongue is inconceivable—one assumes one can always return to it. But that is not so. Language is not a dead body of knowledge; language changes year by year, minute by minute; it lives and grows. In order to remain adequate it must be spoken and it must be read. When you lose your language, you lose the sound, the rhythm, the forms of your unconscious. Deep memories, resonances, sounds of childhood come through the mother tongue—when these are missing the brain cuts off connections. Language communicates much more than literal meaning. It gives us timbre, tone, a rich undercurrent of resonances and shadings, multiple and ambiguous crosscurrents. But in the early years of speaking the learned language one knows nothing of those complexities; the new language stays linear and flat. Inflection adds layers of meaning to what is spoken, but the immigrant has no ear for inflections. Translating meaning from another circle of culture, she constantly makes mistakes and is given to misperceptions.

German, like most European languages which developed through centuries of feudalism, has a rich variety of dialects and intonations, which mark not only region but also class. British English of the upper classes and the cockney speech of the lower classes retain that function, but English in America reflects region more than class. Still, there are class markers in speech, but they are immensely complicated by the effect of immigration—the millions of Americans who speak English as a second language have created a number of creolized varieties of speech. In all this the newcomer finds it hard to become oriented.

I was always aware of the awkwardness of my position as an immigrant. Normally, I'm quick to a fault—I catch the meaning of what a person says often before the speaker finishes, which leads me to interrupt the speaker with my answer. A very unattractive trait, one that over the years I have tried to unlearn, but it is indicative of the way my mind works. Living in translation I usually could not catch the exact meaning without doing the translation. Therefore, from being fast to a fault, I now appeared slow, if not slow-witted. Lacking the information usually transmitted by dialect or speech patterns and body signals, I had to guess at the whole meaning or rather I had to be satisfied with an approximate meaning. For a person like me, who is committed to precise definition and precise expression, this was a form of torture.

Living in translation is like skating on wobbly skates over thin ice.

There is no sure footing; there are no clear-cut markers, no obvious signposts. It helps to trust in one's balance, to swing free and make leaps of the imagination. I suppose what I am saying is that it is immensely strenuous. Quite apart from being alienating.

Two years after I came to the United States, the country was at war. Speaking German in public exposed the speaker to hostile looks and remarks. I'm a nonconformist by inclination, so public disapproval would not have been enough to discourage me from speaking German. The truth was, I no longer wanted to speak German; I was repelled by the sound of it; for me as for other Americans it had become the language of the enemy. These expressions of mindless patriotism are not sentiments of which, in the abstract, I can approve. In practice, however, they were just what I felt. I ceased speaking German altogether.

By then, I was married to an American-born man and all my friends were American-born. Still retaining enough of my European heritage to think that every child should learn one or more foreign languages, I wanted my children to be raised in such a way that they would easily learn foreign languages. Yet I did not speak German to them, because of the attitude I held at the time. I did sing them German lullabies, because they were the only lullabies I knew. Later, I taught them the rudiments of French.

It took several years before I began to think in English. It was exciting when it actually happened and it made a qualitative difference in the way I lived. I began to be able to express myself with the speed and precision characteristic of me and most of the time I could find the word I needed without resorting to a dictionary. There came a night when I dreamt in English and after that, I thought I had made it.

But it is one thing to speak and think and even dream in a second language; it is quite another to be able to write in it as a creative writer. My decision to become "an American writer" had been made long before my language proficiency entitled me to such a claim. Nevertheless, I wrote short stories and articles, although I felt quite inadequate to the task. I had great difficulty getting dialogue right; my characters all talked the same way, since I was incapable of creating individual speech patterns. Awareness of my shortcomings was of little help. I felt like a tone-deaf person trying to compose a symphony. Carrying a notebook with me everywhere, I jotted down the speech fragments I heard. I read books on the craft of writing and on "style." Nothing seemed to help. One of my favorite exercises was to compose a paragraph in the style of a famous writer. That was useful, but I still had no style of my own. That should not have surprised me—I already knew then that form is the shape of content. But it is not some ideal abstract "shape"—it is content as shaped by the creating artist, content filtered through the prism of the artist's entire life experience. And I was then a broken prism—a refugee without language, between cultures, belonging to neither the old nor the new.

I took another translation job which I found quite satisfying. I translated the jacket copy and the texts of a collection of German folksongs appearing on a two-disk LP. The folksongs were all well known to me; to give a poetic and not just a literal translation was a challenge, which in the end I felt I met. I contemplated a career as a translator, but I quickly gave it up. What I wanted to be was a writer.

At one point during this initial apprenticeship I decided to stay with my Austrian culture, to write only of what I knew. My first two short stories written in English were descriptions of my experience in Nazi Germany. In one of the stories, I did the interior monologues of five Nazi soldiers, caught in a tense battle situation on the Russian front. In both stories I avoided having to do English dialogue. Both were published immediately: the first one in a small, cultural journal, the second one in the best fiction magazine then in existence, *Story* magazine. This quick and unexpected "success" spurred my literary ambition but did nothing to improve my language skills. Daringly, I wrote three short stories with American locale and characters—none of which aroused the slightest interest in publishers. Once again, I returned to my earlier decision to write about what I knew best and I began to work on a semi-autobiographical novel. It described the four years 1934–1938 in which Austria made the transition from a democracy to an authoritarian clerical government and finally to Nazi fascism, as experienced by a teenage girl.

In a sense, this novel was my apprentice work as a writer of English. It took nearly twelve years to complete it, because I did seven rewrites. Over and over again, I transformed the text from a translation to an original work in English. Even so, the final version still has traces of German syntax and style. Writing is learned by doing; there is no escaping that. My Sisyphian labor at last produced a book with which I was satisfied, but by then the topic of antifascism, which had been of such paramount interest in the early 1940s, had become a drug on the market. I have readers' reports from the various publishing houses that could break your heart. My work was compared to that of Thomas Mann and Thomas Wolfe and the readers expressed high hopes for my literary career, but they did not want to publish this book. In yet another ironic development of my career my novel *No Farewell,* in which I had invested all my best effort to mastering the English language, was first printed in Austria in a German translation in 1954. It was very successful there and this success inspired me to take part in a cooperative publishing venture in the late 1950s, which finally resulted in American publication of the book.

*

Recently, in trying to think about some of the long-range effects of my refugee status I became aware of something as a problem which I thought was not really a problem for me. I have a German name which is unpronounceable by English speakers and thus is inevitably mispronounced. I accepted that mispronunciation as the proper form of address for me, came to use it myself and have done so for fifty years. I became aware of the disjunction only when I spent some time in German-speaking countries and heard my name pronounced correctly. Each time that happened, it gave me pleasure. That made me realize that it pained me that my own children, my husband, my best friends could never really pronounce my name. I had buried that pain and refused to acknowledge it. It was, so I thought, a trivial matter. I no longer think so, and an examination of my relationship with my only sister confirmed my new insight.

My sister Nora and I were separated through emigration when she was twelve years old and I was eighteen. While I emigrated to the United States, she spent the war years in a school in Switzerland and then settled in England. She eventually became a British subject, but never really felt at home in England. Early in the 1960s she emigrated to Israel, where she still lives.

We were separated by continents, by warfare and finally by poverty. In 1948, when I for the first time after my emigration returned to Europe, we met briefly in England. By then she was twenty-three years old, independent, self-supporting. I was twenty-eight, married and had a baby and a toddler in tow. Our meeting was difficult, first because of the presence of two overtired and cranky children. We also had trouble communicating with each other—she spoke English with a pronounced British accent; I spoke American English; both of us no longer spoke German. I remember coming away from that meeting with a sense that she had become a stranger to me, in more ways than one, and that she had become "stuck up," different. What I probably reacted to was not a change in her attitude, but the persona she presented to me, that of a young proper English lady. From later conversations I know she had similar feelings toward me.

We met again in 1957, when she came to visit us in New York. We both wanted very much to have "a good visit," to recapture our old intimacy. By then both of our parents were dead, we were the only close family for one another and we sincerely wanted to find a common ground for friendship. We loved each other and showed it in many ways, but our daily interaction was stiff, formal and full of mutual irritation. We simply seemed to get on each other's nerves—and ostensibly there was no good reason for it. From my point of view, I found her mannerisms, her mode of behavior, difficult and in some profound way incomprehensible. The fact that my beloved little sister had turned into a cultural stranger never ceased to outrage me, but I could not learn how to deal with it.

It was on her second visit to New York, eight years later, that an incident occurred which suddenly illuminated our difficulties. We were in my apartment, washing the dishes after dinner. My husband and the children were not with us at the time, and so perhaps we had a moment of quiet. One of us, I don't know which one, began to hum an Austrian folksong, and then to sing it, in German. The other chimed in, and we found ourselves singing in two voices, the way we had often sung in our childhood. One song followed another—from somewhere long forgotten by both of us, the childhood songs welled up and broke to the surface. We were not doing it consciously; we were not even aware of what was happening, but when we finished we were smiling and hugged each other with the spontaneity that had been missing all those years. I felt as though suddenly all the barriers between us had broken down; we were children together, as we had always been, and what separated us—the shifts in cultures, the different lifestyles, the separate hard struggles for survival and reconstitution—all of that fell off our shoulders as the common language at last united us.

Nevertheless, during our infrequent visits—about once every two or three years—and in our correspondence we mostly stayed with English. I think this was largely due to my often expressed insistence that I no longer thought in German and therefore could not express anything significant in that language. I lacked the facility, I said. I would often start a letter to Nora in German and give it up after a few lines, switching to English. Nora spoke German continuously with her close friends in Israel, even as she tried to make the language switch to Hebrew, which she found very difficult. So English seemed a mutually satisfactory compromise. I marvel at the fact that even after the incident with the songs, we did not seem to understand the significance of the language barrier between us. It took another incident to make it crystal clear.

This occurred in 1973, in Sicily. My husband had died a few

months earlier, and I wanted and needed to be with my sister. We had a wonderful week together in Sicily, and most of the time that week we spoke in German. We celebrated our feeling of closeness by a fine dinner in a fancy restaurant. My sister has never learned to be a social drinker, and at the most will take a glass of wine. That night I insisted on her drinking along with me and between us we emptied a bottle of fine wine. I was pleasantly warm and lively, but she was definitely tipsy. Two middle-aged women in a foreign city, we left the restaurant noisily chattering and decided to rest by sitting down at the curb of the street. We were giggling and laughing and suddenly my sister started telling jokes—ancient jokes which we used to tell each other as children. They concerned a male figure famous as the butt of Viennese humor, a certain mythical Count Bobby. Count Bobby was stupid, arrogant, self-satisfied and endlessly duped by others. He spoke Viennese dialect in the nasal twang characteristic of the nobility and that was the way my sister told the joke. I immediately topped it with another Count Bobby joke, also in dialect and we both fell into a fit of uncontrolled laughter. The jokes were not that funny and we were not that drunk, but, once again, language unlocked the gates and memory took over. In the Vienna of our childhood, we had learned at least three different ways of speaking German—High German, which was school German, the language one spoke to strangers and to parents; the kitchen dialect one spoke to cooks, servants and lower-class people; and Count Bobby's Viennese dialect, which was both accurate and a mockery of the real dialect spoken by upper-class people trying to be "just folks." It is just these kinds of distinctions which are lost in translation. Nora and I finally made it home and into our separate rooms, joking in dialect and getting more infantile with each step, but when we said goodnight to each other there was a deep transformation of feeling between us. Nothing needed to be said; we both knew we had found each other, after all those years. What had done it was the mother tongue, the language going even deeper than formal speech, the actual spoken dialect of childhood.

In the years since then our relationship has improved and deepened. Now we speak German almost all the time; in fact, for nearly a decade, my correspondence with Nora and our biennial meetings were the only times in which I did speak German. It would be nice to be able to report that all estrangement and all difficulties between us have ceased with the change in language, but life is never that simple. Our relationship has remained complex, but deeply meaningful to each of us. We have learned the cost to our intimacy created by cultural separation and by language differences. Our lives have been deeply marked by our fate as refugees and by the happenstance of landing on different shores, on different continents. Each of us paid a heavy price for assimilation into a foreign culture and part of that price was that we, loving sisters, were for decades strangers to each other.

*

Gradually, assimilation was completed; the past drifted out of sight. There came a time when I felt secure in my command of English, in speech and writing. I did the acrostics in the *New York Times* successfully and usually won at games of anagrams with native English speakers. I proudly developed tricky skills, like being able to read a poem or passage in German, while reading it aloud in English. With a little more effort I might have become a simultaneous translator at the United Nations. But my denial of German had by then gone too far. I never read any German books or newspapers and I lost touch with decades of development in the German-speaking realms. As for my reading in English, I had broadened out to a good knowledge of basic English fiction, poetry since Shakespeare, and modern American literature. I had by then been an "American writer" for fifteen years, but after that short spurt of early success with the short stories, I had published nothing. Two finished novels and eight or more short stories lay dead in my files, and for the first time in my life I seriously considered giving up writing. Acting in a numb sort of desperation, I decided to take some college level courses and see what would happen.

Looking back on it, there is more than accident in the choice of the first course I was taking at the New School for Social Research. That institution, turned into a university-in-exile by refugee scholars in the late 1930s, is well known for the broad range of scholarship in its faculty. I selected a course in English grammar, taught by a Yugoslavian emigrant with an unpronounceable name. My husband thought I had temporarily lost my mind. As far as he could see I knew more about English grammar than anybody else he knew and why I wanted to take a course in it was beyond his understanding. He kept suggesting other nice courses I could take, but I was unresponsive. "I need to be absolutely certain I know the grammar," I explained lamely. "There are still a few things I'm unsure about and I'm tired of it."

There were seven students in the course, only two of them native-born Americans. The others were one Hispanic and three Chinese. The Americans were the poorest students, while one of the Chinese and I excelled. I enjoyed the course and it gave me a sense of competence and self-confidence which I had lost in my unsuccessful efforts as a writer. In some incomprehensible way it marked the close of one period of my life. The next course I took was in seventeenth-century British poetry, and after that I decided to resume my academic training and work toward a B.A. This led, by almost imperceptible small steps, to the decision to become a historian and therefore to graduate study. It took me four years of part-time study to earn the B.A. and three years of full-time study to earn the Ph.D. As I now see it, my mastery of the English language had to be followed by mastery of American history before I could truly cease being an immigrant. As a shining reward for all this strenuous effort my writing career began to flourish as soon as I was an academic. It was then by way of American History that I became a successful "American writer."

The story should close with this happy ending, but it does not.

In 1984 I was invited to participate in an international congress of women historians held in Vienna, my hometown. I accepted with many mental reservations and much anxiety. One aspect of it concerned language. I had been asked to offer two papers, but I felt so incompetent in German that I hired a student in the German department of my university to translate my speeches into German. These translations I read from the podium, feeling somewhat like an impostor. My conversational German seemed equally inadequate, since I lacked most of the vocabulary of my recently developed field, Women's History.

In 1986 my book *The Creation of Patriarchy* was published in Germany in translation. My contract with the publishers specified that I had the right to make editorial suggestions in regard to the translation. My editor and the translator were most generous in interpreting this right, and so it came about that I carefully edited the German version, first in manuscript and then again in galleys. The process was very difficult for me and renewed all my insecurities about my knowledge of German. I felt totally incompetent in the academic languages of the various fields on which the book is based – paleontology, anthropology, Ancient Near Eastern studies. Similarly, most of the words for concepts in feminist discourse of the past twenty years were unknown to me. So I sat, once more, surrounded by dictionaries, learning my own mother tongue all over again.

Yet there was something else happening. My "feel" for the language was quite intact and manifested itself in an uncanny sense of style. I always knew when something was wrong in a sentence, but, often, I did not know enough German to fix it. I worked closely with my patient and skillful translator, and I learned a lot in the process.

The publisher invited me for a two-week-long promotion tour in Germany after the book came out. This time, emboldened by the translation work, I decided to attempt to speak about my book in German. I did so with trepidation, and prepared for it as though I were lecturing in a foreign language. Every speech was written out in advance and I mentally prepared answers to the questions I expected would be asked. I always prefaced each public appearance with a statement, which served both as an explanation of my refugee status and as a hedge against linguistic failure. "You may wonder at my peculiar accent, and often at my choice of words. Although I am a native German speaker, I have not really spoken

German in fifty years, and I have never before lectured in German." The audience response was good, even though there were moments when I had to use an English word and ask the audience to help me with the translation. After one lecture a woman came up to me and complimented me on my German. I thought she was merely being polite and demurred, but she insisted. "Of course you speak a competent German, but what I admire is that you speak the purest German I have ever heard." "Pure?" "Yes," she said, "uncorrupted by Nazi language and by all the abominations of modern usage." Rip Van Winkle, being complimented on his "pure" speech. How odd. . . .

After that lecture tour my interest in German was revived. For the book on which I was then working, *The Creation of Feminist Consciousness,* I made use of many German sources, a few of them in medieval German. As I worked over these sources my old proficiency returned. After all, what I lacked was only the vocabulary of the past fifty years. By the time my work on the translation of the second book started, I felt quite adequate to the task. Now I had many more suggestions for my translator and most of them concerned style. The content was right, but the style was not mine, but hers. We worked on that and corrected it. When my work on the translation of the second book was finished I felt I was truly bilingual.

My new confidence found expression during my second book tour in Germany. While I again carefully prepared my lectures in writing, I soon felt free enough to answer all questions without preparation. In a three-week intense teaching situation in a German university, I taught with only an outline of notes in German, and finally, looking at some of my American teaching notes in English, I lectured in German from them.

*

The Nazis robbed me of my mother tongue, but the rest of the separation, of the violent severing of culture, was my own choice. My writing, my intense drive to become an "American writer" had pushed me into leaving the language of my childhood behind, never counting the cost. Through my writing, I had found the way back, but now the cost seems enormous. The return of the mother tongue has brought some healing of the other losses, but memory is different now. Before, what was lost sank into a deep hole of oblivion – one covered it up and built anew forgetting the cost. Now memory includes what was lost and what it cost and what might have been had I been able to be a writer in my own language. Healing the split between feeling and thought, between the conscious learned faculties and the rich vibrations of the unconscious, I might have "tapped my way along the guiding rope of language" and found a richer, more poetic form for what I had to say. In translation, one becomes a trickster, too clever by far and too concerned with mastery. I envy those who live in the power of their own language, who were not deprived of the immediacy by which creativity finds its form.

There are works that cannot be translated. There are wounds that can never heal.

ARTHUR KOESTLER (1905–1983)

Born in Budapest in 1905, Arthur Koestler switched languages twice, from Hungarian to German and then from German to English. After studying at the University of Vienna, he worked in Palestine, France, and Germany as a journalist for German-language newspapers. While covering the Spanish Civil War, Koestler was captured by Franco's forces and sentenced to death. After extricating himself from Spain, he was arrested and interned by Vichy officials in France. Koestler settled in England and became a British subject during the 1940s.

Koestler was a member of the German Communist Party, but his best-known work, the political novel translated as *Darkness at Noon* (1940), was inspired by his repudiation of Stalinism during the Moscow purges. Other novels include *The Gladiators* (1939) and *Arrival and Departure* (1943), which was the first book of fiction he composed in English. After abandoning fiction, Koestler wrote on scientific subjects, in books including *The Act of Creation* (1964) and *The Ghost in the Machine* (1967). His memoirs are composed of *Arrow in the Blue* (1952) and *The Invisible Writing* (1954). An advocate of euthanasia, he ended his own life, in a double suicide with his wife, in 1983. This passage from Koestler's autobiographical collection, *From Bricks to Babel* (1980), illustrates how translingual authors cannot take their chosen medium for granted.

From "Becoming Anglicised"

The reasons why all the places where I have lived long before England have now become "abroad" – which is the ultimate test of belonging to a country – are difficult for me to analyze. There is, for instance, language. Since 1940 I have been writing in English, thinking in English, and reading mostly English literature. Language serves not only to express thought, but to mold it; the adoption of a new language, particularly by a writer, means a gradual and unconscious transformation of his patterns of thinking, his style and his tastes, his attitudes and reactions. In short, he acquires not only a new medium of communication but a new cultural background. For several years, while I thought in English, I continued to talk French, German and Hungarian in my sleep. Now this occurs only rarely.

The process of changing languages is a fascinating one, and as I have gone through it twice (first from Hungarian to German, then from German to English) I hope to give one day a detailed account of the psychological problems that it involves. One curious aspect of it, from the writer's point of view, is what one may call "the rediscovery of the cliché." Every cliché, even the broken heart and the eternal ocean, was once an original find; and when you begin writing and thinking in a *new* language, you are apt to invent all by yourself images and metaphors which you think are highly original without realizing that they are hoary clichés. It is rather like the sad story of the man in a remote village in Russia, who just after the First World War invented a machine with two wheels and a saddle on which a person could ride quicker than he could walk; and who, when he rode to town on his machine and saw that the streets were full of bicycles, fell down and died of shock. Something similar happened to me when I finished the first novel that I wrote in English (*Arrival and Departure*), with a sentence whose poetic ring made me rather proud:

> . . . at night, under the incurious stars.

It is still there, on the last page of the book, a verbal bicycle.

GUSTAVO PÉREZ FIRMAT (1949–)

Born in Havana in 1949, Gustavo Pérez Firmat left his native Cuba shortly after Fidel Castro came to power in 1959. He received a B.A. and an M.A. from the University of Miami and a Ph.D. from the University of Michigan. Currently a professor of Spanish at Columbia University, he has also taught at Duke University. As both a poet and a critic, Pérez Firmat has made translingualism a central theme. He published his memoir, *Next Year in Cuba: A Cubano's Coming-of-Age in America* (1995), in English and recreated it in Spanish in 1997 as *El año que viene en Cuba.* Other nonfiction by Pérez Firmat includes *The Cuban Condition: Translation and Identity in Modern Cuban Literature* (1989), *Do the Americas Have a Common Literature?* (1990), *Life on the Hyphen: The Cuban-American Way* (1994), and *My Own Private Cuba* (1999). "Dedication," which characterizes the poet's translingualism as an impossible necessity, comes from his 1995 collection, *Bilingual Blues (Poems 1981–1994).*

Dedication

The fact that I
am writing to you
in English
already falsifies what I
wanted to tell you.
My subject:
how to explain to you that I
don't belong to English
though I belong nowhere else.

Resistance

ELIAS CANETTI (1905–1994)

Born in Ruschuk, Bulgaria, in 1905, Elias Canetti grew up in a multilingual family of Sephardic Jews whose neighbors included Bulgarians, Turks, Greeks, Albanians, Armenians, Gypsies, Romanians, and Russians. Canetti's earliest languages were Ladino and Bulgarian. "To each other," he wrote in the first volume of his memoirs, "my parents spoke German, which I was not allowed to understand." Canetti's command of German eventually became adept enough to earn him the Nobel Prize in Literature, in 1981. Though he lived in England for more than fifty years, he did not employ English as his literary medium.

Canetti was educated in Zurich, Frankfurt, and Vienna but settled in England shortly before the start of World War II. His writings include the 1935 novel *Die Blendung* (*Auto-da-Fé*); a nonfiction study in the psychopathology of mobs, *Masse und Macht* (Crowds and power, 1960); and plays such as *Hochzeit* (The wedding, 1932), *Komödie der Eitelkeit* (Comedy of vanity, 1950), and *Die Befristeten* (Life-terms, 1964).

In the following passage, taken from *Das Augenspiel* (The play of the eyes, 1985), the third installment – after *Die gerettete Zunge: Geschichte einer Jugend* (The tongue set free, 1977), and *Die Fackel im Ohr* (The torch in my ear, 1980) – of his three-volume autobiography, Canetti links the death of his father to his own adoption of German. German had been the special language of intimacy between his mother and father, and when Canetti's father learned that his wife had spoken German with a flirtatious doctor, it convinced him of her infidelity and led to his sudden heart attack when he was only thirty and his son was only seven. Here Canetti recounts, in German, how, twenty-three years after the fact, he finally learned that linguistic treason was what did in his beloved father.

From *The Play of the Eyes*

In her high-handed way she [my mother] had shown me recognition. The book, she said, was just as if she had written it, it could have been by her, I had made no mistake in wanting to write, I had done right to put everything else aside. What could chemistry mean to a writer? Bother chemistry; I had fought resolutely against it, shown my strength even in opposition to her. With this book I had justified my ambition. This was the kind of thing she wrote me, but then when I saw her in Paris and tried to defend myself against this new submissiveness, which I had never met with in her and found hard to bear, more and more followed.

Suddenly she started talking about my father and about his death, which had changed our whole existence. For the first time I learned what ever since then – more than twenty-three years had elapsed – she had concealed under frequently changing versions.

While taking the cure in Reichenhall, she had met a doctor who spoke *her* language, whose every word had its hard contours. She felt challenged to give answers and found within herself daring, unexpected drives. He introduced her to Strindberg, whose devoted reader she had been ever since, for he thought as ill of women as she did. To this doctor she confided that her ideal, her "saint," was Coriolanus, and he had not found this odd, but admired her for it. He didn't ask how she as a woman could choose such a model, but, moved by her pride and beauty, avowed his tender feelings for her. She adored listening to him, but she did not give in to his pleas. She allowed him to say what he wished, but she said nothing relating to him. He had no place in her conversation, she talked about the books he gave her to read and about the people whom he as a physician knew. She marveled at the things he said to her but made no concessions. He persisted in urging her to leave my father and to marry him. He was entranced by her German, she spoke German, he said, like no one else, the English language would never mean as much to her. Twice she asked my father to let her prolong her cure, which was doing her good, and he consented. She blossomed in Reichenhall, but she knew quite well what was doing her so much good: the doctor's words. When she asked for a third extension, my father refused and insisted on her coming straight home.

She came. Not for a moment had she thought of giving in to the doctor. And not for a moment did she hesitate to tell my father everything. She was with him again, her triumph was his. She brought herself and what had happened to her and laid it – those were her very words – at my father's feet. She repeated the doctor's words of admiration and couldn't understand my father's mounting agitation. He wanted to know more and more, he wanted to know everything; when there was nothing more to know, he kept on asking. He wanted a confession and she had none to make. He didn't believe her. How could the doctor have proposed marriage to a married woman with three children if nothing had happened? She saw nothing surprising because she knew how it had all developed from their conversations.

She regretted nothing, she retracted nothing, she told him over and over again how much good the doctor had done her; her health was restored, that's what she had gone there for, and she was glad to be home again. But my father asked her strange questions:

"Did he examine you?"
"But he was my doctor!"
"Did he talk German to you?"
"Of course. What would you have him speak?"

He asked if the doctor knew French. She said she thought so, they had talked about French books. Why hadn't they spoken

French together? This question of my father's she had never understood. What could have given him the idea that a doctor in Reichenhall should speak any other language than German to her, whose language was German?

I was amazed at her failure to realize what she had done. Her infidelity had consisted in speaking German, the intimate language between her and my father, with a man who was courting her. All the important events of their love life, their engagement, their marriage, their liberation from my grandfather's tyranny, had taken place in German. Possibly she had lost sight of this because in Manchester her husband had taken so much trouble to learn English. But he was well aware that she had reverted passionately to German, and he had no doubt of what this must have led to. He refused to speak to her until she confessed; for a whole night he kept silent and again in the morning he maintained his silence, convinced that she had been unfaithful to him.

I hadn't the heart to tell her that she was guilty in spite of her innocence, because she had listened to words she should never have allowed, spoken in this language. She had carried on these conversations for weeks and, as she owned to me, she had even concealed one detail – Coriolanus – from my father.

He wouldn't have understood, she said. They had been so young when they talked about the Burgtheater together. When they were adolescents living in Vienna, they hadn't known each other, but they had often attended the same performances. They had discussed them later on, and then it had seemed to them that they had been there together. His idol was Sonnenthal, hers was Wolter. He was more interested in actors than she was; he imitated them, she preferred to talk about them. He hadn't much to say about the plays, she read them all over again at home; he liked to declaim. He would have been a better actor than she. She *thought* too much, she preferred to be serious. She cared less for comedies than he did. It was through the plays they had both seen that they got to know each other well. He had never seen *Coriolanus*, he wouldn't have liked it. He had no use for proud, heartless people. He had a hard time with her family because of their pride; her family had opposed the marriage. He would have been hurt to learn that of all Shakespeare's characters Coriolanus was her favorite. Only when she suddenly started talking about Coriolanus in Reichenhall had it dawned on her that she had always avoided mentioning him in conversations with my father.

Had she been dissatisfied in some way? Did my father hurt her feelings in some way? I didn't ask many questions, she needed no prodding, nothing could have diverted the flood that had been storing up inside her for so long. But this question tormented me and it was good that I asked it. No, he had never hurt her feelings, never once. She had been bitter about Manchester because it wasn't Vienna. She hadn't said a word when my father brought me English books to read and discussed them with me in English. That was why she had withdrawn from me at that time. My father had been enthusiastic about England. He had been right. There were distinguished, cultivated English people. If she had only known more of them. But she lived among the members of her family with their ridiculous lack of education. There was no one she could have a real conversation with. That's what had made her ill, not the climate. That is why Reichenhall, especially her conversations with the doctor, had helped her so much. But it was a *cure.* It had served its purpose. She would have liked to go there once a year. My father's jealousy had ruined everything. Had she been wrong to tell him the truth?

She meant the question seriously and wanted an answer from me. She put as much urgency into it as if all this had just happened. She retracted nothing about her meeting with the doctor. She didn't ask whether she should have refused to listen to him. She thought it enough that she had been deaf to his entreaties. I gave her the answer she didn't want. "You shouldn't," I said, "have shown how much it meant to you." I said it hesitantly, but it sounded like blame. "You shouldn't have bragged about it. You should have said it casually."

"But I *was* glad," she said vehemently. "I'm still glad. Do you think I'd have come to Strindberg otherwise? I'd be a different woman, you wouldn't have written your book. You'd never have gone beyond your wretched poems. You'd never have amounted to anything. Strindberg is your father. You're my son by Strindberg. I've made you into his son. If I had disowned Reichenhall, you'd never have amounted to anything. You write German because I took you away from England. You've become Vienna even more than I have. It's in Vienna that you found your Karl Kraus, whom I couldn't bear. You've married a Viennese woman. And now you're even living in the midst of Viennese vineyards. You seem to like it. As soon as I'm feeling better, I'll come and see you. Tell Veza she needn't be afraid of me. You'll leave her just as you left me. The stories you made up for me will come true. You *have* to make up stories, you're a writer. That's why I believed you. Whom is one to believe if not writers? Businessmen? Politicians? I only believe writers. But they have to be distrustful like Strindberg, they have to see through women. One can't think ill enough of people. And yet I wouldn't give up a single hour of my life. Let them be bad! It's wonderful to be alive. It's wonderful to see through all their villainy and yet to go on living."

From such speeches I learned what had happened to my father. He felt she had deserted him, while she thought she had done no wrong. A confession of the usual sort might not have hit him so hard. She was not fully aware of her own state of mind; else she wouldn't have bludgeoned him with her happiness. She wasn't shameless, she wouldn't have spoken so freely if she had seen any impropriety in her behavior. How could he have accepted what had happened? To him the German words they used with each other were sacred. She had profaned these words, this language. As he saw it, everything they had seen on the stage had turned into love. They had talked to each other about it innumerable times; these words had helped them to bear the narrowness of their daily lives. As a child I was consumed with envy over these foreign words, they made me feel superfluous. The moment they began talking German, no one else existed for them. My feeling of exclusion threw me into a panic; in the next room, I would desperately practice saying the German words I did not understand.

Her confession left me embittered, because she had deceived me. Over the years I had heard version after version; each time she seemed to give a different explanation for my father's death. What she represented as consideration for my tender years was in reality a changing insight into the extent of her guilt. In the nights after my father's death, when I had to restrain her from killing herself, her sense of guilt was so strong that she wanted to die. She took us to Vienna to be nearer the place from which her first conversations with my father had drawn their nourishment. On the way to Vienna she stopped in Lausanne and hit me over the head with the language which up until then I had not been allowed to understand. On the evenings when she read to me in Vienna, the evenings that gave me my being, she recapitulated those early conversations with him, but added *Coriolanus,* the mark of her guilt. In our apartment on Scheuchzerstrasse in Zurich she drowned herself every evening in the yellow Strindberg volumes I presented her with one after another. Then I would hear her singing softly at the piano, talking with my father and weeping. Did she pronounce the name of the author whom she read so avidly and whom he had not known? Now she saw me as the child of her infidelity and threw it up to me. What was my father now?

In such moments she *tore* everything, she was as reckless as she would have been if she had been leading her true life. She had a right to see herself in my book, to say that she herself would have written like that, that she *was* my book. That was why she recovered her magnanimity, why she accepted Veza and forgot that I had deceived her for so long about Veza. But she combined her magnanimity with a dire prophecy: just as I had deserted her, so I would desert Veza. She couldn't live without thoughts of revenge. She said she would come to see us, imagining that she would then see her prophecy come true. She was quick and impetuous and took it for certain that with the publication of my book, which obsessed her, a time of triumph was sure to set in. She saw me surrounded by women, who would worship me for the "misogyny" of *Auto-da-Fé* and long to let me chastise them for being women. She saw a fast-moving procession of bewitching beauties at my home in Grinzing, and in the end she saw Veza banished and forgotten in a tiny apartment just like her own in Paris. The inventions by which I had taken her mind off Veza had come true; the chronology didn't matter. I had merely predicted something, I hadn't deceived her and she hadn't let herself be deceived; no one could hide his wickedness from her, she had the gift of seeing through people, and she had passed it on to me. I *was* her son.

ASSIA DJEBAR (1936–)

One of the most prominent and prolific of contemporary Algerian authors, Assia Djebar focuses on the situation of women in a post-colonial society, one that, after a long and violent struggle, achieved independence from France in 1962 but remains beset by tensions between secular and Islamic cultures. Though Djebar, who was born Fatima Zohra Imalayen into a Bedouin family in Cherchell, Algeria, writes in French and has lived for extended periods outside her troubled native country, her books are layered with traces of Arabic and Berber. Her most notable novels include *La Soif* (The mischief, 1957); *Les Enfants du nouveau monde* (The children of the new world, 1962); *Femmes d'Alger dans leur appartement* (Women in Algiers in their apartments, 1980); *L'Amour, la fantasia* (Fantasia: An Algerian cavalcade, 1985); and *Ombre sultane* (A sister to Scheherazade, 1987). Djebar's work as a poet includes *Poèmes pour l'Algérie heureuse* (Poems for a happy Algeria, 1969). She has also been active as a filmmaker and stage director. She is currently professor of French and Francophone Literature at New York University. In the following excerpt from the chapter "Ecrire dans la langue de l'autre" (Writing in the language of the other), in *Ces voix qui m'assiègent . . . en marge de ma francophonie* (These voices that besiege me . . . from the periphery of my Francophonia, 1999), Djebar examines her linguistic situation.

From "Writing in the Language of the Other"

1. *A novelist of the French language* – It is thus that I could introduce myself today, hands held out in presentation, and what is it that I have to offer after having entered literature more than thirty years ago now, if not six novels, a collection of short stories, a play, and a short collection of poetry, a copy of each of these works in one hand (let's make it the right hand since, while writing, I am not a "left-handed woman") and in the left hand two rolls of 16 millimeter color film (1,500 meters and 800 meters), the two feature films that I have written and directed. . . .

Such is the small harvest of this mature woman, distinguishing me from any other woman of the same age who could introduce herself with, for example, four grown-up children and two or three younger ones, even perhaps with one or two grandchildren standing at the front of the group; there would be her human progeny. . . .

But today, my words are present – and my words are in the French language. I am a woman, and "a French speaker." My speech might certainly have been deployed in another register – in Arabic, or eventually in another language. The bottom line is that my writing, in its original form, could be only French.

Thus my words, which might be double, and perhaps even triple, participate in several cultures, while my writing is exclusively French.

One used to say: "I am a man (or woman) of my word." One also maintained: "I say only one thing," and the meaning was taken as an affirmation of honor. Well, I choose to present myself summarily to you through this affirmation: "I am a woman of writing." And I add in a tone blending gravity and love:

I have only one writing: that of the French language, with which I trace each page of each book, whether fiction or reflection.

2. I am an Algerian woman, though instead of my native land I ought to make reference at least to the language of the men and women who were my ancestors: "I am an Arab-Berber woman," and, in addition, "of French writing."

Since my first novel was published, thirty years have gone by, altering nothing in my identity, if it consists of paper, passport, blood, and soil.

However, thirty years later, I declare: I present myself above all as a writer, as a novelist, as if the act of writing, when it is daily, solitary to the point of ascetic, has come to modify the balance of belonging. Because identity is not only a matter of paper or of blood but also *of language.* And if it seems that language is, as is so often said, "a medium of communication," it is above all for me, a writer, "a medium of transformation," to the extent that I engage in writing as *adventure.*

In May 1982, in Ottawa, during my first trip to Canada, I was set to give a talk at a conference on French literature. As I recall, I had begun thinking about it early in the morning, until just before the time scheduled for my presentation.

I had, under pressure of my public talk, suddenly realized this truth:

I had until then utilized the French language as a veil. *A veil over my individual person, a veil over my woman's body; I might almost say a veil over my own voice.*

And I had evoked (the energy of anamnesis releasing itself that morning in Ottawa) my experience as a little girl going out into the street with a lady (my mother), a city woman enveloped in her white silk veil, a small gauze covering embroidered across her face, and I a little girl with her hand clinging to the rough surface of the immaculate silk, becoming aware of the prying eyes that the villagers cast on that veiled city woman who came every Thursday to the public bath. . . .

A veil that was neither a disguise nor a mask but that offered suggestion and ambiguity, a veil that certainly blocked out desire, but also a veil that subsumed the desire of men. . . .

So for me, in the first stage of my trajectory as a writer, I wanted to keep writing far from me, as if in its spirals, its upstrokes, and its downstrokes, I was hiding myself in it, aware of the extraliterary curiosity that my writings might arouse in advance – in all, a little like my urban mother's silhouette parading through the center of the village, in front of the country folk. . . .

I had then attempted to explain, for those who had read my most recent books (notably *Femmes d'Alger dans leur appartement*), what price I had paid for that ambiguity: for about ten years of nonpublication, experienced like a kind of voluntary mutism, I might almost say like a sudden aphasia. . . . As if, symbolically tangled up in this silk veil, I were attempting to step outside the French language without, however, abandoning it! To tour it from the outside and then to choose to reenter.

To penetrate it again as a guest, if not as a resident with hereditary rights.

French is thus becoming for me a veritable guest house, perhaps even a permanent place from which to observe each day the impermanence of occupation. Yet in the end, I performed the prophetic action of crossing the threshold myself, I, freely, no longer submitting to colonial conditions.

So much so that this language has come to seem to me a house that I inhabit and that I try to mark each day – while knowing that I have no right at all to the ground on which it stands. But if I make no claim according to *jus soli,* at least, risking a facile play on words, I can look for my right not in the soil but in the sun! . . .

For, while my characters, in *Femmes d'Alger* as much as in the novel published most recently (*Ombre sultane*), struggle against the traditional veil, try to remove it and yet bother with it, I as author have found my space in this writing.

Woman's space that inscribes at will both its inside and its outside, its intimacy and its unveiling, its anchorage as well as its navigation. . . . Writing that could signify historically my extraterritoriality, and that little by little, however, becomes my own only true territory.

3. *"Language of the other,"* I have declared. After 1982, while spending two years writing *L'Amour, la fantasia,* the first installment in a novelistic tetralogy that aims to be a "search for identity" and that is admittedly semi-autobiographical, I asked myself: This language of the other, what does it represent for me? How did it enter so deeply into me? Is it at the point that I become "the other" in my society, is it at the point that I take on the part of "the other," the strangeness inevitably included in a group of origin? . . . Yes, what is for me that language of the other, I who, precisely at the age of twenty, enter into literature as if blindfolded yet feeling overwhelmed with light?

The first sentence of that book, *L'Amour, la fantasia,* is an immediate response – and of course to every question about foundations multiple answers arise and disappear, successive waves over the sands of the shore, without exhausting that interrogation. Yes, my first response, obviously, was the hand of the father:

> A little Arab girl going to school for the first time, one autumn morning, her hand in the hand of her father.

If I myself could recall the situation of every child immigrant today, in Europe or in Canada, going to school and assimilating into the language of the host country, into "the foreign language," I would say: That child returns home every day and finds her mother most often, her father sometimes as well, speaking the *language of elsewhere,* that of rupture and separation. It is in that language that the child *hears* the mother, in the sound of their origins, sometimes without being able to answer. . . . As if Absence, as absence in the child herself, interrogated her. . . . For she has been plunged too hastily into the *ambient language* – language of the other, foreign language, and by an intimate contrast, a language that has become that of "here and now."

Let us imagine what subtle lurch, what imperceptible equilibrium, at times what cunning risk of vertigo – if not schizophrenia – enters into this precocious identity. . . .

My childhood, I wanted to recount it, shared equally between two languages, my interior partition paralleling the division between the world of cloistered women and the world of men, native men as much as foreigners. . . . I discovered then that, for me, a nubile girl who would never be cloistered, French which was throughout a century the language of conquerors, of colonizers, of new owners, that language was silenced for me in the *language of the father.*

4. *"Linguistic territory between two peoples."* Have I noted: that communal language shared with other migrants, those who come from other cultures and other languages, how – when one chooses or when one is pushed to write – yes, how that language thus appropriated "conforms," so to speak, to usage in the hands of a "professional" writer?

I answer by advancing the idea that, when one is a writer but a newcomer to the language – without, let's say, cultural baggage that it carries – to write in the language of the other is very often to use all the resources of language to convey, to make visible "the other," its power of alterity.

Let me explain. In 1982, I was finishing up a second, very unusual film project: using archival footage to reconstruct the recent past of the Maghreb. . . . Not another simple illustrated history, not an audio commentary accompanying images arranged in chronological order. No.

I sensed rather quickly that those who photographed, who recorded the images of the past brought to it the glance of an "other" (the glance, might I say, of a "tourist"). They photographed everything – in other words, nothing essential. Because the essential was then clandestine, hidden, out of range. . . .

To reconstruct on a screen several decades of a colonized people was to make palpable how much, in every image, the real was in the margins, how everything in the past was barely seen, emptied of its meaning. . . . In sum, those images concealed the past, projected it onto a deforming, illusory screen. . . .

How then does one attempt to approach that "identity" of a bygone past? The sound, *under* the images, could not be commentary; it had to fill a vacuum, make that vacuum felt. . . . It had to "denounce," alert, without being polemical or even "committed." So I understood that, by means of sound, I had to retrieve, suggest, perhaps resuscitate *the invisible voices,* of those who had not been photographed, because they were lurking in the shadows, because they were spurned. . . .

> Memory is a woman's voice,
> night after night
> we strangle it
> under the bed
> of a leaden sleep!

sang an actress, heard over the bodies of the first North African women photographed in color, at the beginning of the 1920s. . . .

5. And I return to this "other" in all writing.

Thus, from this work on visual memory (nine months in post-production, editing the footage, but also getting musicians to sing, to recover in fragments the anonymous popular tunes . . .), I understood that similarly in literature the excluded, the forgotten of my native group had to be brought back into the light, particularly through the French language.

Throughout Algeria's nineteenth century, a century of confrontations, of violence, of ferment, no combat artist had attended to the struggles of the ancestors who pranced about in the sunshine defying and dying. . . . I felt in myself an urgent need to resuscitate those images and yet to use French words.

Thus, in the language considered another's, I found myself

obliged to fulfill a mnemonic responsibility, a mission of recalling an elsewhere, an extinct Arab-Berber past, my own. . . . As if bloodlines needed to be conveyed through the host language; and that is indeed the true hospitality, not merely being able to cross the threshold of the other. . . .

So, for me, my Ariadne's thread was becoming my ear. . . . Yes, I was hearing Arabic and Berber (the lamentations, the cries, the ululations of my nineteenth-century ancestors), I was really hearing them and, in order to resuscitate them, the savages, in the French language.

So much so that writing became inscribing, transcribing, writing in depth, retrieving into the text, the paper, the manuscript, the hand, retrieving simultaneously funeral chants and buried corpses: yes, retrieving the other (previously the enemy and unassimilable) into the language.

Have I succeeded in conveying what was for me this labor of exhumation, of disinterring what the language treats as "other"? Perhaps that is what a writer does first: always bring back what is buried, what is shut up, the shadow engulfed so long in the language. . . . Bring the obscure into the light.

6. In conclusion, I might interrogate myself: to live in two cultures, to lurch between two memories, two languages, to retrieve in a single writing the black part, the repressed – ultimately, what transformation does it lead me to?

Am I committed to being a woman of transition, the writer of passage, to deliver a message on two channels (so that instead of double fidelity it is double drift or even double "treason" that awaits me)? . . . To cease writing, because of the risk of, little by little, no longer speaking *the words of the tribe* (according to the very beautiful Italian novel by Natalia Ginsburg), would that mean no longer belonging to any tribe, to any group, without being able in fact to blend two pasts, two treasures?

Progressive displacement, slow and infinite deracination, no doubt: as if it were necessary to uproot incessantly. To uproot while rediscovering myself, rediscover myself because I am uprooting. . . .

Who am I? I had answered at the beginning: first, a novelist of the French language. . . . Why not finish by asking myself the question again? Who am I? A woman whose culture of origin is Arab and Islamic. . . . So, let me underline this: in Islam, the woman is a guest – in other words, temporary; risking, every moment, unilateral repudiation, she cannot truly claim any permanent location.

Thus, in a religion that begins with an emigration virtually sacralized, the woman becomes an eternal emigrant, with no point of arrival and for that a creature deserving both the best and the worst! The best symbolically, the worst historically.

For my part, though I write daily in the French language, or precisely because of writing thus, I am in fact only one of the women of that multitude. . . . Simply a migrant. The most beautiful designation, I believe, in Islamic culture.

Translated by Steven G. Kellman

MARJORIE AGOSÍN (1955–)

Marjorie Agosín's grandparents emigrated from Europe to Chile, which is where, though born in Bethesda, Maryland, she grew up. In both *A Cross and a Star: Memoirs of a Jewish Girl in Chile* (1995) and *The Alphabet in My Hands: A Writing Life* (2000), Agosín recounts a privileged childhood in Chile. Yet her Jewishness set her apart from the largely Catholic population and made her the object of anti-Semitic comments and actions. After the overthrow of President Salvador Allende, a family friend, the Agosíns fled Chile, settling in 1974 in Athens, Georgia, where Marjorie's father, a medical researcher whose story she recounts in *Always from Somewhere Else: A Memoir of My Chilean Jewish Father* (1998), continued his work on infectious diseases. Agosín earned a Ph.D. from Indiana University and has, since 1972, served on the faculty of Wellesley College. She has been active in the campaign for human rights in Latin America.

Agosín's poetry includes *Conchalí, brujas y algo más/Witches and Other Things* (1984), *Women of Smoke* (1988), *Zones of Pain* (1988), *Hogueras/Bonfires* (1990), *Sargasso* (1993), and *Toward the Splendid City* (1994). Despite long residence in the United States and fluency in English, she writes in Spanish, though her work is more widely known in translation than in the original. In this (translated) excerpt from her memoir, *The Alphabet in My Hands*, Agosín explains how, accepting her identity as "a Jewish writer who writes in Spanish and lives in America," she could not possibly switch languages.

From "Words: A Basket of Love"

Books

Leaning against the books we played at spelling their textures. Before we knew how to read, books were paths, premonitory routes to happiness, invention found between the words. Everywhere books were alive. According to my grandmother, some of the books in our house in Santiago had been saved from the treacherous bonfires of Berlin. It was still possible to feel in them the presence of terror, the savage, sad skies between certain notched pages, pierced by fear. At times I would spread myself out on all the books that my grandmother left behind, Rilke's and Goethe's poetry, the family Bibles, and the books my father and grandfather burned in the bonfires of 1973 in Chile, books about the brain, Freud, and anything written by a Jew. Now I think about the shattered poets of Sarajevo, tearing the pages from beautiful books in order to warm their souls during winter nights. Books have been my traveling companions because I am from nowhere, and they provide me with the transfiguration of memory. Books help me to invent countries that I have visited in the forests of my dreams, to have certain faceless friends who, in the storm of exile, I took for my own.

In books, words are landscapes, prairies, steep mountain paths, and forests where a girl dressed in red inquired about her dead mother. So many books written to rescue and invent memory, so many books like slices of pain among the shadows, so many useless attempts at storytelling. One day, when I was still very young, I discovered geography books. There were books that seemed forbidden, dangerous books with drawings of the human body. Other books were birthday gifts, still books bearing witness to events beyond time and words. Impulsively, it occurred to me that I should leave the books propped up on the immediacy of the night table. Then I caress them, wish them good night, and imagine them dreaming in those cities where someone wrote a story for them. Books sleep in children's dreams. I dream the dream of stories not yet told and my lips begin to tell them out loud.

Silences

The silence. The austerity of my dead words could no longer be my language. The silence. I learned English like a person feeling her way, on the sly and in the shadows of rented rooms. I reviewed the words, repeated them out loud: sun, light, peace. At times I hid in the closet with my pet, a flying squirrel, and cried.

The English language never took on the texture of my soul, the feel of my skin. It showed me the precision of detail, the melody of never-before-heard consonants, and I still must pause before uttering "th." After a long while I was able to love this language, because it belongs to my children, and I am amazed to see them love me and I them in that language. I speak to them in English about black angels and iguanas. I was never bilingual or bicultural. I let each language have its own soul, changeable and warm, free to embark on the dizzy tongues of mad poets.

I could not be in English what I am in Spanish, and yet I never tried. I never sought similarities between words or cities. I lived and live in North America as if by chance, as if my time here were borrowed, and at any moment I might strike out for a country where people speak not my exact language, but one close to it. To go to that land where nothing would surprise me, not the names of the streets or rivers. Then at last I would cease to exist in two languages, in two classrooms, split in half and belonging to no one.

Languages

What does it mean to live in two languages, to exist on the border, not knowing when to cross from the realm of the mother tongue to the realm of the acquired language? Living through two languages is a marvelous thing, say the guardians of order, not memory. I only lived in one because the other did not adjust to my feelings or my skin. One language insisted on forgetting, the other on memory. The privilege of being bilingual and bicultural has its dangerous side. My mother's language I identified with love. English meant codes of silence. Spanish was silence and words. With it we invented parties that no one attended. We imagined the night wind blowing through the empty, frozen house. We found ourselves without a history, with no similarities to those around us. Mirrors returned the moisture of our faces, the austere solitude of our lives as strangers.

My mother taught me to speak the little English I still know. The two of us began with Shakespeare's tragedies and Milton's *Paradise Lost.* I repeated out loud after her. Sometimes the silence, that which wasn't said, my inability to recite names of friends, made me believe I would never master English. So I lived with homework in other languages, autumn games, and a constant homesickness like a tingling in the body. I lost familiar objects and sounds in order to learn English, and realized that I existed outside of time. For me, life between two cultures was no life at all.

Spanish

How I love my language. It is like the sky, high rooftops, and elongated words. Always in transit, all I was able to carry with me were my words. I took care of them, placed them in the moist womb of my pillow. I communed with them. Sometimes they made noises, like a garden, a threshold, lace and nighttime fragrances. I like my language. Looking up words in dictionaries made me happy and I found myself in words, because I, too, wandered lost along the avenues. I did not recognize myself, and no one recognized me.

Who was I in any other language?

Who called my name in Spanish?

Why did they make fun of my accent?

Why could the mere act of speaking out displace my tongue and brand me an outsider?

By contrast, my language loved me, sheltered me from the gray wind of deformed cities, of locked doors. I lost my keys and wandered among the omens of return. My language defined my past, it was relaxed and brave. The words, such ample, respectable ladies, were fraught with the possibility of love beyond diminutives. I never stopped writing in Spanish because I could not abandon my essence, the fragile, divine core of my being. It would have meant becoming someone else, frequenting sadness, losing a soul and all the butterflies. I always spoke Spanish, even in my most solemn dreams. I did not want to translate myself. I was Hispanic to the core and when, on the first day of school, I heard them tell one another not to speak to the Latina, I took a sip of water and wrote a line of poetry in Spanish. The line was so ancient, the words so deep, that I survived.

My Accent

How could someone not want to lose this accent, want to cling to it as to life itself? I loved my accent. As far as I was concerned, it embellished the sound of English, softened words, warmed my lips with each emitted sigh, preserved the things I loved: angels, everyday words, sleepy mornings when I greeted my people in my language. Of all my belongings I was able to keep my accent, and to know that despite its strangeness, I am myself and my voice, looking toward the sun.

Why Do I Write?

Writing is bewitching, like a song or cadence. I arrive at words the way one arrives at spells. Poetry is a story that attaches itself to my feet, my being. Sometimes I will lie down on the earth, invent poems about lost love and fear. Writing is a form of love, of loving and being loved. These aren't words, syllables, or useless alphabets launched by change or an obsession with speech. Each word wants its own freedom to transform reality into wonder, to create another story, to uncover longings, happiness, the astonishing world between the pen and the shattered paper, limber and fragile. Writing is a way to truth, to telling the truth and tying it to books, to stone walls.

As a child I wrote songs, poems, legends. When I was eight, I dictated my first novel to a friend twice my age, Elly Goldschmied. Every summer afternoon on Isla Negra, she faithfully transcribed *The Adventures of Rita,* and from then on, I could not stop writing. To have done so would have meant not to love, to exist, to breathe. I wanted to write about things invisible, nightfall in every desert, intrepid night and the silence of the syllables on the sand. I wanted to be faithful to the language that germinates and blooms like grass above the bodies we love. Then I captured in writing a taste of the country, the voices of women who speak as they fasten their skirts and carry fruit on their swaying heads like words.

Writing was a way to save others and myself. We were transparent in our invisibility. I wanted to know about each one of them, how and who they loved, what they did, where they lived. My words were like signs that led me to inhospitable, but always the most beautiful, regions. Then I encountered the memory of the dead in the Atacama Desert, and he told me: Yes, madam, I am also Jewish, and I know about prisoners. And he showed me the dwarfed bush growing on the Atacama Desert, where men had so often become inhuman, and had carved their history into dead trees.

To write meant to always be awake, willing to take risks, full of magic and happiness, eager to create and undo, because life was that way, like words. I wanted to be a word, that is, to be whole, making my life one with words, and so I speeded up my writing between dreams. I could not stop writing. I rushed toward the realm of words because they were like the blood pulsing uncontrollably through my hands. Writing was my bride, my vocation, my liberation, and above all, my story.

Then, when I left my language behind, and felt that loss like a mutilated body, I wrote about what was missing. I wanted to capture the pain of those who had been evicted from their lives. I wanted to tell about those who close their eyes. I wanted to speak of those places of honor where nothing blooms, yet suddenly the word, the disquieting voice of human life, surprised me and became audible. My work sprung from places occupied by outsiders, strangers, and absences. I revisited the past with obsession. My alphabet was made up of poems in search of a country. My passion was not nostalgia, nor the prudence of days gone by. My passion was writing because it allowed me to commemorate the faces of the disappeared. I did not want to disappear. Blindfolded, I could always find my way to the place of words, to the music of being or not being, to the zones of love within the circle of knowledge where time, seasons, and alliances coincide. Words gave me back my imagination. Words were fireflies, threads of transgression, of faith. Writing was not a hopeless return to the realm of enchantment or the silence of magic and mist that uncovers the light, but above all else the most intense pleasure, the brightest of all lights. Writing saved my life.

My writing and I were allies, companions, words formed concentric rings around me to combat the silence of what was the other. I wrote in order to feel the warm surface of my skin, to recall a lost voice, so that someone might tell me they loved me, or to invent another truth. Who was I in this human groundswell of diverse and secret, as well as open, hatreds? Was I so unlike the refugees from every war, those women on the street, proud and fierce about their belongings in small cardboard boxes?

Then I understood, and the revelation became my dwelling place on the golden thread that liberates me from all labyrinths: I am a Jewish writer who writes in Spanish and lives in America.

Source Acknowledgments

Achebe, Chinua. "The African Writer and the English Language." In *Morning Yet On Creation Day,* 89–103. Garden City NY: Anchor Doubleday, 1975. Copyright © 1975 by Chinua Achebe. Used by permission of Chinua Achebe and Doubleday, a division of Random House, Inc.

Agosín, Marjorie. "Words: A Basket of Love." In *The Alphabet in My Hands: A Writing Life,* 142–47. Translated by Nancy Abraham Hall. New Brunswick NJ: Rutgers University Press, 2000. Copyright © 2000 by Marjorie Agosín. Reprinted by permission of Rutgers University Press.

Alvarez, Julia. "My English." In *Something to Declare,* 21–29. Chapel Hill NC: Algonquin, 1998. Originally published in *Brujulla/Compass* (fall 1992). Copyright © 1982, 1998 by Julia Alvarez. Reprinted by permission of Susan Bergholz Literary Services, New York. All rights reserved.

Antin, Mary. "Initiation." In *The Promised Land,* 163–68. New York: Penguin, 1997.

Anzaldúa, Gloria. "How to Tame a Wild Tongue." In *Borderlands/La Frontera: The New Mestiza,* 53–64. San Francisco: Spinsters/Aunt Lute, 1987. © 1987 by Gloria Anzaldúa. Reprinted by permission of Aunt Lute Books.

Baal-Makhshoves. "One Literature in Two Languages." In *What Is Jewish Literature?* Edited by Hana Wirth-Nesher, 69–77. Philadelphia: Jewish Publication Society, 1994.

Brink, André. "English and the Afrikaans Writer." In *Writing in a State of Siege: Essays on Politics and Literature,* 96–115. New York: Summit, 1983. Copyright © 1983 by André Brink. Reprinted by permission of Georges Borchardt, Inc., for the author.

Buruma, Ian. "The Road to Babel." *New York Review of Books,* 31 May 2001, 23–26. Reprinted with permission from the *New York Review of Books.* Copyright © 2001 NYREV, Inc.

Canetti, Elias. *The Play of the Eyes.* In *The Memoirs of Elias Canetti.*

Translated by Ralph Manheim, 754–59. New York: Farrar, Straus and Giroux, 1999. Copyright © 1999 by Farrar, Straus and Giroux, Inc. Translation copyright © 1979 by Continuum Publishing Corporation. Reprinted by permission of Farrar, Straus and Giroux, L.L.C.

Das, Kamala. "An Introduction." In *The Descendants.* Calcutta: Writers Workship, 1967.

Djebar, Assia. "Ecrire dans la langue de l'autre." In *Ces voix qui m'assiègent . . . en marge de ma francophonie,* 41–50. Paris: Albin Michel, 1999.

Eighty-First World Esperanto Congress. *The Prague Manifesto.* July 1996. Courtesy of the Universala Esperanto-Asocio, Nieuwe Binnenweg. E-mail: uea@interl.nl.net; *http://www.uea.org.*

Ferré, Rosario. "Statement." *Review: Latin American Literature and Arts* 54 (spring 1997):62. Copyright © 1997 by Rosario Ferré. Reprinted by permission of Susan Bergholz Literary Services, New York. All rights reserved.

Firmat, Gustavo Pérez. "Dedication." *Bilingual Blues: Poems, 1981–1994.* Tempe AZ: Bilingual Review Press, 1995. Copyright © 1995 by Bilingual Press, Arizona State University, Tempe AZ. Reprinted by permission of the Bilingual Press/Editorial Bilingüe.

Koestler, Arthur. "Becoming Anglicised." In *Bricks to Babel: A Selection from 50 Years of His Writings, Chosen and with New Commentary by the Author,* 218–219. New York: Random House, 1981. Copyright © 1980 by Arthur Koestler. Reprinted by permission of Random House, Inc., and by PFD on behalf of the estate of Arthur Koestler.

Lam, Andrew. "My American Beginning." Original contribution by author.

Lerner, Gerda. "Living in Translation." In *Why History Matters: Life and Thought,* 33–49. New York: Oxford University Press, 1997. Copyright © 1997 by Gerda Lerner. Used by permission of Oxford University Press, Inc.

Ngũgĩ wa Thiong'o. "Imperialism of Language: English, a Language for the World?" In *Moving the Centre: The Struggle for Cultural Freedoms,* 30–41. Portsmouth NH: Heinemann, 1993. Copyright © 1993 by Ngũgĩ wa Thiong'o. Published by Heinemann, a division of Reed Elsevier, Inc., and by James Currey Publishers. Reprinted by permission of the publishers.

Okara, Gabriel. "African Speech . . . English Words." *Transition* 3, 10 (1963): 15–16.

Rao, Raja. Author's Foreword. *Kanthapura,* vii. New York: New Directions, 1967. Copyright © 1963 by New Directions Publishing Corp. Reprinted by permission of New Directions Publishing Corp.

Rushdie, Salman. "Damme, This Is the Oriental Scene for You!" *The New Yorker,* 23 and 30 June 1997, 50–61. Copyright © 1997 by Salman Rushdie. Reprinted with permission of the Wylie Agency.

Sante, Luc. "Dummy." In *The Factory of Facts,* 261–85. New York: Pantheon, 1998. Copyright © 1998 by Luc Sante. Used by permission of Pantheon Books, a division of Random House, Inc.

Santiago, Esmeralda. "Introducción." *Cuanda Era Puertorriqueña,* xv–xviii. New York: Vintage, 1994. Copyright © 1993 by Esmeralda Santiago. Reprinted by permission of Perseus Books Publishers, a member of Perseus Books, L.L.C.

Senghor, Léopold Sédar. "Le Français, langue de culture." In *Liberté I: Négritude et humanisme,* 358–63. Paris: Editions du Seuil, 1964. © 1964 by Editions du Seuil.

Stavans, Ilan. "Lost in Translation." *Massachusetts Review* 34, 4 (1993–1994): 489–502. Copyright © 1994 by the *Massachusetts Review,* Inc.

Wallia, C. J. S. "Response to Salman Rushdie." *IndiaStar Review of Books: http://www.indiastar.com/wallia6.htm.*

Willemse, Hein. "The Black Afrikaans Writer: A Continuing Dichotomy." In *From South Africa: New Writing, Photographs, and Art.* Edited by David Bunn and Jane Taylor, 236–46. Chicago: University of Chicago Press, 1988.

Index

Index

Index